D0970644

"*The Night Wanderers* is a literary masterpiece."
—*Wiadomosci24* (Poland)

"Currently there is no better book about the latest history of Uganda."
—*Süddeutsche Zeitung* (Germany)

"Jagielski's moving, beautiful, and winding account of Uganda's sad history of multiple conflicts leaves one mourning the suffering so many have endured and questioning to what extent the current government can provide long-term solutions for the generations who survived."
—Maria E. Burnett, senior researcher, Africa Division, Human Rights Watch

the NIGHT WANDERERS

———◄◦►———

Uganda's Children and the Lord's Resistance Army

WOJCIECH JAGIELSKI

Translated by Antonia Lloyd-Jones

Seven Stories Press
NEW YORK

Copyright © 2009 by Wydawnictwo W. A. B.
English Translation © 2012 by Seven Stories Press

Originally published in Polish by Wydawnictwo W. A. B. under the title *Nocni
wędrowcy*, 2009.

First English-language edition.

All rights reserved. No part of this book may be reproduced, stored in a retrieval
system, or transmitted in any form or by any means, including mechanical, electronic,
photocopying, recording, or otherwise, without the prior written permission of the
publisher.

Seven Stories Press
140 Watts Street
New York, NY 10013
www.sevenstories.com

College professors may order examination copies of Seven Stories Press titles for a
free six-month trial period. To order, visit www.sevenstories.com/textbook or send a
fax on school letterhead to (212) 226-1411.

Book design by Elizabeth DeLong

Library of Congress Cataloging-in-Publication Data
Jagielski, Wojciech, 1960-
[Nocni wedrowcy. English]
The night wanderers : Uganda's children and the Lord's Resistance Army / Wojciech
Jagielski ; translated by Antonia Lloyd-Jones. -- A Seven Stories Press 1st ed.
   p. cm.
ISBN 978-1-60980-350-6 (pbk)
   1. Children and war--Uganda. 2. Child soldiers--Uganda. 3. Lord's Resistance
Army. 4. Uganda--Social conditions--21st century. I. Lloyd-Jones, Antonia. II. Title.
HQ784.W3J3413 2011
967.6104'4--dc23
                              2011039871
Printed in the United States

9 8 7 6 5 4 3 2

FOR MY PARENTS

CONTENTS

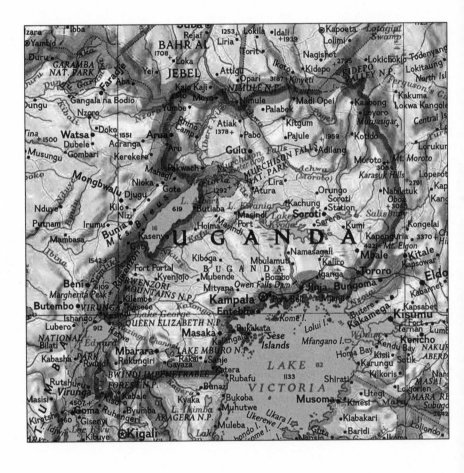

THIS IS A TRUE STORY, and its setting, the town of Gulu, is a real place. The main characters in the story are also real people, possessed by various spirits, including guerrilla leader Joseph Kony, failed rebel Severino Lukoya, former guerrilla commander Kenneth Banya, the king of the Acholi, their chiefs, the priests, the soldiers, and also the children whom the spirits make into cruel, merciless guerrillas by night.

For the purposes of this narrative, the characters of Nora, Samuel, and Jackson have been created out of several real people.

ONE

IN GULU THE DAY WAS ENDING.

The town was hurriedly preparing for sleep, as usual in the rainy season, trying to get everything done in time before the storm erupted, which had been gathering in the darkening sky in swollen, angry clouds, only waiting for dusk to release all the rage accumulated during the scorching day.

Blazing hot, the town was dropping, starting to cool down and go quiet. Now with no regret the weary storekeepers were putting away the goods they hadn't managed to sell in the course of the day. Grimy hired hands from the vulcanization workshop were swearing as they struggled to roll some gigantic tires the size of mill wheels back indoors. Set out on the sidewalk, they blocked the way, forcing passersby to slow down and stop for at least a moment, long enough to plant the seed of temptation to buy some new car wheels.

In the downtown area the offices were closing up. With a rattle and a bang, one after another the shutters were coming down on the stalls and workshops, hidden in the deep shade of arcades running the length of the low-rise buildings on the main street. The innkeepers were starting up their electricity generators, and the noise of them could be heard from all directions.

The imminent cloudburst was already palpable. It was as if heavy drops of warm rain were hanging in the air, ready to fall at any moment onto the dusty red earth and change it into slippery mud the color of blood. The sky was thundering louder and louder, bolder and nearer, and short, bright streaks of lightning were cutting across the clouds as they closed in on the town.

The citizens were vacating the downtown area to get home before the storm and the night. During storms the power supply was usually disconnected. Also, the troops stationed in the town preferred people not to hang around after dusk for no reason. It was easy to mistake them for guerrillas, who on dark, cloudy nights in the rainy season sometimes ventured out of their hiding places in the bush and came all the way into Gulu.

Jackson was waiting for me, as usual, at Franklin's Inn on the main street. There he sat, perfectly still, leaning against a stone column. He was a journalist from the local radio station, King FM. Its office was located opposite the Acholi Inn where I was staying. In the afternoons, when he finished work we would meet at this place. I would order the beer, and Jackson would tell me things—about the wars, about kings past and present, good and bad, and about sorcerers and the spirits that interfered in people's lives and influenced their fate. On Saturdays and Sundays we used to come to Franklin's to watch soccer matches from the British league on a large television screen hung from the ceiling in the crowded, smoky bar.

Jackson didn't move an inch, not even when I came up to his table. He looked tired and was plainly in no mood for talk.

The storm was circling above the town now, waiting for the right time and place to lunge and stun it with thunderclaps, lightning, and lashings of rain. The town was frozen still, as if afraid of being too distracted by the usual hustle and bustle to notice the tempest's first strike. Crushed by its own weight, the sky was sinking lower and lower, as if trying to touch the ground.

Suddenly the wind, which was tugging at the palm trees just in sight beyond town, blew sand along the main street. Abruptly animated, shreds of old newspaper, bits of colored plastic, and yellowed grass went whirling across the cracked asphalt.

Jackson remained motionless, like a predatory animal holding its breath.

"Did you see that?" he asked.

I shrugged.

"But he flew past just over your head."

"Who did?"

The first raindrops fell, spattering noisily on the roofs and the ground.

◄◦►

Then the children began to come into town.

They appeared suddenly, almost imperceptibly. They loomed out of the darkness, from under the ground like apparitions. They were heading on foot, by the dozen, from every direction, toward the almost deserted town, now plunged into silence before the storm. They walked confidently, not in a hurry, like someone repeating for the thousandth time an act that's entirely familiar and no longer holds any mystery.

Some were dressed in school uniforms and had satchels full of textbooks and notepads on their backs. Others, in rags and barefoot, were carrying blankets, bundles and parcels of some kind, as well as sheets of newspaper and pieces of cardboard picked up from roadside ditches or gutters. The older children were leading smaller ones by the hand, and the girls had babies strapped to their backs, like village women on their way to work in the fields.

In the market square the gray river of children, quietly murmuring in the darkness, divided up into several smaller ones. The biggest offshoot turned toward the bus station, while a smaller one ended its journey in the courtyard of the large red-brick church of the Blessed Virgin Mary. Others continued to the yards of local schools and hospitals. The rest of the children ended their march on the main street, in the arcades outside the buildings, where they spread their makeshift beds on the ground.

Most of them were looking for a place to rest, and lay down to sleep at once before dusk fell, plunging the town into darkness. But some of the boys, yielding to the temptations of unlimited freedom, spent a long time running about shrieking, accosting the girls, and playing in the deserted streets, whose masters they became as soon as it was night.

Almost completely obscured by the increasing gloom, the street buzzed with chatter again. The voices wandered, now coming closer, now moving away. Outside the hardware store opposite someone burst into tears. In the empty bar at Franklin's the television was on low, and through the open kitchen window you could hear the proprietor hustling the dishwashers, who after a long day's work had no strength left to hurry.

Out of the pitch darkness of the street, some little girls appeared right by our table. Like moths, attracted by the dim streaks of light trickling from the bar, they quietly started laying their makeshift beds on the sidewalk, part of which Franklin's had taken over. Ignoring the last late clients, they spread their bits of cardboard and blankets on the ground and lay down to sleep.

At the sight of them Jackson looked around vacantly, like someone who has lost his sense of time and stayed up terribly late. He put down his half-drunk bottle of beer and nodded to suggest we leave. Without even waiting for me to settle the check, he rose from the table and vanished into the night. As I followed him out of the circle of light, it took me quite a time to fish his figure out of the dark.

He was walking quickly down the middle of the street, facing ahead without glancing to either side, where the children were bedding down in the arcades. He didn't look round at me or wait for me. As he passed the first cross street he increased his pace. Only then, as if lured by the sound of footsteps, several small figures loomed out of an arcade. Someone shouted insistently in a high-pitched child's voice, and someone set off in pursuit, but almost instantly abandoned it. Jackson disappeared at the top of the street, and once again the sidewalk fell silent.

◄◦►

The next morning there wasn't a trace of the children left.

The earth was going red in the sun again, but there were still some steaming puddles after the nocturnal downpour. Following the storm the air was crisp, bright, and translucent, and the green of the leaves and grass washed clean of dust was bursting with freshness, purity, and life.

Like every day, the main street was full of pedestrians and vendors, in a hurry to get the most important things done by noon, before
everything surrendered to the heat again and was plunged into numb
immobility—right through to evening.

At the street market by the church the village women, who flocked
to Gulu at daybreak, were noisily touting fruits and vegetables set out
for sale. From the nearby square, which was occupied by transport firms,
buses full of passengers and luggage were setting off.

In the arcades outside Franklin's Inn, waiters in aprons gone gray
with age were putting out the tables and washing down the concrete
sidewalk with buckets of water. At the bar, which could be seen from
the street and where the television was on as usual, the first clients were
already drinking coffee and smoking cigarettes.

I found Jackson at his office, where he was reviewing the morning
cables from Kampala and the world outside. When I asked what was
new he replied that there had been another bomb attack in Baghdad,
and that as far as he could see, it looked as if things were getting worse
there. But there was no news from Congo, where they'd just elected a
new president and where I was meant to be going from Uganda. Neither
bad reports of riots and armed rebellion, nor any encouraging ones
either. This lack of news augured well for Congo, in Jackson's opinion.

When I asked about last night and about the children in town, he
didn't seem to understand what I was talking about.

"Why do you think that's strange?" he said, shrugging, without taking
his eyes off the computer screen. "Are you going to Atiak today?"

That was the village he came from. He had been a teenager when
the guerrillas, led by his favorite uncle, Vincent Otti, a former Ugandan
army officer, attacked it ten years ago. Jackson remembered how Otti
used to come to the village in full dress uniform, sit him on his knees,
and let him try on his soldier's cap with the stiff peak. When the rebels under his command attacked the village and murdered 350 of its
inhabitants in the marketplace, Jackson's parents sent him to relatives
in Gulu, and themselves fled to one of the camps set up and protected
by government troops. Otti's brothers had fled from Atiak too, in fear of
their neighbors' revenge.

"Who were those children, the ones we saw last night?" I asked again.

"Children like any others," he replied. "Do you want me to go with you? Because if I'm going, I must ask the boss if it's all right with him ..."

"I'm not going to Atiak, but to Palenga. You know that. So where did those children come from?"

"They came to town for the night, that's all. What's so strange about that?"

"They frightened you."

"You're talking crap."

"It was plain to see. Were you really scared off by those children?"

"You don't get it. Children are different here."

"What does that mean?"

"They're different. That's all."

◄◊►

At the Acholi Inn Hotel, past the lawn where dinner tables were put out in the evenings, there was a small swimming pool. Officers from the local garrison spent their Sunday afternoons there. They were small, with such youthful faces that in peaked caps sunk over their eyes, colored shirts, and light linen pants they looked nothing like soldiers. Rocking on wobbly high stools at the bar, they drank beer, smoked cigarettes, and chatted, louder and louder with every hour and every bottle, entirely absorbed in their conversation.

They only looked up and stopped talking when white women from the many charities based in Gulu appeared at the swimming pool. But the unconcealed, lustful curiosity they aroused soon made the women feel awkward; usually, after a short bathe and a few minutes in the sun on an uncomfortable recliner, they retreated to their hotel rooms.

Sitting nearby under a mango tree, I was waiting to be summoned by the adjutant of an important colonel from the garrison command. Whether I could meet with one of the guerrilla leaders who'd been captured and was reportedly being held in Gulu depended on his consent. Promising he'd introduce me, the adjutant had emphatically advised me not to set foot outside Gulu without arranging it in advance with the colonel. Although allegedly the guerrillas had slipped past the army and made their way as far as Sudan, they were conducting armed raids from there, and the district was still regarded as restless. He had told me to come to the swimming pool toward evening.

The important colonel I was supposed to meet was swimming in the pool. The rest of the soldiers were watching their commander swim and responding to the questions, comments, and jokes he offered from the water.

The colonel was a large, well-built man with a shaved head and very dark, almost black skin. His long gray shorts clung to his massive buttocks and thighs. He swam from end to end at a leisurely pace, hardly moving, as if floating on the water. Now and then, snorting and panting noisily, he turned from his belly onto his back, or from one side to the other, only to return to his former position a few minutes later.

Tired of waiting and of the murmur of conversation in a language I couldn't understand, I started watching some gray bats hanging from a branch. At dusk they started waking up and breaking free of the tree like overripe fruits. But instead of falling heavily to the ground, they soared into the air, slashing it with their wings, suddenly spread for combat. They spun low, just above the ground, as if trying to spot something in the grass. They kept flashing past like desperados drunk on speed, unafraid of death, or entirely oblivious of it.

From under my tree I noticed the adjutant signaling to summon me for an audience. Once I was standing by the edge of the swimming pool, with a single mighty stroke of his arm the colonel turned in my direction. Briefly he circled on the spot, then stopped on bent knees, submerged up to his neck in water.

"So you're a journalist. And what exactly brings you to our parts? There's been nothing interesting happening here for ages. Or maybe there's something we don't know about?"

The soldiers laughed out loud and pricked up their ears. Even the adjutant, who was standing next to me, smiled, slugging beer from a bottle.

"I've been told I'll find everything out from you."

"From me? Who said so? I don't know anything. We soldiers are just simple folks. Attention, at ease, reveille, retreat."

Propping himself on one leg, the colonel turned onto his back.

"I'd like to do a bit of traveling around here, find out some more about your war."

"Our war? So you think we've got a war going on here?"

The officers burst into noisy laughter again; as if bored with the conversation, their commander vanished underwater and slowly swam off to the other end of the pool. There he surfaced and hoarsely called the adjutant over. Left on my own, I gazed at the sky. After yesterday's storm the night looked set to be sultry, with no chance of respite.

Soon after, two girls in bathing suits appeared at the pool. One of them went to the bar, while the other sat down not far from me, plunged her legs into the water, and paddled her feet up and down.

"Watch out! We've got crocodiles here," called the colonel from the other end.

"I'll give you a shout if one appears," she replied, without raising her head.

"Just you call and I'll be right there. You won't find a better man for the job."

At the bar the soldiers roared with laughter. The colonel dove back toward me. He didn't swim up to the edge, but stood nearby with his legs astride.

"I'd advise you not to head for Kitgum or Pader without soldiers. Besides, why trail about for no reason?" he said to me, but kept looking toward the girl, who was engrossed in staring at her own feet, as they grew harder to see in the darkness. "But do go to Palenga, the road's open. It's not far from Gulu, there shouldn't be any trouble in the daytime. But better not wait for nightfall to come back."

For a while he disappeared underwater, and when he emerged he added that I should watch out for children on the way.

"If you see them coming out of the bush, please tell your driver to turn back immediately. And if they show up close to you and it's too late to turn around, tell him to keep going at full speed ahead. Under no circumstance should you stop," he said, brushing drops of water off his face. "Please don't forget—it's good advice, and straight from the heart. With children there's no joking."

And although I got the impression that he uttered these final words in total earnest, the soldiers at the bar whooped with laughter.

◄○►

Palenga was wreathed in white smoke which was emerging from the damp thatched roofs in a large, shapeless cloud, then sinking heavily to the ground before trailing and wandering among the cone-shaped huts. The dwellings were almost on top of each other, densely positioned with no space between them. Because of the rain the women couldn't cook outside, so the entire village was obscured by clouds of stagnant gray smoke from their hearths.

The place was also smothered in the odors of food cooking and a foul smell of garbage and filth. Split in two by the asphalt road from Gulu to Kampala, it stretched on either side all the way to the horizon, marked in one direction by a thicket of small, twisted trees that looked murky in the bad weather; in the other it merged with the sky above a plain covered in tall grass.

I never heard any of Palenga's more than 10,000 inhabitants call it a village. On the whole they rarely and reluctantly talked about it, and if they did mention it, they used the word "camp." They said "I live in Palenga," but never "I am from Palenga." They refused to call it a village, as if unwilling to come to terms with its existence. They were afraid they had only to utter its name, and at once the thing they preferred to perceive as an apparition, an illusion, would become real and irreversible.

They wouldn't have been here, nor would Palenga have existed, if not for the war, which had drifted onto their territory more than twenty years ago. It wasn't the first time the turmoil of war had rolled across Acholi-land. But this time, having had its fill of misfortune and destruction, instead of moving on, like an uninvited guest tired of wandering, the war had made a longer stop among the Acholi. It hadn't left them for such a long time that the young people had no idea what life was like without it.

Only the old people could still remember. And when asked about their homeland, it was they who recalled the names of long-gone villages.

They did it reverently, as if uttering magic spells that would resurrect those villages, turn back time, and reverse the course of history. Either the soldiers had destroyed their old life, homes, and villages, or else the guerrillas had sent them up in smoke. And finally the greedy, ever-insatiable jungle had devoured what was left of them.

The guerrillas used to call at the villages for food and recruits. They told the villagers they owed it to them, because they were fighting in their name and for their cause. If anyone refused, they killed them in the marketplace. After that the soldiers would arrive. Only a few of them knew the Acholi language. Most of them were from the south of the country, all the way from the shores of Lake Victoria, and Lake Albert in the west. They questioned the peasants about the guerrillas and said they needn't be afraid of vengeance because they would protect them from it.

Not knowing what to do or which evil to choose, the villagers kept silent. The soldiers got angry and pounded them in the face with their fists, or knocked them to the ground with blows from their rifle butts. They called them traitors, dragged them off to the cities, and shut them in prisons.

Until finally the war drove the Acholi out of their homes. Oppressed by soldiers in the daytime and by guerrillas at night, they abandoned their huts, their graveyards, and the plots they had wrested from the bush and escaped to the cities, which the rebellion hadn't occupied. Those who stayed behind were forcibly moved out of their villages by government troops.

The military declared that in view of a lack of adequate forces to protect the Acholi from the guerrillas, they had to resettle them from villages scattered all over the country and put them in special camps, close to government garrisons where they'd be safe. Herding the Acholi into camps also meant a death sentence for their villages and fields, which, once abandoned, were reclaimed by the jungle. However, the soldiers didn't seem concerned about that. By dooming the villages to destruction, they hoped they would not just deprive the guerrillas of the opportunity to take recruits, but also condemn them to gradual death by starvation.

For days on end the local radio stations kept repeating government announcements saying: "All law-abiding Acholi from villages in the Gulu, Pader, and Kitgum districts must leave those lands without delay and make their way to special camps under military protection. You must do this or else fall victim to criminal rebels who don't dare confront our soldiers and are treacherously hiding from them in village huts."

In this way the entire Acholi people—two million of them, not counting those living in cities and 100,000 killed in the war—were driven out and settled in two hundred crowded camps such as Palenga, which were not only a place of salvation for them but also a prison.

The soldiers announced that no one was allowed to leave the camps after dark, and that anyone who disobeyed this order would be regarded as a guerrilla and shot without warning.

However, even when they strictly observed the military rules and guidelines and locked themselves in their huts after dark, the Acholi got no peace at all. The villages and plots they had left behind didn't satisfy the guerrillas for long. Once they had plundered the abandoned huts and vegetable patches where the crops had gone wild—manioc, corn, sorghum, and sunflowers—once they had stripped the rotting fruit from the mango and papaya trees, the ravenous guerrillas headed straight after the villagers. They came right up close and lurked in the bushes near the camps guarded by the military, or even in the grass surrounding them, which was tall enough to hide adults.

By day, like predatory wild animals, they lay in wait in their hideouts for stray victims, foolhardy people who had drifted too far from the camp. After dark they crept up to the huts and market stalls, or even to the granaries and stores the soldiers were minding. They stole food and kidnapped children. They set fire to the straw-thatched huts and killed their inhabitants. Thus they needlessly inflicted a cruel death—these were crimes out of nightmares, as they derived sensual pleasure from burning people alive or butchering them with machetes.

They attacked at night, unafraid of the soldiers on guard. Their hunger, exhausting and dizzying, was always greater than their fear. Before the watchmen were alerted and could run to the rescue, the guerrillas would take their plunder and vanish into the bushes and the darkness, where no one was going to pursue them. Once night had fallen, the army never set out against them.

There were always very few soldiers to guard the camps, and in view of the attackers' numerical advantage over them, they had no intention of risking their lives. The army had crammed almost 70,000 people into the biggest camp, Pabbo—more than the combined population of the local towns, Gulu, Pader, and Kitgum—yet only six policemen were assigned to guard it. Not surprisingly, in the course of a single month the guerrillas managed to attack Pabbo several times.

Badly remunerated and robbed of their pay by the officers, the soldiers themselves were desperately poor and homesick for their native lands in faraway Buganda, Toro, and Ankole. They weren't too bothered about the fate of the Acholi—not enough to die for them. So they pretended not to believe the villagers who came running to them with news of guerrillas in the bush, or else they were so slow to come to the rescue that the attackers had time to get away.

The guerrillas were perfectly aware of this. They had their spies in Palenga and the other camps, who informed them how many soldiers stayed on duty for the night and whether they'd been seen boozing that evening in one of the roadside bars. The inhabitants of Palenga even claimed that more than once on the day preceding a nocturnal attack they had seen the soldiers guarding the camp chatting and drinking with outsiders, and even playing cards or soccer with them.

The sight of strangers, especially children, whom the guerrillas also sent on spying missions, made the villagers panic. Not trusting the soldiers to protect them from danger, some of them banded together in the evenings and posted watchmen outside the smallholdings on the edge of the camp. The rest would sink into unsettled sleep that didn't bring relief, not knowing what the night would bring; frightening and inevitable, it robbed their days of value and their lives of joy.

Maybe that was why life in Palenga couldn't advance. Time never seemed to move forward, but just trickled by; no one regretted its passing, and no one felt nostalgia or cherished any memories.

◄◦►

Hiding from rain and sun inside their thatched huts, the men leaned against the rough clay walls, smoking tobacco in silence. They sat like that for days on end, deprived of any occupation, not knowing what to do with their time, or with their idle hands, which were large and gnarled from hard labor in the fields. Joints cracking, they made them into fists, stuffed them into their pants pockets, straightened their bony fingers, laced them across their chests, or snatched blades of grass and stones from the ground. Sooner or later, those hands would be hanging awkwardly in a gesture of capitulation, as if ill-fitted, ill-suited to any purpose, of no use at all.

They also stood around by the road, outside the few stores that jostled among the cone-shaped huts. Here you could buy food past its sell-by date, cigarettes, lemonade, and beer. The beer was warm, because in Palenga the power was still not connected, but even so there was never a lack of willing takers.

Soldiers from the local post and truck drivers heading for Kampala sat perched on wooden crates, with open bottles in their hands. They drank the beer slowly, with their eyes half closed, appearing not to notice the men gathering around them in a timid, hesitant, but tightening circle. They came and squatted right next to the soldiers and drivers, as if ignoring them, but actually on the alert, their bloodshot eyes watching for the tiniest gesture of encouragement, any opportunity for a chat, which with a bit of luck might even turn into an invitation to a nice, free feast.

The bottled beer sold in the stores was too expensive to get drunk on. So those of Palenga's inhabitants who could no longer endure the daily hopelessness in a sober state intoxicated themselves with *kwete* brewed by the local women—a beer made of sorghum, bananas, and corn. They also got drunk simply because they had nothing better to do.

The first thing they had lost in the wars was their herds of long-horn cattle, which for the Acholi were a symbol not just of wealth but also of dignity, a source of pride. Then their land was taken from them, their villages, and even their graveyards, where the dust of their ancestors lay.

After losing their final sources of income, they could no longer keep their families, and after fleeing from the guerrillas, driven by the soldiers into the roadside camps, they couldn't even secure their own children's safety. They hated their fate, themselves, and everyone around them. With no way of changing the life they found so unbearable, they had renounced it and were wasting it away, very slowly dying, going to seed like their abandoned plots of land.

The last emotions that still lay dormant within them were anger and desire. Their anger was helpless, vengeful, and blind, turned not against the perpetrators of their misfortune—those people were powerful, unreachable—but against anyone who out of the goodness of their heart tried to help them. By helping they were bearing witness to their decline and humiliation, and that made them guilty.

The desire too was born out of anger, not love. There was no ardor in it, no affection or concern, but there was violence, a wish to destroy, to inflict pain, to lose themselves in causing harm and deriving strength from it.

Abola Imbakasi, the headman of Palenga, reckoned these negative emotions came from the fact that the local men owed too much to the women and had become too dependent on them. Unable or simply unwilling to break free of their refugee torpor, they had let the women take on the burden of keeping the families and bringing up the children. The women fired bricks and charcoal, brewed beer and then sold it at roadside stalls. They had to hide their income carefully from the men so they wouldn't steal and squander it on cheap, bitter gin, or on the girls from Gulu, who for a handful of shillings would go into the woods beyond the village with the soldiers.

The men from Palenga had no money and couldn't buy themselves love. So they took women by force, as if only by inflicting rape could they come alive and shake off their inertia—then instantly sink back into it.

Headman Imbakasi also suspected there was a dark force underlying the division between the men and women of Palenga. Evil did not just come out of nowhere. It was something that turned the natural order upside down.

"Among us it is accepted that when a man is talking, a woman should keep quiet," he said, shaking his head in disbelief and helplessness. "But our women have stopped listening to the men."

◄◦►

Headman Imbakasi walked briskly between the huts, which were packed together so tightly that on emerging from one, you stepped straight inside another. It was the soldiers who had told the Acholi to build the houses like that in the camps. The closer together, they said, the safer. But the proximity had proved a curse. A fire only had to start in one house for the flames to shoot up into the thatch, jump across to the neighboring ones, then race on and on, driven by the wind, marking their path with fiery trails across Palenga. The thatched roofs burned brightly, with a snapping sound, as the heat made the clay walls crack and crumble. Violent and unstoppable, the blaze would travel from hut to hut until finally it grew weary and put itself out. Infectious diseases made pilgrimages across Palenga in a similar way.

Having close neighbors also meant that no one in Palenga was ever alone for a moment. Everything happened in full view of others—indoors, in view of wives, children, parents, and cousins; and outside in view of near and not so near neighbors, passersby, and strangers. Being so close to each other, almost face to face, feeling the neighbors breathing down their necks, the people of Palenga were always falling over each other, jostling one another, pushing, touching, tugging, squeezing, and stroking. It was impossible to break free of this embrace, and there was no escape into solitude.

A visit to an African village starts with an audience with the local leader, headman, or chief. I found Imbakasi, the headman of Palenga, in a warehouse converted into a church, a whitewashed brick barrack underneath the only surviving tree in the area. Instead of a church tower, on the tin roof there was a crooked cross made of planed planks.

Abola Imbakasi had just said goodbye to a priest in a dirty cassock, and was going home. He beckoned for me to follow him, and quickened his pace. Like an experienced tracker, he could find the right way through the muddy, stinking tangle of alleyways and backyards without having to look for it. Noticing that I couldn't keep up with him, he grabbed me firmly by the hand and led me between the huts like a child. The procession was brought up by Robert, Imbakasi's son, who stuck close to his father.

The reason for the headman's nervous haste was the news he'd been brought. A dozen women had taken their children into the woods to fetch firewood, wild fruits, and water from a stream. They had set off from the village at daybreak and still weren't back, although it was now past noon. On the advice of the elders at Palenga, Imbakasi had long since forbidden his people to go beyond the stream. The guerrillas liked to hide in the bushes along its banks, lying in wait for victims like predatory animals by a watering hole. In addition, the soldiers had occasionally mistaken civilians rummaging in the bushes for guerrillas and fired at them from machine guns deployed in the village.

◄◦►

But there was something else which Imbakasi was clearly most unwilling to talk about, or else he saw no point in initiating me, an outsider, in matters so foreign to me. As we emerged from the cluster of huts onto the road leading to Gulu and Kampala, without slowing down, he muttered that the war people had provoked in Acholi-land had disrupted the natural order.

"Those who used to live together in harmony have now turned on each other and become enemies," he said, frowning.

We walked along the damp asphalt through the camp, where beyond the last huts the road took a broad turn and disappeared behind a hillock sparsely covered in small trees. Further on, as we moved down the hill toward the plain, the trees started bunching together, until at a certain point they changed into black forest, whose boundary was apparently marked by the small stream, invisible in the tall yellow grass.

"It's better not to go there," sighed Imbakasi heavily, glancing at his son walking beside him. "To avoid getting drawn in."

He said you only had to stand by the water's edge to feel something take hold of you, telling you to do what you didn't want to, something you knew you shouldn't. The trees and the river beguile and tempt you to go in further and further, but you mustn't listen. One day, a while from now, maybe it'll be safe. But not now, not today, when people cannot even get themselves straight.

Fools disregard what they're told, he said. They enter the stream, or go among the trees, and vanish. Some of them are found, but so changed that they are no longer themselves—they're like strangers. But most of the people who disappear never come back again.

Over a hillock, on a path trodden into the grass that led to the stream, stood a group of people. The men were holding machetes with silver blades coated in wet grass cuttings. They greeted Imbakasi, who engaged them in conversation. His son Robert stood beside him, not saying a word, as if absent, as if his soul and his thoughts were in another world entirely.

Imbakasi said that Robert was fifteen, but he seemed much younger. Small, slight, and meek, he was nothing like a boy on the threshold of manhood. He could speak English, but when addressed he smiled uncertainly and gave quiet, one-word answers.

The men at a roadside bar whom I had asked how to find the headman had told me his son had been in the guerrillas.

"Is that true?" I asked him. "Were you really a guerrilla?"

The villagers on the path started hollering and pointing toward the forest. A sudden wind arose and tugged at the branches, bending the treetops to the ground as if feverishly searching for something among them. Then out of the woven wall of forest, one after another some female figures emerged, dark against the grass. As they headed back to Palenga, bent low by the burden of firewood on their backs, the women seemed to be bowing.

◄◦►

Headman Imbakasi's hut was in the middle of the village. It was slightly bigger than the others, but not at all grander. Only a small, tidy yard distinguished it from the neighboring ones, and some wooden stools set before the door, where the headman held his audiences.

Inside, curled against the clay walls and crawling with flies, lay some thin, tawny dogs; they glanced at us timidly, and occasionally one of them leaped up to run away. A small flock of hens, a few goats, and a spotted piglet were grubbing in the garbage behind the house.

Apart from Robert, the headman's son, I saw hardly any children in Palenga, though usually in African villages the children immediately spot a newcomer, surround him in an intrusive swarm, and never leave his side.

"Many people have sent their children away to relatives or friends in the city to be educated," said headman Imbakasi. "Here there is no occupation for the adults, even less for the kids. This is no place for them. So they are sent away, and the ones who remain are kept in the church in the daytime. There the priest, who comes to us from Gulu, teaches them reading, writing, and religion, including how to pray to the Lord God and sing hymns. At least that is of some use. And the priest has his eye on them, so we don't have to be afraid they'll get into mischief, or that something bad will happen to them. Or that they'll go where they shouldn't, like across the stream, among the trees."

It was two years ago when Robert, the headman's son, went to the stream with his friends to knock ripe wild mangoes off the trees with stones. The trees grew on the other side, so—although the adults had warned them not to—they went into the water. On top of that they crossed the stream without removing their sandals.

Toward evening, four of the boys came back to Palenga, but Robert and two others had vanished into thin air. The adults, who went to look for them the next day, found neither their corpses nor any trace of them. In Palenga people started saying the boys had been taken by guerrillas, who had been seen by the stream. And although there was no proof, every time news went round of another attack and another slaughter committed by the guerrillas, people glared at Imbakasi, afraid to fling a direct accusation at him by saying: Maybe your Robert did it! Maybe it was he who did the killing, burned people alive, slit their throats, or chopped off their hands with a machete!

Three months later Robert was found. The guerrillas had indeed captured him by the stream. They had seemed not much older than he was—they only looked older because of their guns and torn, oversize army clothes. They had herded the prisoners through the forest for days and days on end, until one evening, when they had stopped for the night, the boy had managed to escape among the trees. No one had come after him. The guerrillas were so exhausted by their endless trek and by hunger that they hadn't had the strength to chase the runaway.

"You'll die anyway! Wild animals will eat you," they cried after him. "We'll find you yet, and then you'll be sorry!"

For some time he had wandered about in the bushes, until finally he happened to emerge onto a road running through the forest. There some soldiers found him and took him to Gulu, to a special center where they treat children who have been in the guerrillas against their will, heal them spiritually, and restore them to life.

Headman Imbakasi learned that Robert had been found when he was sent for from Gulu. There he was told that before his son could return home, first he had to be treated. Until that was done, his father could only visit him. After a while he was sent for again and told that the boy had now been healed and was ready to go home.

But back in Palenga Imbakasi sensed that Robert was not yet entirely cured. He was like a terrified animal, shouting things in his sleep at night, but in a strange, alien voice, and uttering words in a language no one could understand. Sometimes he behaved like a madman. The headman had been planning to take him back to the center in Gulu for more treatment, but first he had summoned the priest. The priest shut himself in a hut with the boy and had a long talk with him. Since then Robert had calmed down; the phantoms that had haunted him had disappeared as if by magic. On parting the priest had advised Imbakasi not to let the boy out of his sight, at least for some time, to be sure he wouldn't do any harm to himself or others. He should also be on his guard in case those in Palenga who had been hurt by the guerrillas did or said something to Robert that could change him again, or arouse the demons that lay dormant inside him.

Headman Imbakasi firmly assured me he wasn't upset by the wicked people who maligned his son behind his back and called him a guerrilla.

"What if he chose to go into the forest? What if he joined them of his own will?" He shrugged and added that the one hundred days his son had spent in the guerrillas was too little for him to have been able to do anything really evil, one of those terrible things they talked about in Acholi-land.

"It was too short a time—he didn't do anything bad, he couldn't have. They never even gave him a gun," he said, glancing at the silent Robert, sitting on a stool beside him. "The boy just worries that the guerrillas will come to Palenga and punish him for running away by burning down the village and killing us all, the entire family. He's afraid they'll recognize him by the brand they marked him with after kidnapping him. They said it could never be erased. I keep telling him the doctors in Gulu are stronger than the guerrillas and they'll wash it off."

A small group of children spilled out of the church, onto the asphalt road.

"In the evening they are sent off to town, to avoid tempting evil."

◄०►

On the way back from Palenga to Gulu we passed some soldiers on the road in wet waxed capes, brought out of storage with the onset of the rainy season. The rain was streaming down their faces but they didn't seem to notice. Only when it got worse, lashing them in the cold wind, did they shelter among the banana and mango trees. Hidden in the bushes, they blended in with the leaves and the foul weather.

Gulu loomed from around a bend, looking wet as it huddled beyond the railroad tracks. The center where the children were kept and cured of their nightmares was set back from the main street, halfway between the Acholi Inn Hotel and Franklin's. As I drove down that way, I thought I caught a glimpse of Jackson among the arcades.

The children's center was amid some large, flat-roofed bungalows. It was fenced off from its neighbors by a high whitewashed wall. The gray cast-iron gate was closed, and the watchman roused from his sleep by my knocking was unable to dredge up a single word of English. Through a small window cut out of the metal he kept repeating something in his own language. Finally, more and more tired and fed up, he waved a hand at me and disappeared. I realized he had gone to fetch help.

Through the little window I could see a large courtyard covered in reddish gravel and some white buildings with barred windows set in a square around it. There were some girls in orange skirts sitting on benches made of wooden planks placed against the walls. Some of them were nursing babies, either breast-feeding them or rocking them to sleep on their knees. The boys were standing still, idling under the one and only tree, bunched together as if they found the open space offered by the yard unsettling or intimidating. Dressed identically and of a similar age, they looked like prisoners brought out of their cells for a walk.

The watchman still hadn't reappeared, and I was getting ready to leave when from one of the buildings a small, thin boy emerged, and at a determined though unhurried pace came walking toward the gate.

"He doesn't speak your language," he said.

"Where did you learn it?"

"At school," he replied. "Formerly I used to go to school."

I gave him not more than ten years old, but Robert didn't look his fifteen years either.

"Are you a father?" he asked.

"A father? No, I'm not a priest."

"Then what are you doing here?"

"I'm a journalist."

"What does that mean you do?"

"I write about how people live. And who are you?"

"I am Samuel. Come and see me tomorrow—there's no one here now."

"What about you? You're here, you're talking to me."

"There's no one here now. The adults have already gone. It's late today. Come tomorrow when it's daytime. Come tomorrow when Nora will be here."

The sun was slowly fading, and the sky had gone navy blue. The town had vanished in a gray gleam.

◄•►

The next day began wet and gray with rain again. The sun, which most mornings dispersed the heavy, gloomy clouds like a playful puppy, had given up this time and was barely brightening the sky. Drops of water sparkled on the long ribbons of banana leaves, and the brick-red earth felt slippery underfoot.

The solid gate in the wall around the children's center seemed to be shut tight, just like yesterday evening. But on a small grassy square in front of it, there was a group of children buzzing about. I noticed the girls' orange skirts from afar. They were gathered around a large tree growing by the wall, waving their arms and jumping up to the branches as if trying to take off into the air. From a distance they looked like dolls at a puppet theater, being yanked upward by invisible strings. They kept dropping clumsily to the ground, tripping and falling over. Then they got up, tilted their heads, stared into the sky, and took off in brief, awkward flight again, without making any noise—none of them were shouting or even laughing as they did this wild dance around the sacred tree.

Only when I came closer did I notice a cloud of cockchafers hovering low among the branches. That was what the girls were looking for—they were jumping up to catch the lumbering insects, or at least knock them to the ground and then look for them in the grass. They were tossing them into plastic bags proffered by their younger friends, their hunting assistants.

I went closer. At some point a cockchafer flew over my head, buzzing loudly. Automatically I stretched out a hand and caught it. It was large, gray and brown, and had a hard carapace. It looked like the ones I used to catch as a child among the willow trees.

We used to go hunting for cockchafers at dusk, once it was a bit too dark to play soccer. The twilight made it hard to catch them, and made the game more interesting. Until night fell, we would chase after the low-flying insects, jump up and try to catch them in flight, rolling about with laughter in the wet grass. We used to stuff the captured cockchafers into bottles, and once it was dark, we'd count up our prey. Then we'd shake the insects out of the bottles and watch as the stunned creatures regained consciousness, mistrustfully opened their wings, and took off at high speed, as if keen to escape pursuit.

One of the girls watching the hunting offered me her plastic bag. I opened my hand and tossed the cockchafer into it.

"Who's winning?" I asked.

Without answering, she dropped her gaze.

"Who has caught the most?" I repeated the question, pointing at the bag she was clutching.

She shook her head and pointed at the gray locked gate.

"Will you show me how many you've caught?"

The children under the tree stopped their hunting and stared at us in silence, as if reproachfully. I felt as if I were obstructing them in some way, spoiling something. The girl thrust a hand into the bag and fished an insect out of it. With a swift, practiced movement she ripped off its wings and carapace and put it in her mouth.

I felt someone seize me by the hand. It was a young woman in a light dress made of cheap printed cotton. At the sight of her the little girl squealed and cuddled up to her.

"I am Nora." She had a low, husky voice. "It was you who came yesterday, wasn't it?"

"Yes, but too late. I came in the evening when everyone had gone."

"Sam told me."

"Sam?"

"The boy you spoke to yesterday. His name is Samuel."

Still squeezing my hand, she led me through the gate. In one corner of the yard some girls were leaning over a fireplace where there was some oil sizzling in a black frying pan.

"I thought they were playing a game," I said. "I know that one from childhood."

"No, they eat them. They fry them and eat them. They call it *nsenene*. They say they like it," she replied. "And if they play games, they only do it here, inside the walls."

◄◦►

In the yard, inside the walls, the children had started playing a war game.

First, pushing and falling on top of each other in line, they were waiting for the teacher in charge to fetch out and distribute some guns, machetes, and clubs carved from pieces of wood. Once armed, but still arguing with each other, they divided into those who were going to play the guerrillas, those who were to play the soldiers, and those who would be people living in the village under attack. None of the boys wanted to be included in this third group. They scampered away from the teacher and tried hiding behind one another, like kids in a school yard forced to play with the weaklings on the team that's doomed to lose. Finally some of the older girls, who were holding babies and watching the squabbling from the sidelines, agreed to be the inhabitants of the village under attack.

The boys assigned to play the role of soldiers went off to the gate, leaving the girls with babies in the middle of the yard. The guerrillas, who were in the majority, gathered under the solitary tree. I sat down in the shade on a bench with Nora and Samuel, who never left her side.

The leader of the guerrilla detachment was a stocky boy in a baggy cotton shirt. He lined up his men and gave them a speech in an imperious tone. Then he went up to each of them in turn and drew signs on their foreheads with his finger. Once he was done, he threw his hands in the air and began chanting a song. It sounded sad and familiar. I was sure I had heard it somewhere before. When the singing stopped and the boys, their heads lowered in concentration, cried "Amen!" I remembered that the children's choir at the cathedral in Gulu had sung a similar song during Sunday mass.

Then the leader in the red shirt gave a signal and the guerrillas started moving toward the village girls. Stooping low, they crept along slowly and silently, communicating through hand signals. Once they were close, the commander raised his arm and the boys, lying in ambush, froze to a stop outside the village.

At the sight of their persecutors' fierce faces, the girls—their future victims—started choking with laughter and pointing at them. Nora was laughing out loud too, and was holding Samuel's hand.

Suddenly the commander let out a high-pitched, piercing shriek, ringing with threat, but also alarm and terror. Petrified until now, as if released from a magic spell, the boys rushed at their chosen victims, waving their guns, clubs, and machetes. They let out loud screams too, copying their leader, as if trying to drown out everything around them, including their own fear and doubts. The noise also seemed to be aimed at shocking and overpowering the people on whom they were going to inflict suffering, so they wouldn't defend themselves, beg for mercy, or try to avert their inevitable fate.

A cloud of red dust rose in the yard, hiding the swarm of children from view. As it slowly dropped, it revealed the battlefield. The girls attacked by the guerrillas were lying still, faces to the ground, pretending to be dead. Some were trying to slip away, but they were pursued and brought down. Now the guerrillas were dragging the one who had run the furthest into the middle of the yard by her arms and legs. Pulled up high, her skirt exposed thighs marked with livid scars.

Nora was still laughing. The boys were standing over their victims, mindlessly meting out pretend blows with their clubs and machetes. The smallest of them, a barefoot little kid of about six, pushed his way between the older ones shouting loudly. The children on the bench whooped with laughter. They were behaving like the audience at a show, applauding the most successful performances.

"What's the little one shouting?" I asked.

"He's saying, 'Me too! Me too! Let me kill someone too!'" replied Nora, turning her gaze from the children to look at me.

Then the guerrillas scattered dry leaves and grass on their victims' bodies and pretended to be setting them alight. Some of the girls taken prisoner had their hands tied with string, and the rest were ordered to pick up the toys scattered on the ground—the guerrillas' war trophies. Then they lined up the prisoners and were getting ready to march off when from round a corner out ran the soldiers and rushed to the attack.

Another battle began, a new show. The army quickly got the upper hand over the guerrillas, who took off, desperately trying to escape. The soldier boys raced after them all over the yard, and even among the buildings. The chase no longer resembled a game, but a contest fought in deadly earnest, where no one was willing to concede defeat.

The captured guerrillas did not surrender like the people in the village they'd attacked, but fought to the bitter end, when they were pretend-killed by the soldiers. Only the smallest ones let themselves be taken prisoner. The guerrilla commander in his baggy red shirt refused to be captured for the longest time. More than once his pursuers caught him, but he tore free like a wild animal and went on running, damp with sweat and covered in dust and earth.

Finally they cornered him by the gate. Even though it was open, from there he had no escape route, because the game was only played in the courtyard. Assailed by lots of attackers, he struggled and fought back, but was now reconciled to defeat. They threw him to the ground right by the bench on which Nora, Samuel, and I were sitting. The fighters didn't seem to notice us at all—we simply didn't exist in the world they were now inhabiting.

Pinned down by the knees of four enemies, the guerrilla commander was panting heavily.

The teacher ended the game with a loud whistle. Shaking off the dust and discussing the course of the battle, the children went to an arithmetic lesson.

"We encourage them to play this game," said Nora. "Sometimes it's the only way we can find out what really happened to them."

Whenever battles like the one I saw were enacted in the yard, the teachers and caregivers kept a close eye on each child, examined their faces, and listened to what they were shouting. Nora said that during the war game the children repeated events they really had seen, and had often taken part in, as if returning for a while to their previous incarnations.

"Sometimes they are incapable of talking about it," she said, exposing her face to the midday sun.

"The fact that they killed people?"

"Uh-huh," she muttered idly, without opening her eyes.

I asked if any of the children playing in the yard had killed people.

"Yes, except for the very youngest, all of them."

◄◦►

Samuel never joined in with the war games in the yard, but he did draw pictures of them.

Maybe that was why he stuck so close to Nora, who taught the drawing classes. She handed out paper and colored pencils, and encouraged the children to draw whatever they remembered best, whatever they thought most important. She took me to a dayroom where the white-washed walls were covered in pictures of burning huts, corpses in pools of blood, guerrillas killing people with machetes and axes or shooting from guns.

Nora praised Samuel for his drawings.

"He has a sense of composition. His drawings are alive. He paints not just the foreground but also a second or third plane. Look at this one, for instance." She pointed at one of the pictures on the wall. Three guerillas were clubbing a man who was lying on the ground, covered in blood. Behind them there was a hut with a burning roof, and next to the hut a chained dog trying to break free. "And look how he mixes the colors."

Nora said most of the children at the center weren't able or refused to talk about what had happened to them when they disappeared from their villages and ended up at camps in the bush, in the guerrillas' world. Some were afraid, bound by a sense of guilt, suspecting that if they revealed the whole secret they'd be punished. Others were incapable of choosing the right words and broke off their story at the first incident that was too hard to describe. They didn't know how to express what they had seen, let alone what they thought or felt about it.

Even when they tried to talk, the thoughts, memories, and fears they named and uttered aloud seemed deficient, inappropriate, not right. Afraid of being misunderstood and judged, they would fall silent.

The war games and drawings were intended to provide help and relief. It was easier to talk about events drawn in colored pencil on paper or reenacted in the dusty courtyard. Samuel willingly spoke about the war and everything he had experienced—or so at least Nora assured me.

"He'll tell you all about it," she said. "But don't ask him to."

However, many days went by before he first told me he had killed people. He had killed ten, or maybe more. Lots, lots more. Too many to remember each one. Too many to remember at all.

I had been expecting this confession. I had only come in order to hear it. And yet, when it finally came, I was at a total loss.

⤙⊙⤚

I have never felt awkward encountering people who have killed or given orders to kill—soldiers, guerrillas, their commanders, or the political leaders who have incited war in the sacred belief that it was the only possible way to establish justice, their only salvation.

In my experience they rarely see themselves as the perpetrators of crime. They seek justification and mitigating circumstances, they make light of the harm they have caused and blame it on others. My conversations with them have been like a simple duel of shrewdness and competence, a game in which deceit is often a principle, and outsmarting your rival means winning.

I have found it harder to talk to the victims of war crimes, who are always their only witnesses. By telling a journalist the story of the misfortune they have suffered, they are usually hoping to get help and to change their fate. They regard the harm that has been done to them as the greatest, most unfair injury of all—and it is the only thing of value they have left. They are sure that as soon as the world hears about their miseries, it cannot possibly remain indifferent. But when nothing changes, they become embittered and feel an even greater sense of injustice.

Then they are reluctant to tell their story again, and keep the rest of the treasure represented by their memory of what they have seen and suffered to themselves. They don't want to talk about it, because they are afraid of the pain, regret, and sense of guilt. Why didn't I run away sooner? Why did I open the door? So in my experience, while conversations with people who have killed are like an interrogation, encounters with their victims are like a confession, but not one that leads either to penance or to absolution. This kind provides no consolation or relief.

Moreover, for my report to be as good as possible, as true as possible, I have always had to find out as much as I can—ask questions about the details, tiny things that might seem irrelevant or inappropriate. What time was it when the guerrillas entered the village? Was the sun shining? What were you doing just then? Was the radio on? Can't you remember what time it was when the bomb fell on your house? And what did the man who shot your husband look like? Do you remember his face? How was he dressed? How many shots did he fire? What was it like? Please say, please tell all.

◄○►

The problem with talking to Samuel lay in the fact that he was both victim and executioner all at once. I wanted to get to know him in both roles, to understand how he had passed from one into the other, and then back into the first, original one.

I kept putting off the conversation, although I knew I had to have it. And that it was what I wanted. Each morning when I arrived at the center, I would look out for Samuel among the children in the yard. I would smile and wave, and when my gaze fell on him he would turn his head. He would reply with a greeting but wouldn't come up to me, nor would I call him over.

I'd sit on the bench waiting for Nora, and when she came Samuel would instantly appear too. Sometimes, he would scramble onto her knees like a small child, ignoring her protests and anguished complaints.

"Sam! What are you doing? Get off me at once," she'd say, rubbing her aching thighs. "You're too heavy, you'll squash me. What sort of a guerrilla are you?"

Then the boy would spar with her, deliberately poking his elbows into her legs.

But usually at the sight of Nora he would come and sit near the bench with a toy. Then he would keep glancing in our direction and listening to our conversation, which he couldn't understand.

Although he looked ten, in fact he was thirteen. Yet there was something about him, maybe the solemn expression in his eyes, which at times made him seem even older than he really was. He had a large shaved head, veinous hands covered in scars, and cracked feet as big as an adult's. He was no different from the other children at the center, and his story was in no way more dramatic or more unusual. It was Nora who chose him for me from among the rest. Or maybe he made the choice himself? As he never left Nora's side, he became my companion too.

"Sam, show us how you caught a snake in the bush," said Nora, and the boy acted out a hunting scene for me. "Can you believe it? He crept up behind the snake, grabbed it with his bare hands, and threw it live into a pot of boiling water. It was delicious, right?"

Samuel nodded and grinned at us.

"And tell us how you got lost at night. Tell us how they gave you a gun."

He didn't know many English words, which meant that his accounts were matter-of-fact and simple. He spoke slowly and clearly, choosing his phrases carefully like a good, well-prepared pupil being questioned by the teacher. Nora listened to him attentively. He fixed his gaze on her, and took her nods of assent as praise and encouragement.

"The main thing is to ask a good question. He has to know what I'm asking about. If he can't understand he'll get scared and clam up," said Nora. "Right, Sam? You clam up and then you're as silent as the grave. Or you start crying like a little kiddywink."

"Nora's a kiddywink," he cried, laughing and pointing at her. "Nora's a kiddywink! Nora's a little kiddywink!"

"Samuel! Stop it or you'll be sorry!" she threatened. "Ask him about school."

I asked about his favorite subjects and teachers at school, and about the soccer teams whose names and colors he knew from the television.

"I like drawing and I like Nora," he replied solemnly.

"What about math? I didn't like math."

"I don't like math either."

"What about gymnastics? Do you like it? I loved it."

"I like gymnastics too. And I like nature."

"I loved nature too."

One day, after classes, the three of us were sitting on the rough concrete steps outside the dayroom. We were watching the rest of the children running about the dusty yard playing soccer. A phone rang in the office.

"Nora!" someone called. "It's for you!"

Nora hauled herself up and disappeared behind the door.

I had never been left on my own with Samuel before. Nora had always been with us, and in any case, Sam only showed up when she was in the vicinity. Her presence was the condition for my meetings with the boy, but at the same time it was an obstacle.

So there we sat, side by side, watching the boys kicking the soccer ball about. The silence was becoming awkward, unbearable. We could hear Nora laughing through the half-open door.

"Do you play soccer?" I managed to croak, glancing at Samuel.

"Yes," he replied. "But right now I'm talking to you."

"That's right," I agreed.

Samuel drew a circle in the sand with his toe.

"And which soccer player do you like best?"

Sam rubbed out his sand circles.

"Ronaldo from Brazil," he said.

I thought he had guessed what I really wanted to talk to him about. Lots of journalists had been to Gulu before me, and each one had wanted Samuel and his friends to tell how they had been kidnapped from their villages and taken into the bush by the guerrillas, and how, having no alternative, they had joined the rebellion and killed people themselves. Sometimes I thought Samuel was waiting for the moment when I too would finally question him about it. But he didn't look surprised or disappointed when I didn't ask.

◄०►

I preferred to talk to Nora about Samuel—she was his teacher, caregiver, confessor, and healer. She knew everything about the boy.

In the morning I would come to the center and wait for Nora. She made coffee and then, before going to teach classes, she took me to her office and opened a large safe where the children's records were kept. Gray cardboard files tied with tape held the secrets not only of the boys and girls playing in the yard like Samuel, but of all the children who had been kidnapped and taken into the bush, ended up at the center, been treated, and then gone back to their families and villages—like Robert, son of the headman from Palenga.

Their accounts of everything they had seen and experienced had been written down by their new caregivers and kept locked in the safe. Nora took notes by hand, with a ballpoint pen. She reckoned the clatter of a typewriter keyboard intimidated the children, took away any courage they had left, and damaged their fragile, newborn trust. To facilitate the confession and the therapy that followed it, a list of questions had been drawn up which the children were meant to answer.

Were you forced to kill any of your relatives or neighbors?

Were you forced to chop off people's hands or feet with a machete?

Were you forced to gouge out people's eyes?

Were you forced to rape women?

Were you forced to burn people alive?

Most of the questions were answered with the word "yes." There were photographs of the children attached to the completed questionnaires, just like the ones on student ID cards.

After that Nora and her colleagues talked to each child dozens of times. Some answered willingly, others brushed off the questions with a denial or a nod, and yet others refused to speak at all. Nora never pressed them but waited patiently for the opportunity to question them again. And again—until finally she broke through the fear and mistrust that were blocking their words and discovered the whole truth.

Before allowing me to rummage in the safe, she fetched out the gray files herself and spread them on the desk for me like photographs from a family archive.

"This is Roger. He was with us for over a year, and this is Emma and her daughter. They look alike, don't they? Emma died a few months ago. And this is Richard—you saw him this morning. He's the goalie. Or this one! Do take a look at Benjamin's story. It's hard to believe it really happened. And here's our Samuel!"

Our Samuel! That's what she had called him ever since I started coming to the center and questioning her about the boy. She burst into laughter, a little flirtatious, and a little provocative. I thought I could even sense a note of irony in it.

"Our Samuel, our boy," she said. "Our common cause."

Samuel stared at me out of the photograph. The poor-quality paper and shades of black and white made his face disappear behind his large, wide-open eyes, their whites shining.

When a bell rang, Nora stood up, smoothed down her skirt, and went to the drawing class, leaving me with the pile of photographs and life stories on gray paper scattered on the table.

◄◦►

Samuel was nine years old when the guerrillas captured him.

He had run into them in a copse near his village. He had gone into the forest with an uncle and several cousins to fetch firewood, wild bananas, and mangoes. The sun was starting to set, though it was still quite high in the sky. They were on their way home, and were already close to the village. They could even hear their mothers calling through the bush, and they could see smoke rising above the straw roofs. They weren't in a hurry, and were sure they'd make it before nightfall, when under the cover of darkness the guerrillas came out of their hiding places to hunt.

Samuel knew about the guerrillas. In the village no one really talked about anything else. The adults implored the children not to venture too far from it even by day, and under no circumstance were they to go to the forest alone, where the guerrillas were said to be lurking among the trees and bushes.

According to rumor, they captured not just children who disobeyed their parents and elders by unwisely going too far from the houses, but even attacked schools to drag the children straight from their benches. It was said that the guerrillas themselves had originally been kidnapped and taken into the forest, where from children they had changed into cruel wild beasts, feeding on human flesh and blood. It was also said that whenever they wanted, they could vanish like ghosts, and appear in several places at once—not just in the Gulu area, but also in the Kitgum and Pader districts. They had even been seen in Lira, Soroti, and Teso. They knew spells that protected them from bullets and made them invincible. Before he met them, and then became one of them, Samuel had often played at being guerrillas with boys his own age in the village.

They had sprung up all of a sudden like forest phantoms. Wearing torn uniforms, they were long-haired and dirty, with their guns aimed and machetes raised to strike. Samuel and his relatives were so surprised and terrified that they hadn't put up the least resistance, nor had they tried to escape—none of them could even have thought of it, although that was the only moment when it had been remotely possible.

The guerrillas threw them to the ground and tied them up with ropes. Samuel was amazed to find he could understand what they were saying. In muffled voices they were giving orders in the Acholi language. They told the prisoners to get up, and herded them toward the forest. Only then, as they were getting further and further from the village, did Samuel hear the loud, shrill whistle the adults sounded as a warning against danger. Then a few shots were fired from the direction of the village.

He couldn't see what was happening in the village, which the guerrillas had attacked. He couldn't hear any screams, and didn't see any fire consuming the straw roofs, or anyone being murdered. Stumbling and falling, hounded in the darkness by the guerrillas, the captives had spent a long time wandering through the bush, until they emerged into a small clearing full of people. The abducted villagers were gathered under an old mango tree. Now and then another group of guerrillas came out of the forest with new prisoners and plunder.

Night had fallen; to find their way through the undergrowth, the guerrillas had lit torches. Seeing this, Samuel remembered how his older cousins had explained to him that the flickering pillars of light from their torches provided the easiest way to spot them at night.

⟵⋄⟶

That was what it must have been like. That's how I imagined it, as I read the accounts Nora had recorded, and heard her stories about the children at the center and about the ongoing war in the district.

Gradually I started asking Samuel questions too.

"Were you afraid?" I inquired, when he told me his story of being abducted from the village.

"They were small boys, those guerrillas. Just as small as me. Smaller than most of the children they took captive," he said, staring at me searchingly, as if trying to guess whether the fear I was asking about was similar to the kind he had felt. "Yes, sure I was afraid. But I didn't cry."

"Did they hit you?"

"Only later. Then I was afraid."

"Did they hit you a lot?"

"Yes. But not too much."

He answered every question, concisely and directly, which I took for defenseless, sincere frankness, and which made the conversation even harder for me. It was I who was having trouble formulating my questions, to which, like a model student, Sam was instantly giving the answers. I just couldn't find the right words; they all seemed inappropriate to what I wanted to ask, not the ones I needed.

In fact I had already met boys who'd been kidnapped and had fought in all sorts of armies and guerrilla units before now, in Sudan, Rwanda, Burundi, West Africa, and the Congolese cities of Bukavu and Lubumbashi. I well remembered the underage soldier I had met years ago in Kisangani, Congo. In green drill clothing and huge rubber boots, he was standing on guard outside the headquarters of commander Joseph Kabila, the son of Laurent-Désiré Kabila, who led the guerrilla army that raised a rebellion against President Mobutu. The boy was called Claude and he was eleven years old. He was clutching a large machine gun and told me how he had fought in the guerrilla troops against Mobutu's soldiers. When I was finally summoned inside, he asked me to leave him some cigarettes.

The Chechens who had guarded me at night in Duba-yurt to make sure I wasn't kidnapped by slave traders were certainly not adult men either. They kept watch outside the room where I slept and never left my side. Although I never asked my host, I knew he had bought rifles for them with the money I had given him earlier for expenses connected with my visit. I had also seen child soldiers in Afghanistan. The sight of them neither surprised nor shocked me, and talking to them didn't make me feel awkward, maybe because they seemed adult, or maybe because they were taking part in wars, which we are used to regarding as a matter for adults. Or maybe because in their parts of the world, even when no war has erupted, life goes by more quickly—in places where people die before fifty, youth is much shorter, and children grow up earlier. Teenage girls are already mothers, and teenage boys are supporting families—or killing, fighting wars.

I only remembered Claude from the Congo River because as I listened to his tales about war and guerrilla marches I had realized he wasn't much older than my son, whom we were still afraid to let go to school on his own.

Maybe if I had met Samuel in his previous incarnation—as a guerrilla from the forest—it would have been easier to talk to him. But by now he had returned to the form of a child, or rather he had been transformed back into a child again. The more he became a new person, the more unreal his previous incarnations seemed to me.

Another reason why I was unable to talk to the boy was that I was less concerned about what he had experienced, done, or seen, and more interested in understanding, virtually feeling, what he was like then. Samuel couldn't help me with that. His terseness was of no use here, and all my questions were clumsy.

"Can you remember how you felt then?" I asked, when he told me about his first night in captivity.

"I was hungry," he replied.

Nora reckoned people don't always feel something. Sometimes something inside a person dies, and if nothing can ever revive it again, they can't feel anything.

From Samuel's words, looks, and gestures, from Nora's account and his own, written down and stored in the safe, I put together a moving image in my mind. Then I tested the truth of it by talking to the boy, asking him about the details of its composition, its proportions and shades of color, and the thickness and shape of its lines.

⟶⟵

Samuel was nine years old when he killed for the first time. It happened in the clearing under the mango tree, that same night when he was taken captive by the guerrillas.

Not even years later could he explain why he hadn't cried that night.

"I just didn't cry, that's all," he said, shrugging, when I asked him about it.

Sheltering from the fierce afternoon sun, we were sitting in the shade on the steps outside Nora's office. A while ago she had finished classes and was drinking Coca-Cola from a bottle, which she used now and then to wipe the sweat from her brow. At the sight of her Samuel ran up and kneeled beside her, playing with a car cobbled together from a flat piece of wood and some rusty wire.

"Have you already described how they told you to kill that boy?" she asked. "He was called Wilson, right?"

Samuel turned around and said no. Without interrupting his game, he glanced at me, as if trying to guess whether I was now ready and willing to hear his story.

"Tell him," said Nora.

I was grateful to her, but at the same time annoyed. I thought she was unnecessarily speeding up his account, and that by urging the boy on she would only frighten him.

"How do you intend to find anything out if you don't ask him questions?" she kept saying. "Don't be afraid, he won't eat you. Do you want to stay here forever?"

"I don't want to ask him," I explained. "I want to talk to him about it."

"But it's one and the same thing."

Once again I sensed in her voice a note of superiority and a hint of mockery, which often appeared when she listened in on my conversations with Samuel.

"Did you really not cry, Sam?"

"No, I didn't. I was too scared."

All he could remember was acute, cold fear. And probably the shock stifled everything else in him, thoughts, doubts, and memory. He clearly saw and understood what was happening around him, but he felt as if he weren't actually taking part in it. As if he were just watching it.

He felt as if he were asleep, and having one of the bad dreams that occasionally made him feel anxiety, but he couldn't dispel it or change the course of events in any way. He could only wait until the nightmare ended, because like any dream, even the worst kind, it was bound to end.

He knew the boy whom they told him to batter with a large wooden club. They lived in the same village, and he knew the boy's name, though he couldn't remember ever having played with him. He was a few years older than Samuel, taller and stronger.

The guerrillas had dragged him out of the group of prisoners and beat him because he was crying. They knocked him to the ground and hit him with clubs and rifle butts. They screamed that they would kill him if he didn't stop it at once. But the boy couldn't restrain his sobbing. Then the guerrillas stepped away from him. They chose a few boys from among the prisoners, pressed wooden sticks into their hands, and ordered them to batter the crying boy. They warned that anyone who disobeyed the order would die with him. Or instead of him.

At first Samuel tried to hit the boy gently, on the legs, arms, and shoulders, to inflict as little pain as possible. But the boy kept moving and was still sobbing. So he started to hit blindly, harder and harder to make him stop. Only some time later, after further executions, did he realize that by taking pity on Wilson and wanting to save him pain he had only prolonged his agony. The boy had to die in any case. That was what the commander had ordered, and now nothing could change it. So it was better for him and for everyone for death to come as quickly as possible. He could only do him this one service—hit him on the head with all his might and kill him as fast as possible.

If he had had to, that was just how he would have killed his own relatives. He never stopped thanking God for showing him mercy and making sure the first person he killed was not his father or his brother.

Other prisoners kidnapped by the guerrillas from the villages were not so lucky. Fathers were forced to kill their sons, and children to kill their parents, brothers, and sisters. Friends had to murder friends and neighbors—neighbors, in the sight of other guerrillas and prisoners, so there wasn't the faintest hope that this blackest of all secrets wouldn't ever be revealed.

These executions at the guerrilla encampments, in forest clearings, and even in the marketplaces of villages under attack were almost ritual murders, a macabre initiation, inducting the prisoners into a new life. They were a frontier, a sharp, bloody line cutting them off from the past and everything it contained. There was no way back to their old, familiar way of life.

And if they still fostered some illusions, the guerrillas soon shattered them.

"You have no other way now. No one will accept you in your villages and homes anymore," they said. "No one there wants you anymore, no one is waiting for you, no one will love you. You have killed, and killers are cursed. But you mustn't escape or cry. Rejoice, because now you've become soldiers in the Lord's Army."

◄◦►

"So what's he like, your Samuel?"

Jackson didn't think much of my familiarity with the boy at the center from the start. In the evenings, when we met as usual at Franklin's bar, not only did he never try to hide his carefully practiced, disdainful amusement at my new acquaintance, but in fact he did everything he could to make sure it didn't escape my notice. Whenever I started to talk about the boy and his stories, Jackson went quiet or suddenly changed the subject, pretending he'd remembered something important that he had to mention before it slipped his mind again.

He gave the impression of being amazed at my interest in Samuel's case, and that I was wasting my time on it. Spending days on end with Sam and battling through his feeble English to understand his story was in Jackson's view an obvious waste of time. He made it plain to me that he could no longer see what exactly I had come to Gulu for.

"Do you really want to write about that for your paper?" he asked, pretending to be having a hard time suppressing his mirth.

"I might even write it up for one of the papers in Kampala," I replied.

"I don't write for the papers, and we don't bother with things like that on my radio channel," he said. Suddenly irritated, he kept folding and unfolding a paper napkin lying on the table. "You think you understand everything, you think you know everything. But in fact you only see very little, and only what everyone else can see," he soon added. "But the really important things, without which you can never understand, will remain invisible to you. And you can't change that, just as you can't change yourself." For a brief moment the grimace of feigned contempt and indifference left his face. "But maybe that's how it should be. Maybe it is others who should judge us. Since we are unable to get to grips with ourselves, maybe it's better to observe ourselves through the eyes of others."

Jackson found it unpalatable that thanks to my friendship with Sam and Nora I had become independent of his views, judgments, and stories. My self-reliance took away his sense of importance and his role as an authority. In trying to convince me of the impossibility of ever knowing somebody else's truth, he wanted to put me off working on something over which he had no influence, and in the face of which he felt a sort of fear I couldn't fully understand.

Deep in thought, he was mindlessly turning an ashtray full of cigarette butts in his fingers. When he looked up, once again he was wearing the mask he had put on when I first met Sam.

"So come on, what's he like, your Samuel?"

He described the boy as "your Samuel." His words carried not just the usual note of forbearance, but also of reproach, for devoting time and attention to Sam, and thus distinguishing him from the others, though he had done nothing to deserve it.

Nora, by contrast, was pleased by the attention I devoted to the boy. "Your Sam is already waiting for you"; "That Sam of yours has been asking about you"; "Take your Sam home with you and you can chatter on for the rest of time," she'd say to me. "Or maybe you'd take me away from here too? Then you'd have the whole flock."

"Samuel?" I replied, turning to Jackson. "He's a nice boy."

"But didn't he say he killed his father or brother?" he asked. "They do that."

In my conversations with Sam never once had I asked him about his family. Nor could I remember if there was anything about his relatives in the cardboard file lying in Nora's safe. However, I did remember that when he talked about being kidnapped from the village, Sam had said what a mercy and relief it was that the first person he killed was not his father or brother. But I had never seen Samuel have any guests on one of the Sundays designated as visiting days.

No one ever came to see him.

◄◦►

"Does Samuel have any family?" I asked Nora.

"Yes, and no." She looked up from the morning paper, which she was browsing without particular interest.

The presidential elections were fast approaching, and among the color photos on the front pages of the papers, the contenders for the most important post in the country were vying for votes and attention. But Nora wasn't interested in politics. She was sick of reading articles about election campaigns and political rallies. It's a waste of time, she said. She quickly turned the front pages, which were always given over to descriptions of political events, and only stopped at the foreign news columns. But here too she usually just cast an eye over the headlines, and only became absorbed in the paper when she found pictures of local or, best of all, foreign actors and singers, articles about fashion, or the gossip column.

"What do you mean, yes and no?"

She smiled mockingly, haughtily, as she always did when she caught me being careless in some way. Without a word she put down the paper and reached into the safe. Samuel's cardboard file was lying on a separate shelf. His life story covered a few scant pages of yellowing paper.

"Samuel's mother died while he was in the bush. Of syphilis," said Nora, running her eyes down the lines of script. "After her death Sam's father went away. Apparently to Kampala, but no one knows for sure. He has shown no sign of life. No one knows where he is, and we don't know how to find him. He hasn't the faintest idea that Samuel has been found. And I'm sure he isn't in the least bit concerned."

Sam's two sisters and brother were taken in by his father's brother, Uncle Anselm, who was living with his own family at one of the camps near Gulu. However, he had refused to take in Samuel too. Nora had gone to inform him that the boy had ended up at the center for treatment. Anselm had replied that besides the three adopted orphans he had five of his own children, for whom he could not provide as it was. The person most set against Sam was Anselm's wife, who thought the boy would bring them bad luck. "I don't want any spirits from the forest in my house," she had insisted, and wouldn't even let Anselm go to Gulu to visit the boy. She also forbade him from telling Sam's siblings that he had been found. They were already used to the fact that he was gone.

Anselm was Samuel's only relative in the Gulu area. His father's two other brothers had been killed in the wars, and his sister had gone away long, long ago; apparently she lived as far away as Juba, across the Sudanese border. Sam's mother didn't have any family in Gulu. His father had brought her here from Kasese, near Lake Edward. It was said she came from Congo. None of her relatives had ever come to see her in Acholi-land, nor had she ever gone anywhere to visit them.

"So that means Sam doesn't really have anyone?" I asked.

"That's what it comes down to," said Nora, tying the tape round Samuel's file. "But actually it's not all that bad. He has got me. And now you too."

"Could you lend me his file for a couple of days? I have nothing to do at the hotel. I'd like to copy it out or at least make some notes. Could you?"

"Maybe I could," she muttered.

◀◈▶

I suspected that with his tales of murders committed by young guerrillas and runaways Jackson was doing his best to scare me, put me off my friendship with Sam, and show me that the boy didn't deserve any sympathy at all. He kept insistently returning to stories about macabre pogroms and massacres. And about their perpetrators—children.

"In the village of Gere Gere they murdered everyone. First they caught all the children, tied up the adults, threw them to the ground, and killed them one by one. They told the prisoners to light a bonfire on the road, put a large cauldron on it, and boil some water. They cut off some of the corpses' heads, hands, and feet and threw them into the pot. Then they forced those they had not yet battered to death to eat human flesh. Finally they killed them too. Another time, in the Agoro hills on the border with Sudan, some guerrillas running away from the army encountered a funeral procession. They ordered the mourners to cook with sorghum and eat the remains they were carrying in the coffin to the graveyard. And in the village of Mucwini, not far from Kitgum, first they ordered parents to kill their children, and then children to kill their parents. Has anyone told you the guerrillas use the same tools for killing that the peasants use for farming the land?"

The sheer, mind-boggling cruelty and boundlessness of the evil committed filled Jackson with disgust and horror. But the more he repulsed these images, because they took away his peace and sense of security, ruining his life, the more forcefully they kept returning, disgusting and disturbing.

"I also knew this one guy who killed his father and his brother," he told me. "He lived in our village, in Atiak. They ran into some guerrillas on the road. The guerrillas announced that only one of the three would survive, and pressed an ax into his hands. Afterward he explained that he was made unconscious by fear, and that they'd have killed his father anyway, because he was old and couldn't have withstood the journey through the bush, but his brother was only four and wasn't fit to be a prisoner. He hacked them both to death with the ax, and indeed he himself survived. Three years later he managed to escape from the guerrillas. He went back to the village, but before then he was treated at the center in Gulu, like that Samuel of yours. Not everyone in the village was willing to accept him, but finally it was decided that he could come and live with his mother. And then sometime later he had an argument with a much older boy in the neighborhood, attacked him with a knife, and killed him. He was taken to prison in Kampala. If you'd like to meet him, I could probably help you."

For some time now Jackson had been planning a trip to Kampala. He said he needed to confer with the owners of the King FM radio station before the presidential elections.

"You can never be sure with them. You can never work out what it is they want, what they like and what they don't like," he complained.

During the last elections he had almost lost his job. His conversations with the voters in Gulu had displeased some officers from the local garrison. In Kampala some officials at the Ministry of Information had written to the heads of the radio station complaining about him and, afraid of losing their license, its owners had told Jackson to apologize to the army people and not get involved in politics anymore. But how could you not get involved in politics when the country was electing a new president?

"I have to know what and how," said Jackson, "so there won't be any problems later on."

He was encouraging me to make the journey to Kampala too, promising to take me to a school where girls who had run away from the guerrilla camps were sent. "They have killed too," he said. "And they didn't just fight in the guerrillas; they were given to the commanders as wives and bore them children. Children, mothers and murderesses."

I thought the suggestion of an expedition to Kampala was Jackson's latest stratagem to lure me away from Gulu and put me off its murky business and my meetings with Samuel, which clearly bothered him.

"I remembered that I know a journalist in Kampala who could tell you about Dominic Ongwen. Now, before the elections, he should be in the city."

⟞◦⟝

Dominic Ongwen was one of the five most important guerrilla leaders. Some said he had been killed in a skirmish with the army in Teso, and there were others who swore they had seen his dead body with their own eyes in Soroti. But shortly after, rumors went round that he had survived, not even lightly wounded, and had managed to get across the Nile and make his way into Congo, where he was hiding in the jungle.

Before being abducted by the guerrillas and changed into one of them, following his mother's death he had lived with his aunt and three brothers in the village of Olwal, near Gulu. As the oldest, ten-year-old Dominic worked in the fields, supported his brothers, and substituted for their father, who had abandoned the family.

One day, when he and some other boys were on their way back from the fields to the village to sit out the afternoon heat, some guerrillas had blocked their way. They had taken him with them, because he was the biggest and strongest. He had had no choice, but he didn't cry like the others, or put up any resistance. Nor did he try to escape.

After twenty years in the guerrillas he had grown up to be one of the top commanders. He was entrusted with a unit, and as a leader he had the right to possess a wife. He was assigned thirteen-year-old Florence, who had also been abducted from her village by the guerrillas. She was nine years old at the time. First she had been given as a wife to another commander, who was killed soon after in a skirmish with the army. Then she was told to move into Dominic's hut. Before escaping from the bush, she bore him two children.

Dominic became not just one of the most important, but also one of the cruelest commanders. While others tried to negotiate with the government, surrendered their weapons, or were killed in skirmishes with government troops, Dominic emerged unscathed from every ambush and never once thought of capitulating. Instead he kept ordering his men to attack and burn down villages, murder people and kidnap their children, so they would become guerrillas, as he had years before. He used to say that when he got into a bad mood he improved it by giving orders to kill people. And by killing them himself.

Finally, the international tribunal at The Hague had declared him a war criminal and issued warrants for his arrest. Never before had anyone so young been accused of crimes against humanity.

"That sort of killing changes people entirely. Apparently it comes from the fact that they order them to drink human blood," said Jackson, gazing at the heavy sun, going red above the town. "I must check at the station to see what time the buses leave for Kampala."

⁓

Despite the fact that no guerrillas had been seen in the area for a long time now, and the army had given assurances that it was in control of the situation, the last bus to Kampala left Gulu in the early afternoon, in order to cross the bridge over the Nile by the Karuma Falls before sunset, and reach its peaceful left bank.

The river formed a natural border between two different worlds. At the falls you left behind the world of the ordinary, safe, and obvious, and crossed to the right bank of the Nile, into a world of destruction and fear, which stretched deep into Acholi-land.

The bus station was located in a small square surrounded by a concrete wall, behind the gas station. As I wandered aimlessly about the town, I had sometimes dropped in there; I liked pretending to be off on a journey, so that I could take a furtive look at the travelers. From scraps of conversations I overheard, facial expressions, clothing, or luggage I could guess where they were going and for what purpose, or where they were coming from.

I like bus stations. I prefer them to soulless airports, and to railroad stations, which are gloomy, ponderous, full of worries and sorrow, and stink of old scrap metal. Railroad stations make you think of goodbyes, parting, and inevitability. Bus stations by contrast conjure up a carefree mood, lightheartedness, promise, and adventure. They fill you with eagerness and hope.

By day the bus station at Gulu was like a crowded bazaar, into which some buses had blundered, clearly by mistake; unable to force their way through the crowd, they had come to a helpless standstill among the market stalls. The stalls were packed so tightly and densely around the bus stops that it was impossible to see the bulletin boards on which the drivers hung up the names of the destination cities.

Clutching the door with one hand and gripping tickets and rolls of greasy banknotes in the other, the conductors called out to the travelers, shouting over the noise of the bazaar and the music booming from all directions. Kampala! Juba! Kitgum! Arua! In all this noise, heat, and dust, among the portable mobile stalls selling fruits, candy, drinks, and newspapers, the colored buses pushed their way pell-mell, anything to get nearer the gate, finally break free of the station, and race their passengers away over open ground.

I would walk across the bus station to take a shortcut to church. I even used to look in there when I had a little time to spare before meeting with Jackson. Franklin's Inn was very close by. In fact in this town everything was close to everything else. They all knew each other here, and they knew all about each other. After a few days in Gulu I felt as if I too had already been everywhere and was familiar with everything. In the streets I kept recognizing and greeting the same people.

Only at Franklin's Inn, when darkness fell on the town and everything lost its daytime color, did it occur to me that maybe it was just an illusion, and at most those I took to be familiar simply reminded me of people I had once known in a similar place.

◄◦►

Someone said that children make ideal soldiers because after a time and the right training they regard war as an amusement, a game they have played or would play in the yard at home or at school.

They don't feel fear of death—their own or anyone else's—because, by contrast to adults, they never think about it. They're not afraid because they've been through so little, they know so little, and have so little to lose. They lack experiences, plans and dreams, commitments and responsibilities.

However, Samuel claimed that he had never liked being a guerrilla, and the gun he was given for his own filled him with fear rather than pride. He hated it with all his heart, but he would never be parted from it.

He was given the gun after a long march that lasted almost a month across savannahs, forests, and mountains to Sudan. In the clearing, where he killed for the first time under the mango tree, he was loaded with a heavy sack of plundered sorghum.

"Just you drop it and you'll rue the day!" threatened the commander, aiming a wooden club at him.

Roped together, the other prisoners had to carry plunder captured by the guerrillas too. Samuel mentioned that they were constantly beaten. The guerrillas kept battering them with their fists, clubs, and rifle butts, and kicked anyone who fell to the ground, regardless of whether or not they had broken a rule.

Nora reckoned this beating and cruelty were a carefully devised method of forcing the prisoners to be obedient, a way of shredding their personality to start changing them from children into killers. Constant punishments, pain, and total helplessness in the face of an acute sense of injustice broke down their remaining resistance.

They weren't allowed to light bonfires that gave off smoke. They weren't allowed to talk to the other prisoners or speak at all without being asked a question. In fact they had to do everything to order only.

They were not allowed to cry. Whenever a prisoner failed to hold back his tears, of pain, misery, or homesickness, the guerrillas attacked him furiously and beat him mercilessly, as fiercely as if a child's sobbing were a lethal threat to them. Indeed, it reminded them of times not so long ago when they themselves were ordinary children, and transported them back to a world to which—although it still existed very nearby—they could never return. The guerrillas killed all runaways. They even killed those who were merely suspected of thinking about escape.

Escape is pointless, and obedience crucial. That was the next rule they quickly assimilated. And another one: Give nothing of yourself away, don't betray yourself in any way. Put on an act before others, and best of all before yourself too. This pretending was the most vital thing of all. You couldn't trust anyone or confide in anyone. Sincerity rashly shown to the wrong person could mean suffering and death. Samuel had seen the guerrillas beat a boy to death when he incautiously revealed to a friend from the same village that he missed his mother.

As they moved across the savannah, the guerrillas spied out white ribbons of smoke rising from the ground, which gave away human settlements. Then they would lie in wait until dusk, and attack by night. Left behind in the camp with the other prisoners, Samuel heard screams in the distance, and sometimes he thought he saw bright flames from burning huts shining through the darkness. The guerrillas would come back with stolen plunder and more kidnapped children. On the first night they were forced, just like Samuel, to commit their first murder, the initiation rite that was to change them forever.

"The smallest ones are best suited to it," said Nora.

Leaning her head back, with both hands she tried to tame her hair, ruffled by a sudden gust of wind. Unlike most of the girls in the town, who braided their hair into cornrows, Nora straightened hers and wore it tied on the nape of her neck. A wide grayish scar cut across the dark, almost navy blue skin on her arm.

Yellow blades of dry grass began to whirl in the yard.

"There's going to be another storm," she muttered.

She turned around and playfully grabbed a small boy who, while sheltering from the wind behind her, had suddenly been blinded by dust and had clutched at her dress. Nora took him by the hand and stood him in front of her.

"The youngest ones are best suited to it, like him," she repeated. She stared at the boy, as if trying to guess his age. "Eight, nine years old, not more. These ones are already independent and strong enough to understand and do what they are told. And at the same time they're too small to tell the difference between good and bad. You can still teach them anything you like."

⟨⟨⟩⟩

Jackson and I left Franklin's Inn before dusk, before the first children from Palenga and the other camps scattered around Gulu had reached the town. They invariably arrived at the same time, as the sun was making its final efforts to remain above the horizon; soon, having over-estimated its own strength, it would sink slowly over the manioc fields, and disappear behind a darkening wall of trees. The children's march into town was repeated like a ritual, like the hands of a clock going around or a daily prayer, uttered mindlessly, just out of habit, as a duty.

By day, in the bright sunlight, Gulu belonged to the adults. With nightfall, plunged into darkness, it passed into the hands of the children. The adults yielded it to them solemnly, without a word, as if that was what the normal, long-established order of events was meant to be. At night the number of children in Gulu was three times the number of adult citizens by day. At dawn the children gave them back the town, and without protest dissolved like apparitions in the growing daylight.

Nora called them the night wanderers.

They came to the town to get through the night safely. Their own parents, adults, had sent them on their way. Only like that, by driving the children out of their homes for the night, could they protect them from a deadly danger—from the guerillas, who like predatory animals set out at night to hunt down their victims, circling the huts in the brushwood and then suddenly launching an attack. No villager would have dared or known how to stand up to them, or refused to hand over everything they demanded. And they usually came in order to take the children.

The guerrillas never came into the town, where the troops were stationed, not even at night, when the soldiers were shut behind the walls of their barracks. In Gulu the children were safe. Here nothing threatened them, and they weren't a threat to anyone else either. To spend the night safely in the town, some of them had to walk over six miles, so they set off straight after school, and got up before dawn to be on time for the first bell. Those with the furthest to go only went home to their parents on Sundays when the schools were closed.

Before the town gave them some old warehouses as a shelter, they would bed down for the night outside, lying on pieces of torn cardboard spread out on the hot asphalt. The rain would drive them under the arcades running along the streets, and they also came down to the bus station, to the bazaar, where they stretched out on the stalls left there for the night by the market traders. When they began climbing over the fence and sleeping in the gravel courtyard outside the church, the local priests, white missionaries, came out to spend the night with them. The priests also brought them food and blankets, and it was they who persuaded the town authorities and the troops to provide the night wanderers with some shelters. One of them was called Noah's Ark.

One Sunday during holy mass, the local archbishop, with the proud name of John Baptist Odama, gave a sermon explaining to the townspeople that the children who descended on them by night deserved the sort of sympathy and support that are shown to families after a death.

"However you look at it, these children are already dead as far as the world is concerned," said the archbishop.

The military from the local garrison soon realized that there was a close connection between the number of children coming into town for the night and the situation in the local area. Whenever the war in Acholi-land died down, the night wanderers became less numerous. But when more of them came for the night, it meant the guerrillas were back in the vicinity. At those times an emergency was declared in Gulu and at the local garrison. Unable to do any more for them, the citizens yielded the town to the children for the night by way of compensation and absolution.

No one had ever made an announcement or reached an agreement on this matter. Quite simply, with the first signs of approaching night the town began to settle down. Looking around and checking to see that nothing had been forgotten, like a traveler before a long and unfamiliar journey, it gradually emptied in the falling twilight. Everyone wanted to get home before night set in for good.

As the town changed hands at dusk, its citizens and the night wanderers seemed to avoid one another, trying not to cross each other's path. The children made their way along the streets and laid out their beds on the ground, mistrustfully at first, casting frightened glances at the departing adults. They too seemed to be feeling a presentiment of evil.

In Acholi-land, children prompted unbounded, though closely concealed fear, especially after dark. At the sight of children, the villagers working in the fields dropped everything and took to their heels. Encountering children on the road, drivers accelerated. In general strangers were greeted here with anxiety rather than the curiosity that was usual elsewhere. People expected the worst of them.

As they let the children into their town for the night, the citizens of Gulu furtively cast fearful glances too. They were unsure if the people they were trying to save might not prove to be their curse. In the fading light they tried to perceive the usual, reassuring innocence in the children's faces—or any sign of the terrible transformation that they found incomprehensible and horrifying.

◄◦►

"Are you sure I didn't give it to you?" Squatting by the safe, Nora was looking for Samuel's file on the shelves.

"No, you didn't—you just said you would."

"Well then, it has to be here somewhere. I've always put it back in here, haven't I?"

Before I asked to borrow the file, Nora always had it at hand. Whenever she was unsure of something and wanted to check a detail or a date, she reached into the safe and immediately had the answer to everything. The file disappeared when I asked if she would lend it to me for a couple of days. First Nora claimed she had to ask the permission of her boss, Mark, head of the children's treatment center. When I said I had already spoken to him, she hissed like an angry cat.

"What do you need the file for? You can have Samuel. Take him with you, and be done with it."

Barefoot, with unruly locks of hair falling on her worried face, she looked like a little girl helplessly searching a basket of toys for a missing favorite doll.

"I have no idea where it has gone. Someone must have taken it."

She got up from the floor and stretched, holding her sides like a weary woman taking a break from work in a paddy field or a manioc patch.

She had several incarnations. Sometimes she was a smart, elegant girl with big-city manners, plans, and aspirations. She wanted to go back to Kampala, find a job at the university, and write academic papers. She said she preferred that sort of life. She had come to work in Gulu to pay her debt to fortune. "Those who have succeeded should do something for those who haven't been as lucky," she used to say. But she didn't want to stay here forever. "One more year, two at most, and I'm going back to Kampala," she would say in a decisive tone, like someone who knows what they want and is sure they're going to achieve it. At such moments she really didn't suit the town of Gulu, lost in the northern savannahs. She seemed like someone foreign, an outsider. Like me.

At other times she seemed to belong here, hardly any different from the local women to be found at the bazaar, with their idle, lumbering movements. Like them she would burst into loud, husky laughter, covering her mouth with a hand as if embarrassed by her own voice and amusement.

"Well, it's not there." She locked the safe, pushing back a lock of hair that was hanging in her eyes. "So what are you going to do at the hotel on your own now?"

"No harm done, maybe I'll do some reading. I'll sort out my notes. And I'll look in on you tomorrow."

"Yes, you do that..."

The guerrilla unit that kidnapped Samuel from his village kept grow-ing by the day. In clearings and gorges it joined up with other ones or acquired new prisoners. One day they turned north. They marched through deserted villages that had been burned down and pillaged, and passed weed-choked bean and manioc fields. The only human beings they very occasionally met were old people who hadn't deserted their villages to escape the war and the guerrillas. Wizened and wrinkled, they looked more like withered wild trees than people.

When the commanders questioned them about military patrols, food, or water, they didn't answer, as if they didn't understand what was being said to them or, after being isolated for so long, had forgotten human speech. They never begged for their lives to be spared, and they showed no sign of fear. It was as if they didn't feel pain when the infuriated guerrillas beat and knocked them to the ground. They didn't even raise their hands to shield themselves from the blows.

The journey through the wilderness seemed endless. On and on and on they marched. Samuel had never walked for such a long time with-out any rest before. He had no idea how far behind he had left his home village. With every day of the march the bush gave way to more and more savannah, and the mango groves changed into acacia thickets.

Loaded down with plunder, dead tired, in total silence they marched from dawn to sunset. Sometimes they only made a short stop at noon for refreshments and a rest before carrying on. When night fell, they stopped and slept at the first suitable place.

Sometimes rivers and streams cut across their route. Then the guer-rillas stopped and spent a long time conferring. Although the forest streams were so narrow and shallow that you could easily cross them by wading up to your knees, Samuel thought he could see uncertainty and fear in the guerrillas' eyes. They would go quiet, and the commanders would mutter prayers. Before finally advancing to the other side, all the guerrillas, and the prisoners too, had to take off their shoes.

Samuel did not recognize the rivers they crossed. Until one day some gray mountains appeared on the horizon, and down in a valley they came to a fairly large river, with clumps of papyrus growing along its banks. Samuel heard the guerrillas calling the river Aswa. They seemed to be overjoyed, as if it were not a river, but a long-lost, greatly missed friend. The river Aswa, fast and mighty in the rainy season, rushing to merge with the Blue Nile, marked the border between Gulu and Kitgum, lying to the northeast. Further on, beyond the mountains, which every day became bigger, more distinct, and more ominous, must be Sudan, where—as the adults used to say—the guerrillas had their hideouts.

Finally, after many days on the move, one morning they reached a village whose inhabitants were children. Samuel thought most of them were older than him, but he also saw boys much younger than himself. They had long, matted hair, and wore outsize calf-length rubber boots, like the ones he had seen soldiers wearing. Some of the boys were dressed in baggy army jackets.

This was to be the end of the journey. First they were herded into the marketplace and lined up in several ranks with the inhabitants of the village before an adult man dressed in a long, flowing robe. They recited a prayer, repeating it after him as he ran his fingers along the beads of a rosary and said: "Our Father, who art in heaven, hallowed be Thy name, Thy will be done, on earth as it is in heaven."

Then the prisoners were untied and told they were in Sudan. From here there was no escape. They didn't know the area, and even if set free they couldn't have found their way home. But in any case, they had a perfect memory of the crimes they had committed on the way, and believed that if they ever went home they not only would be severely punished for them, but would also bring vengeance upon their families.

In the Sudanese village the children abducted from Uganda were divided among the guerrillas' families. The girls, who made up almost half the prisoners, were distributed to the guerrilla commanders and more highly trained guerrillas as wives. From then on they would have to bear their children, take care of their homes, and sometimes fight as well.

Samuel ended up with commander Opiro's family. As well as the commander, it included his four wives, several children who had been born in the guerrilla camp, and two boys older than Samuel who had already become guerrillas instead of prisoners and carried guns. One of them, Vincent, later explained to Samuel that several guerrilla families made up a unit, and several units made up a brigade. There were five brigades, and soon they were going to meet their commander-in-chief, master, and leader.

His name was Joseph Kony, and the guerrillas spoke of him as God the Father.

—◦—

I asked Samuel about Kony more than once. He said that at first sight he looked like one of the children at the Sudanese village.

"He had the same long hair as them. Except that he was taller. He is very, very big."

Whenever he talked about Kony, there was none of the tension in his voice that I could sense when he spoke about his own ordeal. He had no inhibitions holding him back—on the contrary, sometimes, noticing my interest, he would voluntarily steer the conversation round to life in the guerrillas. But once he started to tell his story, he would stare at me, trying to guess if I was interested or bored. I suspected he was doing his best to say what he believed I most wanted to hear. The effort he had begun to put into his tales was causing the tension that now came with them.

He chose his words carefully too, and spoke purposefully.

"Goodness! Sam! How nicely you talk!" Nora once exclaimed, when she overheard our conversation.

The boy was disconcerted, but instantly glanced at me; seeing no hint of mockery, he smiled broadly, very pleased with himself. A few days later Nora told me that he had been asking her how to say certain Acholi words in English.

But when he talked about Kony, he was not as tense, as if he didn't care if the story of the mysterious leader of the murky guerrilla sect would entertain me. He felt free of responsibility for what he was saying. Or maybe he had no doubt it would be interesting.

"I once saw him in uniform, and another time in a white robe, the kind priests wear in church. When he addressed us in the square, he looked like the president or a bishop."

"Have you ever seen a bishop?"

"Once, in church in Gulu. But he was fatter and bald."

◄◦►

Jackson only talked about Kony when we were alone.

At first we used to meet at his office. That was where I made his acquaintance soon after arriving in Gulu. I was walking past on my way back to the hotel from town one evening when Jackson appeared out of nowhere in front of me. Beaming with joy, as if greeting a long-awaited friend, he declared: "You must be a journalist from abroad." When I nodded, he introduced himself, with a look of relief on his face. "Well, you've come to the right place. I'm a journalist too. You won't find a better guide and interpreter than me around here," he said. "Something told me we would meet."

The next day, on my way from the hotel to town, I went to find him at his office. He didn't seem surprised.

He prepared radio news bulletins. He told the townspeople about world events in faraway countries, which neither they nor he had ever seen. I never heard him talk on the radio about the issues he knew thoroughly, the things Gulu and the whole of Acholi-land actually lived with on a daily basis—such as the night wanderers, the war, the soldiers, and the juvenile guerrillas or their mysterious leader.

When we were at his office, he would never even mention Kony's name. He would say "the guerrillas" or "the Lord's Army," but he avoided the name of its leader as if it were a sinister spell that could cause misfortune.

If I mentioned Kony's name while asking him questions about the war and the guerrillas, even though he didn't usually suffer from too much work, Jackson would suddenly be extremely busy, or his memory or hearing would let him down.

"Is it true he's possessed by spirits?" I asked.

"Spirits?" he muttered, without looking up from the morning paper lying open on his desk. At neighboring desks his colleagues were idly looking through the agency wires. "I don't quite understand what you're talking about."

"What about the village he comes from? Is it possible to go there? There must be some relatives of his living there, or people who knew him."

"It's terribly hot in here. Can we talk about it this evening? I have a lot of work to do today."

At Franklin's Inn his memory returned.

"You asked about the village Kony comes from. I've remembered. It's called Odek, it's a few kilometers from Gulu."

"Is it possible to go there?"

"But what for?" He shrugged. "To all intents and purposes it's no longer there."

"What about its inhabitants? Someone must have known Kony."

"No, there's no one there."

"Why didn't you tell me that this morning? I'd have had time to go there and get back before evening. Are you afraid to talk about Kony in front of people?"

"Am I afraid?"

Finally, however, he realized that he did owe me an explanation.

"There are certain matters we do not talk about here," he said, as if it were an excuse. Sensing that it wasn't enough, he thought for a while and said: "In your country you can say those things, right?" He had confirmed his own thoughts, as if declaring himself to be right.

"You mean the spirits that get into people?"

"Do you believe in that?"

"Do you?"

"Who would believe in such a thing . . ."

A fat waitress in tight trousers idly wiped the table with a cloth and put down some frosted bottles of beer.

"And what happens to a person whom a spirit enters?" I asked.

"What would you expect? Some lose consciousness and can't remember anything afterwards, others lose their minds and never come out of their insanity. They say that while a person is possessed he ceases to be himself and only does what the spirit tells him to. Sometimes the spirit chooses the person it wants to possess, but it's also possible for someone to send a spirit after you."

"So the person whom the spirit enters isn't even aware of it?"

"For sure, that can happen. Have you never had the thought: Why am I doing all this? And how do you know the people you meet here aren't possessed, and are only talking to you because the spirits have told them to? Maybe a spirit has entered me too and told me to meet with you. Or maybe it's you that's possessed."

The image conjured by his imagination, of me, possessed by spirits from Gulu, plainly amused him. "Here we have a whole multitude of very weird spirits of every possible kind."

◄◦►

Before coming to Gulu I had gone through lots of old newspapers looking for articles about Joseph Kony, but I had only found two photographs of him. One shows him standing in the midst of his commanders. He has long hair and is wearing an army jacket, and seems to be conferring with his comrades, or maybe the photographer simply caught them having an ordinary chat. Kony is turning his head, as if he has just been distracted from the conversation. He looks relaxed, or even amused. I couldn't find anything sinister or disturbing in his face, expression, or figure.

In the other picture, which came from a Sudanese paper, Kony is with a small group of girls with shaven heads wearing light knee-length dresses. Kony is standing behind them with a scarf on his head to protect him from the sun. He's wearing a loose white shirt and black trousers, and he's barefoot. His arms are stretched wide to embrace the children, as if he were blessing them or asking for them to be blessed. In this pose his figure is shaped like a cross.

"I've seen other ones too," said Jackson, when I showed him the pictures of Kony at my hotel. He scrutinized them, trying to make out and understand new details and signs, and also to check in case the old ones he could remember had changed their meaning. "I think one was from Uganda and the other from Sudan. In the one from Uganda he was wearing a shirt saying: BORN TO BE WILD. In the other he was holding a service at the camp. He looked like a sort of saint. He was in a long white robe, the kind the Sudanese Arabs wear. Or maybe it was a lady's dress? People say he sometimes wears women's clothing. And the last time he had his picture taken he was wearing a green army uniform with a general's epaulets."

Apparently there was another photograph of Kony in motorbike goggles, holding a child on his knees. Jackson also mentioned a movie made by the guerrillas which showed Kony leading the attack on a village. He was waving a rifle and was just about to give his people the order to set the huts on fire. But Jackson had never seen this movie and didn't believe it actually existed.

Perhaps no one knew what Kony was really like. He hadn't met any outsiders for years. And even those who had seen him, like the guerrillas, said that every time he looked different. Sometimes he seemed so ordinary that he could have blended in with the crowd on the street in Gulu without being noticed. But another time he looked different from everybody else, strong and handsome, like a giant, a being from another world.

The doctors in Kampala maintained that Kony was a psychopath, a mentally unbalanced person suffering from a split personality, wavering between fits of paranoia and a superiority complex. From the fact that he used to touch his face while talking, others concluded that he was a shy, unconfident man.

What was known about him was that he was approaching fifty, came from the Palaro tribe, and was born in the village of Odek in the Gulu district. His father, Luwigi Obol, was the village teacher and preacher, and his mother, Nora Anek Oting, took care of the household. As a small boy, after school Joseph Kony used to graze his father's cows by the stream.

He was a well-behaved, quiet child. Among his peers he was only distinct for being fond of the dances held in the village during tribal ceremonies and festivals. He also sang in the church choir and served at mass. He was a poor student who never finished elementary school.

He completed four grades without even learning to speak English well. Those who remember him from that time claim that his parents took him out of school because they had no money for his further education. In an interview for a Sudanese newspaper Kony himself said he had stopped going to school after spirits had begun to haunt him in his sleep, revealing to him the mystery of healing and telling him to cure people of their illnesses.

As a youth he had joined an armed unit commanded by one Major Benjamin Apia, who was fighting against bandits attacking Acholi villages to steal cattle. He had agreed to take Kony on to treat the sick and wounded.

He was twenty-five the first time Lakwena entered him, the "Holy Spirit" who is the most powerful spirit of all and who commands everything. Possessed by Lakwena, Joseph Kony headed into the Awere mountains, where he prayed and fasted for sixty days. And when he came back to the village, he announced that at night Lakwena had entered him again and told him to create his own army; at its head he was to conquer the whole of Uganda, eradicate evil and sin, and establish the righteous order of the Lord. That was why he had decided to call his troops the Lord's Army, before leading them into a war that would be final and definitive.

In the lands of the Acholi in northern Uganda, on the right bank of the Nile, war had been going on for so long that many people thought it would last forever. All sorts of armed factions, with long names that were hard to remember, were endlessly murdering, looting, and destroying the villages.

For centuries the Acholi and their neighbors had fought over the herds of cattle that were their most valuable possession, their source of pride and even identity. They had also fought over grazing land, water holes, and slaves. However, they had only discovered what war is, or rather what it can be, when the British appeared on their lands, white men who came from faraway Europe and declared this part of Africa to be their property, an overseas colony, a pearl in the imperial crown.

The first natives the British took to serve on their estates at the heart of Africa, on the great lake named after Queen Victoria, were from the

Bugandan tribe. They were close at hand, living in a kingdom the British had conquered. Rich, and of a peaceful disposition, they spent their time cultivating the land and fishing. They were used to discipline and obedience to their ruler, the *Kabaka*, or king, so they were ideally suited to becoming loyal vassals of the Crown. They were also the first tribe to adopt the European newcomers' Christian faith.

The British officials made sure that none of the races subject to the Crown ever gained an advantage over any others, and especially that none of them grew so strong in the colonial service as to rebel or demand independence. Seeing the rising influence and wealth of the Bugandans, eventually the British began to discharge them from their colonial troops, the King's African Rifles, and replace them with warriors from tribes living in the north, on the banks of the Nile, including the Madi, Lugbara, Lango, Kakwa, and Acholi. As a result, under the British protectorate in Uganda the officials, teachers, and tradesmen were Bugandans, and the soldiers were mainly from the northern tribes.

After shedding a lot of blood in the world wars the British pulled out of Africa and Asia, and finally granted their colonies freedom. In Uganda they divided power between the peoples of the north and south. The Kabaka of Buganda, Frederick Mutesa II, became president of the country, and the prime minister was Milton Apollo Obote from the Lango tribe.

Though incorporated into a single state and proclaimed its citizens, the peoples of the north and south were unable to live together in harmony. First, with the help of his compatriots from the army, Obote overthrew the Kabaka-president. Then he in turn was deposed by his chief of staff, Idi Amin from the Kakwa people. After each coup the corpses lay thick on the ground, as the new rulers murdered everyone who had served their predecessors, as well as any real or imaginary rivals to the throne, subversives, and rebels.

During the reign of Idi Amin, Uganda gained the sinister reputation of a savage country, out of control, a land of shocking violence and rape that went unpunished. The nightmare appeared to have no limits and no end. They even seemed to have stopped bothering to bury the corpses—there were so many of them that they couldn't keep up with the burials, so the victims' remains were thrown into Lake Victoria and the Nile for fish and crocodiles to devour.

With every coup d'état, as each new ruler came to power, impossible as it might seem, the fighting became even bloodier, even more savage. Under Amin's rule a quarter of a million people were murdered. After Amin, Obote took power again, and under his rule a further half million people were killed.

Obote was overthrown by the rebel generals Tito and Basilio Okello, the first Ugandan rulers to come from the Acholi people. Only when power was taken away from the generals by the next rebel, Yoweri Kaguta Museveni, and returned to the south, did peace finally prevail in Uganda. But in the meantime the war shifted to Acholi-land and dug itself in, as if with no intention of ever leaving the place again.

Disaster struck the Acholi at their time of greatest triumph, when their countryman from Kitgum, General Tito Okello, had gained power in Uganda. Earlier, although their cousins from across the Nile, Obote and Amin, had held power, the Acholi had only benefited from their patronage to a small degree. Obote took them into his army and sent them to the south to crush rebellions in the kingdoms of Buganda, Toro, Ankole, and Bunjoro, loot and burn the villages, kill the rebels, and kidnap the women. But Obote surrounded himself with no one but his own compatriots from the Lango people, and assigned the best and most lucrative positions to them.

Amin, who overthrew Obote, saw the Acholi as loyal soldiers of the man he had deposed. He didn't trust them, and suspected them of conspiring against him, until finally he had hundreds of Acholi officers murdered in their barracks. Then he replaced them with his own Kakwa countrymen and with ruthless killers from Sudan, who were so blindly loyal and obedient to his every nod that he made them his personal bodyguard.

When Obote returned to power after deposing Amin, he took the Acholi into the army again, but only as before to stifle rebellion in the south; meanwhile he continued to favor the Lango people. Soon the soldiers were clashing with each other, participating in rape and murder, and were starting to lose the war against the guerrillas. Finally the army revolted. Though passed over for promotion and higher pay, the Acholi officers had declared allegiance to the president, but now, seeing that no one was defending him anymore, they deposed him and expelled him from the country.

Many of the Acholi believed that their long-awaited destiny had finally come true. While serving in the British army and fighting for it in Africa, Asia, and Europe, they had willingly let themselves be persuaded that they were born soldiers, proud, invincible warriors destined to win wars and rule the country.

But the rebels from the south, who had declared war on Obote, had absolutely no intention of recognizing either their authority or their precedence. On the contrary, they saw the Acholi soldiers not as rulers, to whom they owed allegiance and respect but as hateful enemies on whom they should inflict revenge for past injuries. For serving in Obote's and Amin's armies and quelling several rebellions in the south, the Acholi deserved hatred and retribution. Wasn't it their fault that Uganda had flowed with blood for a quarter of a century? Hadn't they murdered the citizens of the south without mercy, hadn't they raped, looted villages, exterminated the population, and hauled off stolen plunder to the north, to Gulu and Kitgum? But even so, when Museveni, the guerrilla leader, unexpectedly renounced a truce he had signed earlier, and after a short, violent war captured Kampala, the Acholi felt cheated and wronged. "After all, it was we who overthrew Obote," they kept saying. "But Museveni repaid us for that with betrayal."

Anticipating ruthless requital for the years of tyranny, rape, and pillage, in panic the Acholi fled to the right side of the Nile. Terrified by the threat of vengeance, pogroms, tribunals, execution squads, and the gallows, the recent officials and officers who came from the native parts of the former leaders, Okello, Obote, and Amin, incited their compatriots against the new president from the south, threatened slaughter and massacres, and called for rebellion, a new war.

In Acholi-land chaos and lawlessness reigned. Their leader, the overthrown president Tito Okello, fled to Sudan. Taking advantage of the power vacuum, Karamojong warriors started raiding Acholi villages and stealing their cattle. And as if that weren't enough, a terrible drought set in, which scorched the pastureland and dried up the wells. When the first soldiers of the new president, Yoweri Museveni, appeared on the right bank of the Nile, the Acholi saw them not as saviors but as invaders eager for revenge.

◀◦▶

Before thirty-year-old Alice Auma headed the Acholi armed rebellion, she lived in her native village of Bungatira and sold fish at a market barely ten kilometers from Gulu. She wasn't a beauty, but she was a fine, strong, healthy woman. But to the surprise and concern of her neighbors, even though she was twice married she never had any children, so both times she was returned home to her father, Severino Lukoya.

She was different. She was like a giant, a head taller than most of the men. To cure her of her shameful infertility, her father took her to a succession of eleven healers and witches well known in the area, but all in vain. With each passing week the girl became more introverted, until finally she stopped taking any notice of the world around her. More and more often she lost consciousness, but whenever it happened, instead of falling to the ground in a faint, she started muttering mysterious words that other people couldn't understand. Severino Lukoya claimed that his daughter had been like that since the day when, as a very small girl, she had encountered an extremely large snake.

The doctors from Kampala said that Alice was suffering from a hormonal disorder, as a result of which she didn't yet menstruate. But the villagers of Bungatira had a different way of interpreting the cause of her madness. They were convinced she had been possessed by spirits, which had chosen her in order to speak to people and interfere in their lives. They were confirmed in this belief not only by Alice's strange behavior, but also by her sudden, ardent religious devotion. So they were not overly surprised when one day the girl announced that the spirit of a soldier killed half a century ago had appeared to her in the night, through whom in turn the Christian Holy Spirit was speaking. Whenever he entered her, he took control of her body and her mind. When he vanished, Alice could not remember what she had said or done. The girl called him Lakwena, the Messenger, and soon she too was known as Alice Lakwena—Alice of the Holy Spirit.

The spirit told her to go into the Paraa forest near Murchison Falls and submerge herself in the waters of the Nile. She was gone for forty days. When she came back, she said Lakwena had ordered her to drop the fish market in Gulu; from now on she was to cure people, because she had received the gift of healing. Following the spirit's instructions, she left for the nearby village of Opit, where she founded her own temple by the railroad station and began to cure people of madness and infertility.

In Acholi-land the war against the new rulers from the south was already well under way when Lakwena told Alice to form an army and call it the Holy Spirit's Army. At its head Alice was meant to defeat all armed units, not just in Acholi-land but in the whole of Uganda, and establish righteous peace and order there. She was meant not only to rescue the Acholi from destruction, but to liberate them from sin and evil spirits that brought down misfortune; then she would guide them back to the path of good, from which they had strayed. Those who nevertheless refused to be converted would suffer a terrible punishment on Judgment Day—they would be bitten to death by snakes.

Before Alice of the Holy Spirit, Africa had already seen plenty of similar leaders, self-proclaimed prophets, messiahs, and saviors promising to bring an end to misery, compensate for past wrongs, and get rid of slavery. Characters like this have appeared in Kenya, Tanzania, Congo, Mozambique, and Zimbabwe. They have fought wars not just in the real world, but also on a mystical plane full of spells and spirits that are invisible to others, yet determine their fates. They have summoned people to fight against their enemies, and also against their own inadequacies which lead them into evil. According to their claims, only victory in both struggles—against the enemy, on the battlefield, and against their own weaknesses—could bring the ultimate victory and the ultimate solution, freedom, and salvation, or restore the natural order.

Severely oppressed by war and fearing the terrible vengeance the alien government would inflict on them, the Acholi believed that Alice had been chosen by the spirits and was capable of saving them from annihilation. In any case, they didn't have much choice. Their guerrilla factions, led by experienced officers who were army deserters, were being routed by government troops. Beaten again and again, the guerrillas kept throwing down their guns and taking to their heels. Those who still refused to accept defeat went to serve Alice of the Holy Spirit. What did they have to lose? They had already tried everything else. Meanwhile Alice promised that if they came under her command and blindly obeyed her, no one would ever beat them again.

The main thing she demanded of them was faith. As she sent her troops into battle, she told them to sing psalms and anoint their bodies with special walnut oil which would change the enemy bullets into water. She also put spells on stones—when thrown at the enemy they were supposed to explode like grenades, or turn into swarms of stinging bees or poisonous snakes. Her guerrillas were not allowed to aim at the enemy. This was done for them by consecrated water, with which priests appointed by Alice sprinkled their guns and bullets. Once fired, these bullets were supposed to draw the sign of the cross in the air, and then go straight to their target.

All this was ordered and achieved by the spirit Lakwena, who had chosen Alice as his medium and spoke through her. But sometimes, quite often, even the guerrillas who had been smeared in holy oil were killed on the battlefield. Then Alice of the Holy Spirit would explain to those who had survived that death could strike anyone who did not believe strongly enough in Lakwena, or had broken one of the many laws he made and announced through her mediation.

At first, poorly armed but with blind faith in victory and in the righteousness of their cause, Alice's guerrillas carried off some astonishing successes in their war against the Ugandan army. Soldiers sent from the south were seized with alarm as soon as they heard that the Holy Spirit's Army was approaching. These soldiers too believed in spirits interfering in human affairs. At home in Buganda, Ankole, or Bunyoro, they would have known how to deal with them, but in Acholi-land they were helpless and defenseless. It was enough for them to hear the guerrillas singing psalms, it was enough for the first shot to be fired, and they fled in the opposite direction.

⤜◦⤛

So it was no surprise that Alice of the Holy Spirit's guerrilla army began to achieve some unusual victories. News of the invincible warriors ran like wildfire right round Acholi-land. Each day new volunteers turned up at Alice's camp, eager for victory, vengeance, order, and justice. Not only former soldiers came to join her, but also herders and peasants who had lost their cattle, pastureland, and fields, rich traders, school and college students, and even ministers from failed governments.

From 150 guerrillas who defeated the government troops in their first battle at Corner Kilak, the army of the Holy Spirit grew into a force of several thousand, which occupied Kitgum and then headed for Lira, Soroti, Kumi, Mbale, and Tororo, until it reached the city of Jinja, only about a hundred kilometers from the capital, Kampala. But at that point Alice's magic power left her. According to her soldiers, it happened the day she ordered them to cross the Nile. The spirits who had entered her had already been complaining that she wasn't obeying them, and wasn't serving them as before. It may have been that while crossing the Nile, contrary to Lakwena's instructions, Alice's army did not show due respect to the great river and offended it, causing their former ally to change into an enemy. Lakwena himself tried to call his chosen woman to order with severe punishments, but starving and flogging her for disobedience and idleness were to no avail. Alice was losing her power, and her supporters were starting to wonder if she wasn't just one of the ordinary witches so common in Acholi-land.

The Ugandan government sent half its troops against the warriors of the Holy Spirit's Army attacking from the north. It was said that in order to beat Alice, the president had some very powerful witches brought to Kampala from Pemba Island, and from Congo too.

The decisive battle finally took place in the forest near the settlement of Magamaga, on the road from Jinja to Iganga. Deprived of Lakwena's wise orders, Alice's army was routed. Beaten and shocked, as if suddenly awoken from deep sleep, the guerrillas fled to save their skins, and made their own way home. Alice escaped on a bicycle toward the sacred Mount Elgon, visible in the distance, across the border in Kenya.

Ten years later I met her there at a refugee camp outside Nairobi.

Situated among cornfields beyond the town of Thika, the Makengeni camp was no different from similar refugee settlements I had seen in other African countries. It had the same gray tarpaulin tents and huts made of reeds and bamboo, covered in blue plastic handed out by foreign charities.

Alice was spending her sixth year in Makengeni. In Nairobi it was said that the camp near Thika would soon be closed, and its inhabitants would be transported north to Dadaab, in the hot desert part of the country, right on the Somali border. Although they called Alice their guest, the Kenyan government would not allow her any journeys or even visits. Nor would they let her comment on Uganda, so although she came out to greet me, she didn't say a word.

Ugandan president Museveni had tried to have Alice of the Holy Spirit brought back to the country, in an effort to win over the still mistrustful Acholi. The Kenyan president had offered to swap the girl for a Kenyan rebel hiding in Uganda, whose name was "Brigadier" John Odongo. But the plan was dropped when Museveni allowed Odongo to leave for Ghana. Then Alice imposed a condition, warning that she would only return to Uganda if President Museveni paid fifty thousand dollars compensation for cows lost in the war. This plan failed too, because as soon as the Ugandan government agreed to the sum, Alice demanded three times more.

Abandoned and forgotten, she lived with her sister and her last few supporters, who continued to address her as "Your Holiness." Alice of the Holy Spirit still regarded herself as the Christian God's favorite, whom through Lakwena He had gifted with the power of healing. She claimed that she was able to restore sight to the blind, speech to the dumb, and hearing to the deaf. She also claimed that she knew how to cure the fatal illness AIDS, which in her view was a curse imposed by God on sinners.

The doctors from Nairobi who came to examine her called her Alice in Wonderland. They thought her an intelligent person, suffering from a superiority complex and a sexual obsession. She kept repeating over and over that God was telling her to return to Uganda and find a husband who would build an altar for her and father her sons. She also said that no one had yet asked her for love.

She died unexpectedly, after being ill for only seven days. She had suddenly felt a pain in her chest, which grew stronger by the day. She refused to be taken to hospital, insisting that as she could heal, she would cure herself.

"It's a good thing she has died, because like this God's promise has been fulfilled," said Severino Lukoya, when informed of his daughter's death.

◄○►

When the spirits abandoned Alice and stopped addressing people through her, deprived of a commander, her army had been decimated and routed. But then her father, Severino Lukoya, had come on the scene. He declared that the most important spirit had chosen him instead—now Lakwena favored him, would speak through him, and had appointed him as the new commander and leader of the Holy Spirit's Army.

Before discovering that he too possessed the power of healing, old Severino had been a mason. But when Lakwena and the other spirits started to enter him, he dropped everything and founded his own church, where he and his followers prayed for salvation for the Acholi and the world. But although he told them to call him a messiah and swore that every word he uttered came from the Christian God the Father, transmitted to him via Lakwena, the Acholi did not listen to him quite as trustingly as they had Alice. He did not have his daughter's passion or the magic that caused people to place their destiny in her hands and blindly do her bidding.

They didn't believe him as firmly, or at least not with such invincible, indomitable force. Nor did they believe in the need to fight anymore—they were afraid of suffering and death, and doubted the veracity of his assurances that he had the power to save them from misfortune and evil.

So it became harder and harder for him to recruit volunteers for his war against the president in Kampala, even though he claimed victory would open the way to salvation—nothing else could guarantee peace and justice for Uganda and the world. However, weary of endless war, the Acholi refused to do any more fighting, even if this next war really was to prove definitive.

As no one was eager to join his army, he marched into the villages and demanded that fathers hand over their sons to him to be soldiers. When they refused, he took recruits by force. In time he took nothing but prisoners. But the press-ganged recruits did not fight with the same faith as Alice's warriors, and Severino proved a poor commander. He soon lost his army in skirmishes against government troops, and finally let himself be caught and thrown into jail.

Then it was the turn of Joseph Kony, a young man who claimed to be related to Alice of the Holy Spirit and Severino. He now went from village to village, putting it about that the spirits had been let down by old Severino, just as they had been disappointed by his daughter before him. Deserting them for once and for all, they had sought a new medium, and had chosen him, Joseph Kony. They had possessed him, taking control of his body and mind, but in payment they were offering him their power, the gift of leading others. They had released him from the bonds that fetter ordinary mortals. As the spirits' chosen one, Kony no longer had to answer to people, but only to Lakwena, who from now was to be his only master, judge, and confessor.

"The Creator Himself has sent me to govern you," he announced, and warned the Acholi that if they didn't submit to him they would be annihilated and eternally damned. He promised to conquer all of Uganda, or at least break the northern districts free of it and create an independent state for the Acholi, a republic on the Nile. He called the guerrilla army, at whose head he intended to achieve this, the Lord's Army.

This was now the last of the armed factions still fighting in Acholiland. Unable to face up to the government troops or to bear the hardships of army life in a constant state of fear, on the march or on the run, all the others had surrendered and laid down their weapons, dispersed or changed into gangs of ordinary bandits. But there were some people for whom peace meant not just the end of their aspirations and illusions, but also retribution and punishment for the crimes they had committed while at war. For them, Joseph Kony and his Lord's Army offered a last hope and their only salvation. So the worst torturers and outlaws, the biggest killers of all were drawn to the Lord's Army—vile, bloodthirsty, accursed people.

However, there weren't enough of them to pose a challenge to the government troops and, no longer such firm believers in an alliance with spirits, the Acholi were increasingly reluctant to help the guerrillas and refused to hand over their sons as recruits. Kony, through whom Lakwena was now talking, regarded the Acholi as traitors who deserved the most awful death. He decided not to continue asking them to give up their sons for the army, but from now on he would attack their villages and kidnap their children, to transform them at his guerrilla camps into perfect soldiers, blindly loyal, knowing neither fear nor pity.

◄◦►

The Lord's Army was probably the only children's army in the world, or maybe in history, to fight wars against adults and to perpetrate crimes and cruelties that adults would not dare to commit.

In Congo, Sudan, and Mozambique, in Afghanistan, Nepal, Cambodia, and Colombia, everywhere where wars have happened or are happening, children are kidnapped and then used as recruits, porters, workers, concubines, or hostages. But their captors, and then comrades-in-arms, are usually adults.

In the north of Uganda, apart from the few, top leaders such as Joseph Kony or Jackson's uncle, Vincent Otti, almost all the guerrillas in the Lord's Army were children. Like Dominic Ongwen, who changed in the bush from a young boy into a bloodthirsty killer with a warrant out for his arrest, a monster whose name made hearts tremble. In Acholiland the victims became like their oppressors, and turned into torturers. At once they sought new victims too, ones of their own. Passing onto others the curse that had fallen on them was their way of trying to lessen its malevolent force.

One night in the hotel bar I questioned an officer in the government army stationed in Gulu about the war against the children of the Lord's Army. He gave me a withering look and said: "So you're a journalist, I guess?" I nodded, not even expecting a reply. "When we try to spare them, people say we're good for nothing, we're making a laughingstock of ourselves, and we can't even deal with a gang of ragged kids. But when we shoot at them, they start complaining that we're killing children."

After a few days in Gulu I noticed that the soldiers from the local garrison reacted to questions about the guerrillas and the war with antipathy and irritation.

"How do you think we should act toward them?" said the officer angrily. "They burn down villages, they murder and kidnap people, and at the sight of us they immediately shoot. What are we supposed to do, hand out sweets? Like to kiddies in the villages? With guns in their hands they're not children, they're killing machines. They're not human anymore."

I thought of Samuel. I couldn't imagine him with a gun in his hand, ready to kill or even to avoid his own death. Even though he had told me himself what he had done and what he had been through, I saw him as a youngster, a schoolboy, just as when I first met him.

◄o►

"This is a dreadful place," I once said to Nora. "I've never seen anything like it."

"Dreadful?" she said in surprise. "What about Congo? It's really dreadful in Congo, but you're always going there. What are you after? I'd never go there of my own free will. I'd be too scared. Really bad things happen to people there."

Before coming to Gulu, straight after university Nora went to work for a charity in a town called Bundibugyo, very near the border with Congo, on Lake Albert, and not far from the mist-coated, blue and green Ruwenzori Mountains, which Ptolemy called the Mountains of the Moon.

There were refugees from across the Congolese border living as nomads in the area. They had fled war and the grisly murders the rebels were committing there. No one knew who they were, who their leader was, what they wanted, or in what cause they were fighting.

The power of the government in faraway Kinshasa never reached the land of the Ituri. Extending along the Congolese shore of Lake Albert and on the Congolese slopes of the Ruwenzori Mountains, it had become the promised land for various rebels, not just from Congo, but also from Uganda, Rwanda, and even Sudan. By night they would attack remote villages in the hills and bamboo groves, where they would kill, rape, rob, kidnap children, cause a bloodbath and extreme terror. Encouraged by the guerrillas' example, even Pigmies armed with spears and arrows had started making looting raids from their settlements in the jungle. They inspired acute fear because the villagers did not regard them as humans, but as forest dwarves created by evil spirits to look like humans and to destroy them. The garrison commander from the Ugandan town of Bundibugyo even promised to pay the local hunters hard cash for every Pigmy they killed or captured—fifty dollars a head. For three the fee rose to two hundred, which for the locals was a real fortune, enough to change their destiny.

The inhabitants of the Congolese villages fled in their thousands to the Ugandan side of the border. Abandoning their papaya trees, sweet potatoes, tea, coffee, and banana plantations, they ran at full speed to Bundibugyo to find safety. Unaccustomed to the warm, damp climate prevalent in the valley, the refugees from the highland villages soon fell ill with malaria and smallpox, and learned to hate the handouts given to them by foreigners. From then on they were forced to live on charity in refugee huts covered in blue plastic, for which they had exchanged their homes in the mountains.

Nora felt chosen by destiny, and reckoned she owed something to those who had not been so fortunate. She told me that she left Kampala for Bundibugyo in order to help the refugees from Congo. But one of her friends from Gulu once told me she had really gone there because in those days she was living with a doctor, a man old enough to be her father. Nora never told me about that, and I didn't ask.

I still couldn't get her to give me Samuel's file.

"It completely slipped my mind," she explained. "I'll have a look for it tomorrow. First thing."

⤙⚬⤚

"Maybe you'd take him somewhere?"

Nora was sitting under the window on an old couch occupying half of her small office. When she stayed at the center on night shift, or when she simply didn't feel like going home, she slept on it.

"Take him where?"

"This isn't a jail, you know. He doesn't have to sit here all the time. You could talk to each other somewhere else."

There she sat on the couch, like a market trader with her vegetables laid out on the ground. She had her legs folded underneath her, and her slender bare feet tucked into her dress.

"I didn't know he could go out."

"Well, now you do."

The idea that I could take Samuel somewhere surprised me. I had seen girls from the center in town—it was easy to recognize them by their orange skirts. But it hadn't occurred to me that Sam could go out to town too, that I could meet and talk to him away from the center. Above all, coming to see him here was convenient—it allowed me to call the shots. It was I who made the visits, and at any moment, on any excuse, I could say goodbye—I could always escape. Nora wanted to shatter this, to spoil it.

"I guess I'm in your way now?" I asked.

"Not at all. I like it when you come." There was no provocation in her calm eyes, the color of dark gold, but rather the wish to join forces. "It just occurred to me that maybe you'd like to take him somewhere."

She lowered her head, and unconsciously smoothed invisible creases in her dress. Her face was disappearing in the bright, dazzling light pouring in through the window.

"I've never seen your boys in town."

"How do you know the boys you meet in the street aren't from here? Ours are no different from the town boys."

"Where would I take him?" I asked.

"What about me? Where would you take me?"

I turned to look the other way. Through the half-open door I could see the empty yard, flooded with sunlight. We never closed the door when I dropped in at Nora's office. "It'll be better like that," she had once said. "People have all sorts of ideas."

"Well, should I call him?" she asked.

I said yes.

She turned to face the white rectangle of the open door, shimmering in the air, and without getting up from the couch she called: "Samuel!"

"There's no one there," I said.

"No, no," she said, shaking her head. "I know he's there somewhere."

⤙⤚

First we walked down a narrow path across the thick, knee-high grass that grew all round the center's white walls. Never cut or trodden down, it kept creeping closer, getting bolder, like a live creature, just waiting for the chance to push its way through the gate inside, into the red courtyard. Nature was reluctant to yield to people here, and only in places where they had picked a spot for a dwelling, or marked out the route for a road. But as soon as it spotted any human weakness, up it leaped and greedily reclaimed anything it had let them wrest from it earlier. It immediately encroached on any spot that man abandoned.

The tropical climate conceals a special power. It only took three years for the Cambodian jungle to overrun the capital, Phnom Penh, when its one million residents were driven out by their insane rulers, who saw the city as the incarnation of every possible evil. Centuries ago the jungle consumed another capital of the Khmers, the vast city of Angkor, bigger than ancient Rome. The stone palaces are overgrown with trees, and the temples and tombs are home to wild animals, birds, and snakes.

When I arrived in Phmon Penh, the Khmer Rouge had not ruled the country for more than a decade, but they were still hiding in the jungle. People had moved back into the capital, but you could still see trees growing on the roofs. Almost all the houses were stained with dirty damp patches, and had a musty smell of rotting refuse. The jungle had never surrendered. Monsoon rains, sun, damp, and plants were eroding walls, wood, and metal. Only the stone buildings were putting up some resistance to nature.

In Acholi-land there were just three walled cities—Gulu (the biggest one), Kitgum, and Pader. Most people lived in villages, in round clay huts with straw thatched roofs. Abandoned as people ran away from war, epidemics, starvation, or floods, in a flash they became easy prey for avid nature. Grass devoured the garden plots and shot up to the height of an adult man, bushes soon covered the dwellings and farmyards, and banana groves shot up in the small village graveyards, erasing all trace and memory of the life that once existed here. Sometimes it was hard to find or recognize former settlements.

As the caretaker pulled the gate, it crashed shut behind us with a loud metallic clang. Samuel flinched and looked over his shoulder, ready and willing to turn back on a summons he wasn't just expecting but hoping for. But no one called after us. So off we went, down the path across the grass toward the nearby asphalt road, which I took every day to the marketplace. We walked in single file, I in front, Samuel a few paces behind me. Once I turned around to ask: "Everything okay?"

He slowed down to avoid walking into me, and silently nodded.

◄o►

On Sunday mornings the sleepy town was even more indolent than on weekdays. After a violent nocturnal storm, rivulets of rain were running from the deep gutters, picking up bits of garbage and sweeping them down the steep streets. The air was still clean and fresh. The sun hadn't had time to dry up the puddles which had formed on the red earth, or to heat up the damp-stained concrete walls, the cracked asphalt, or the stinking heaps of refuse that would soon dispel the fragile morning freshness, and hold the town imprisoned in stuffy humidity until dusk.

From the open windows of low houses came the sounds of music, scraps of radio shows, and snatches of conversation. At noon, when the sun was already high and was taking possession of the town, the shrill cries of children were audible too, as they played on balconies and in yards. Crawling after the vanishing shade, ugly white dogs were sheltering under the walls.

As every Sunday morning in Gulu, the congregation was on its way to the churches and chapels to praise the Lord—men in dark suits and coiffured ladies in breezy flowered dresses coming along the bumpy sidewalks. The men moved stiffly and awkwardly, as if afraid that bending their limbs would mean crumpling their Sunday clothes too quickly.

Cries of "Hosanna!" and "Hallelujah!" rang out along the streets.

I like going to church on Sunday in Africa. The places of worship here are always full. Attending Sunday mass is not an obligatory ritual, or a habit, but an inner need to be spiritually uplifted, or just entertained by singing and dancing in praise of the Lord. Here people believe in God with an openness that Europeans find embarrassing. They don't shut themselves up in prayer, concentration, or meditation. They flaunt their faith with extreme joy. Here in the middle of the mass, a woman will leap up from her pew, raise her arms, and chant a hymn. Others will interrupt their prayers, listen to the beat, start to clap, stand up, and sing the chorus. Finally the entire church jumps to its feet and whirls into a dance, while pounding out a song which might not appear in any hymnbook.

On the main street, in its festive Sunday mood, we joined in with the devotees on their way to church. Samuel had quickened his pace, caught up with me, and was now walking beside me. He kept looking around, as if trying to spot someone in the crowd. Or maybe he was just checking to see if he recognized anyone, though there was no curiosity in his eyes.

"What shall we do? What do you fancy?" I asked.

He shrugged, the way bored, spoiled children do.

"Maybe we can go to church?" I suggested. "Do you usually go to church?"

He shook his head.

"No, we don't go to church," he said. "Father Cosmas comes to see us when it gets dark."

◄०►

Grateful that I had taken him for a walk, Samuel told me about the second time he had killed.

But first we broke away from the procession of churchgoers and headed up a side street.

"Let's go to the bus station," I said. "I have to check when the buses leave for Kampala."

He nodded.

"I like the bus station. I often go there," I added.

Again he agreed solemnly, without saying a word. In silence we passed Franklin's bar. Outside, one of the waiters was chalking up the program times for the British soccer league's Sunday matches on a blackboard. That afternoon there was going to be a live broadcast from London of a match between West Ham and Arsenal. The match between Manchester United and Aston Villa being played at the same time would only be shown in the evening.

"Who do you support?"

"I don't know," he muttered, as if disappointed.

"I've always been a Manchester fan. I don't know why, but ever since I first watched soccer matches, I've always supported Manchester. Strange, isn't it?"

He agreed.

"My sons like soccer too. I watch all the matches with my older boy. The younger one even plays for his school team."

He didn't reply, but glanced at me with interest. On the corner of the main street and a narrow alley leading straight to the bus station stood a multistory apartment building, painted a faded sky blue. Up on a balcony, its owner, in a white undershirt, was smoking a cigarette and watching the town go by. A pungent, greasy smell of chicken being fried for Sunday lunch came wafting out of the open windows.

There was a small bookstore crammed under the columns on the ground floor, where I used to drop in for notebooks and maps of Gulu and the area. Now it was locked and bolted. Behind the dirty gray display window, under a faded portrait of President Museveni, lay some thick volumes of the Holy Scriptures gone yellow, some postcards showing wild animals and waterfalls that had curled with age, some photo albums, school exercise books, and a few other publications. A boy's face in thick round glasses peeped from under a textbook for learning English. It was the hero of a children's novel, *Harry Potter and the Philosopher's Stone*, the first book in the series.

"Do you know Harry Potter? My son's always talking about him," I said, stopping in front of the store.

"No," he replied.

"He's a young wizard. He lives in London. Lots of children would love to do magic like him."

He stared at the book cover.

"I had a cousin called Harry. But I never saw him because he lived in Gulu."

"Was his name really Harry?"

"Yes, but he's gone now."

We stood outside the dusty window, gazing at the portrait of the president, in unsettling silence again. The thought of asking Samuel what had happened to his cousin flashed through my mind. In Nora's room at the center, where he told me about himself and his life, I definitely would have asked him about Harry from Gulu, but here in the street, outside the bookstore, it seemed patently inappropriate. I remembered that I hadn't asked Nora when I should bring Samuel home.

"Does Nora sometimes take you out with her?"

He shrugged indecisively.

"Are you sure you're okay? You're not saying much . . . At the center you chatter away like mad."

He replied with a hesitant smile.

By now we were just one cross street away from the bus station, literally a few steps. We walked the rest of the way without saying a word to each other.

It was approaching noon when we entered the red-brown gravel courtyard of the Acholi Inn Hotel. When I had asked if he wanted to see where I lived, Samuel had quite readily agreed to come here.

The large room, where apart from a narrow bed, a wooden table, and a chair that went with it, there was no other furniture, not even a wardrobe, made no impression on him. He stood still, patiently. When I pulled up a chair for him he sat down without asking any questions. He didn't show curiosity or disappointment. He was waiting to see what came next. We sat for a while in silence, and then I suggested we move to the hotel restaurant—far more attractive.

Waiters in white shirts were carrying tables outside, setting them up on the grass among the trees, and laying them with tablecloths for lunch—on Sundays the richest and most respectable citizens came here.

There was no one in the bar, which you entered straight from the courtyard. Standing just below the ceiling on top of a glass-fronted cabinet full of colorful whisky and gin bottles, the television brightly lit up the gloom that prevailed in here, even at noon. A boy in a kitchen apron was drying beer mugs, wineglasses, and heavy ashtrays made of thick glass without taking his eyes off the flickering screen.

◂◦▸

Samuel settled into one of the sunken armchairs which were set out in rows opposite the bar each evening, making it look like a movie theater. Years ago when they were ordered in Kampala, they were chosen to decorate the pleasant, elegant lounge that served hotel regulars. British officers and colonial officials used to take their leave of the day here, discussing its main events over a bottle of whisky.

But the war in Acholi-land had scared away travelers, and even many of the local rich, who in view of the uncertain situation preferred not to put their noses out of doors after dark. As a result the hotel bar had passed into the possession of the soldiers stationed in the town; they came here to drink beer and watch movies or soccer matches on television. Instead of being a refined club for the select few, the hotel had become a garrison canteen, a refuge for the bored, the lost, and the doubtful.

Time and dust had long since faded the grand purple cloth covering the armchairs, and dark, greasy stains, rips, and darns had left wounds on the fake satin, stripping it of any remaining dignity or illusions. The damaged, buckled armchairs sagged so low that it was impossible to sit in them and eat, and they were even uncomfortable to sit on to watch the television.

Yet in a loose white shirt and shorts, Samuel looked content. He was sitting up straight, with his hands on his knees, like a model student in the front row. Craning his neck, he was staring at the colorful but silent television screen.

"Can't you make it a bit louder?" I asked the boy at the bar, as I reached for a menu. "And can you turn it to a children's show for a while? We'd like to watch a few cartoons."

The boy at the bar, who was watching a cricket match played a week ago without the sound, shook his head.

"It's broken. There's nothing I can do."

"Can't you turn the sound up?"

"That's what's broken."

"Well, maybe you can change the channel?"

Without a word he rolled up his cloth and put it down, climbed on a chair to reach the right button, and started changing channels. Images flashed across the screen—a pretty girl dancing sensually on the roof of a car, a mute preacher from a religious show, then some women picking tea leaves on a hillside. Finally the screen came to a stop on a cartoon for children.

"Please leave it there! Thank you," I called.

The boy didn't answer, but disappeared through a door behind the bar.

"Or maybe you'd like to watch something else? Maybe you prefer the cricket match?" I asked the reticent Samuel.

He said no.

"What about some ice cream?"

He glanced at me without saying anything, but instantly averted his gaze, as if he hadn't heard or didn't understand.

"What sort do you like best? Let's have a treat today. What do you say?"

He smiled.

"But we mustn't say anything to Nora," I went on. "She'd give us hell if she knew we pigged out on ice cream before lunch."

I looked closely at Samuel, trying to discern some hint or encouragement in his gaze, his facial expression, or even the way he was sitting or folding his hands. The conversation simply wouldn't take off.

I was missing Nora. When I talked to Samuel in her company I never felt constrained. She was the caretaker and guide who made sure none of my words or gestures frightened the boy, allowing me to gain his trust, but not to be overly, unnecessarily intimate, or cross the boundary that set the limits of our acquaintance. Left to myself, on my own with Samuel, I was afraid of going anywhere near that boundary.

"We won't tell Nora. It'll be our secret," I repeated.

But I couldn't find any ice cream on the menu, only some desserts with pretentious names that didn't tell you a thing—"Red Sunset," "Heavenly Sweet," and "Lion's Delight." The waiter who came to take our order admitted that he had never seen them, but was sure they contained ice cream, whipped cream, chocolate, and fresh fruit, and that "Red Sunset" had some liqueur added to it. I ordered all three desserts and several bottles of Coca-Cola.

"Will that be okay?" I asked Samuel.

"Yes," he replied.

"Do you want to eat it here in front of the TV, or shall we move outside to the restaurant, under the trees?"

He cast a glance at the television.

"In front of the TV," he said.

The waiter brought the desserts, which covered an entire small table, and we ate them without speaking to each other. Samuel went on solemnly watching the cartoons, whose heroes, thanks to the broken TV, weren't uttering a word either.

For lunch I ordered fried chicken and fries.

"Let's eat it outside," I said.

Samuel didn't object. And then, when Emma, the petite waitress with the sad, absent, ever-weary face, brought the plates and went back to the kitchen for cutlery, he told me how he had killed for the second time.

"Girls can sometimes be very strong, stronger than boys," he said, watching Emma walk away. "But I wouldn't like to be a girl."

"Sure there are plenty of reasons why it's better to be a boy," I agreed.

He nodded, then looked up and, as if remembering something he'd been wanting to say for ages but that kept slipping his mind, he quickly blurted: "I once killed a girl too."

During the march through the bush, one of the girls had taken advantage of the guards' inattention and hidden in the undergrowth. She thought the guerrillas hadn't noticed her disappearance, but they soon found her.

"They dragged her out of the bushes and tied her to a tree," said Samuel. He leaned over the table and grabbed the straw sticking out of the Coke bottle in his lips, then drained it in a few sips. "Then the commander pointed at me. They gave me a machete and ordered me to kill her. She was crying, but I told her I must do it, because otherwise they would kill me."

Emma came back with the knives and forks.

"Do you want some more?" I asked.

⤙⤚

The lunch hour was approaching, and new arrivals were starting to appear in the hotel yard. They took a quick look at the tables set out under the trees, but seeing no one but waiters bustling about, they soon retreated to the bar, brightened by the television screen.

Apart from us, there was no one in the restaurant except for a few men sitting in a tight circle around a table under a mango tree, off to one side near the fence. They were smoking cigarettes. One of them had a leg missing. Emma was lumbering toward the mango tree, carrying a tray full of frosted bottles of beer and Coca-Cola.

Samuel was eating with his fingers, holding a chicken thigh in one hand while automatically reaching for fries with the other, repetitively, almost mechanically. He no longer seemed lost and uncertain. He was looking around with curiosity, peeking at the swimming pool visible across the hedge, from where we could hear the shouts of children bathing. When he noticed that I was looking at him, he smiled and said: "It's all right. I am okay."

"Do you like swimming? We can come here next time," I said, nodding at the pool. "Did you ever swim in the river?"

"No. The river is bad. Dangerous," he quickly corrected himself. "You have to watch out when you go in it."

"A deep river is a hazard, and you have to be careful, but in a shallow one nothing will happen to you."

"No, no!" he vigorously protested. "The river gets angry when you go into it. If you don't ask it and it gets angry, it can tell the spirits to take you away forever."

Samuel hadn't seen the men sitting under the mango tree. Facing away from them, he only noticed them after lunch, when we got up from the table to return to the center, to Nora. At the sight of them he froze. Suddenly the shy pleasure prompted by ice cream, cartoons, and our time at the restaurant was gone from his ashen face. As I was occupied with paying the bill and chatting to Emma, a good while passed before I noticed the change that had come over him.

He was staring at the men under the mango tree, who were silently listening to a white-haired man in light long pants and a short-sleeved jacket. Only now did I notice that the one with a leg missing had his hair plaited in shoulder-length braids.

"What's up?" I asked Samuel. "Do you know them?"

He said nothing, but kept casting terrified looks toward the men, then averting his gaze again, as if by doing so he could hide, vanish, become invisible.

As we passed their table on the way out, Samuel shrank and stiffened even more. The white-haired man in the light suit and the one-legged man both looked up and swept us with fleeting, unseeing glances.

Without a word we exited the hotel onto the road leading to town.

Samuel walked ahead of me, urging me on and quickening his pace, like someone wanting to elude danger as fast as possible. To my own surprise I felt guilty.

"Samuel?"

He looked back at me. The hotel had vanished around the bend. No one was coming after us. That Sunday afternoon the street was empty, and smelled of soft, warm asphalt.

"They are people from the bush," he said. "They talk with spirits. They see everything, nothing can be hidden from them."

He didn't look terrified anymore, and evidently felt sure he had escaped and left the threat behind him. Nor did he seem disappointed that his Sunday had suddenly been spoiled. I couldn't see any letdown in his eyes or in his face, but just a look of resignation at what fate brings. He reminded me of people who have had bitter experiences in life, over and over, and know we shouldn't expect too much of it, or at best not hope for anything at all. Except that he hadn't even reached the age of fourteen yet.

Nora was sitting in her office, leaning over the desk and filling the columns in a register.

"Where on earth did you get to? You've been gone for ages," she said, looking at me. Then she glanced at Samuel and asked: "Did you have a fun time?"

⟶

I got back to the hotel after dark. The men who had frightened Samuel were no longer under the mango tree. I sat down at the table they had occupied. It was laid with a clean tablecloth, and the previous occupants hadn't left the slightest trace of themselves. Even the ashtray was clean and empty.

When I asked Emma the waitress about the men to whom she had brought the beer and Coca-Cola a short time ago, she was surprised and said she couldn't remember anyone like that—neither the one-legged man in an army jacket, nor the older man with white hair.

That evening I decided to leave the city. I was suddenly filled with certainty that I wasn't needed here, that I had done everything I planned to. I had heard Samuel's story; he couldn't tell me any more, and I couldn't think of any more questions to ask him.

Jackson was right when he said I was wasting my time for no good reason. I was pretending, to him and to myself, that things were different. I had gathered more than enough material to write a report for the newspaper. All the more since it was only meant to be one article—I could only tell Samuel's story once.

I was continuing to visit him without really knowing why. The conversations were heavy-going. To tell the truth, I talked mainly with Nora, and was really just watching Samuel. In time, the only reason for my visits was the feeling that I owed it to him. He had let me coax out confidences, he had shown me sincerity and trust. I also visited him because Nora expected it of me.

But Jackson was right in saying I had forgotten what I came to Gulu for. Or maybe I had forgotten because up against the reality, my reason for coming had proved desperately trivial and petty.

As I was sorting out my notes in the hotel room, the idea of a journey to Lira occurred to me. Lira was the biggest city in northern Uganda, capital of the Lango people, the Acholis' neighbors. It wasn't far from Gulu. Before reaching the crossing over the Nile and the Karuma Falls, you had to turn east onto an asphalt road.

I was curious about Lira. That was where Nora came from. Her mother and two younger sisters still lived there. Her father had left when she was just a child. She hardly remembered him and didn't have a good word to say about him. He had left his wife and children in Lira, abandoned them. First he had gone to Kampala to look for work and a better life. He had promised that as soon as he was sorted out, he'd send for his wife and daughters, but he never got in touch. One of the neighbors assured them he'd seen the man in Mombasa, but Nora didn't believe her father could have gone all the way to Kenya, to the coast. It must have been someone else. No one even knew if her father was still alive. When she finished high school and moved to Kampala to go to Makerere University, her mother asked her to look around the city—maybe she'd run into her father. Nora prayed inwardly for that not to happen.

There was also a Belgian journalist living in Lira whom I had once met in Kampala. She used to work in Nairobi and Kampala as an African correspondent for the Belgian and Dutch press, radio, and television. She had dropped journalism after writing a book called *Aboke Girls*, about the kidnapping and wanderings of some schoolgirls who were taken captive by guerrillas from the Lord's Army.

Saint Mary's, the girls' school in the town of Aboke in the Apac district, was famous throughout the region. It was run by Italian nuns and was regarded as the best, so not surprisingly families in the Lango and Acholi lands dreamed of sending their daughters there.

It was Joseph Kony, leader of the Lord's Army, who gave orders for the schoolgirls to be kidnapped. He had been informed that they came from good families and were very well brought up and educated. Those were the sort of wives he needed for himself and his commanders. Those were the mothers he wanted for the children to be born at the guerrilla camp, who would grow up into a new generation of perfect soldiers.

The guerrillas attacked the school at night, during the rainy season. They abducted as many as 139 students, and then herded them through the bush. They didn't notice that one of the nuns, Sister Rachele Fassera, had come after them. She spent all night and all the next day marching through the bush to catch up with them, then emerged in front of them like an apparition, which may have been the only reason why they didn't kill her. On top of that, in response to her pleas they agreed to release 109 of their prisoners. However, they decided to take 30 with them as plunder for their leader. Sister Rachele decided to devote the rest of her life to liberating the remaining girls. She moved heaven and earth, and appealed to the American, Ugandan, and Sudanese presidents for help. She went to see Nelson Mandela and the pope. But she did not succeed in saving all the kidnapped Aboke girls. After months or years in captivity, where like the other abducted children they were reeducated and forced to kill, some of them managed to escape. Some were killed. Several others disappeared without trace. The book *Aboke Girls* told the story of their fates and of Sister Rachele's efforts to save them from harm.

In the old debate about the nature of the journalist's profession, one school declares that our role is to describe the world, and another says that the journalist can, or even should, change the world. I don't know which is more painful for a journalist—the inadequacy of any description compared with the reality of the horrors of war and the vast extent of tragedy, or the realization of his or her own helplessness and inability to have any influence on the world's fortunes.

I know several colleagues who, after coming up against the cruelties of war, decided to drop the profession. After his umpteenth trip in a row to the war-torn Balkans, one of the British journalists quit his job and went back to Sarajevo in order to adopt several war orphans and take them back to London. Another man I knew who was a South African photographer came home from yet another trip to Sudan and took his own life.

A Czech woman called Petra, who devoted all her time, love, and health to the war in Chechnya, stopped sending reports from the ruined city of Grozny that no one wanted to print, read, or get upset about, and founded an orphanage there instead. Then she left the Caucasus for Afghanistan, not to write articles, but to set up a charity to help the war victims she used to write about. If she becomes disenchanted with Afghanistan, no doubt she will leave. But it will always be possible to find her at one of the refugee camps, in Sudan's Darfur, or in the mountains of Kurdistan. Because journalism, endless traveling, and the desire to be at the epicenter of events all the time is also a form of search. Or escape.

The Belgian journalist whom I had met in Kampala, and who wrote the book about Sister Rachele and the Aboke girls, had also stopped filing news reports from Africa. She had used the income from her book sales to found a charity that aimed to help child soldiers released from captivity. Finally, with Belgian government aid, she was building a center in Lira, where juvenile guerrillas who had run away or been caught were restored to normal life. It was similar to the center in Gulu where Nora worked, and the Belgian woman had named it after Sister Rachele.

The Belgian had just come back from Europe, where she had been persuading people to help children like the Aboke girls, or Samuel from Gulu, by showing them photographs of children from Lira— Bosco Okid, eleven years old, five months in the bush; Geoffrey Omara, twelve, three months in the bush; Wilfred Okodu, twelve, six months in the bush; Sam Eroju, twelve, six months in the bush.

People could choose one of them, and by paying thirty dollars a month for his or her education, become his or her benefactor. "It's like starting life over again," explained the Belgian woman. In exchange for their help, the children chosen by people and by fortune would send photos and write letters. When we met in Kampala she invited me to come and visit her in Lira. She told me about the school she had just finished building, and about the children whose education she was funding. "Five of my girls are at university now," she said with a note of pride.

My girls . . .

Nora kept saying: your Samuel . . .

I called the Belgian woman's number in Lira, but no one answered. It was already late at night, but I tried calling again, once more to no effect—no one picked up the receiver. But I decided to go anyway, the next day, straight after breakfast.

❧

Although several times bigger, after closely built-up Gulu, Lira seemed to me spacious and airy, as spread out as the branches of the old acacias that grew everywhere here. The low-rise tenements didn't get on top of each other like in Gulu, but elegantly made way for one another, and the green of the leaves and grass was deeper and sharper here. Compared with Gulu, Lira was quieter, but hotter.

The war involving the Lord's Army that was going on in Acholi-land had also reached Lira, in the land of the Lango. It had even got as far as the Soroti and Apac districts. Refugees coming into Lira from the villages that were exposed to the worst danger had caused the city's population to double. Accustomed to comfort, the locals regarded the newcomers as pests. But taking no notice at all, they kept arriving in a large stream, because every day brought a reminder that remaining in their villages, or even in the camps guarded by the army, meant taking a lethal risk.

At the Barlonyo camp, located not far from Lira, the guerrillas had massacred 250 people, killing them with machetes or burning them alive, and then sent thousands of thatched refugee huts up in flames. At the sight of the juvenile guerrillas invading the camp, the 300 gendarmes assigned to guard it were the first to take to their heels. At Abia, which is also in the Lira neighborhood, the rebels had killed almost 70 people. Not far away, but in the Apac district, there is also the town of Aboke, from where the guerrillas abducted the schoolgirls.

The ongoing war in the area meant more and more frequent quarrels in peaceful Lira, or even fights between citizens from the Lango and Acholi peoples. The Lango regarded the war as an Acholi issue, and blamed them for the fact that in fleeing misfortune they had brought it down on Lango areas as well. They accused the Acholi of ingratitude—So that was how they repaid sympathy, hospitality, and help! "Get out of here and take your war with you!" they rebuked the Acholi. They also reproached them for their treachery some years earlier, as a result of which not only had President Milton Obote who came from the Lango, been deposed, but power, held until then by tribes from the north of Uganda, had slipped from their hands for good and passed into the possession of the south.

Lira, capital of the north, was the hometown of Milton Apollo Obote, the first ruler of independent Uganda, cobbled together by the British out of several kingdoms and tribes that didn't have much in common. Although she clearly wasn't fond of Obote, in talking about Lira, Nora had said she would show me the house where he used to live. When he died in exile in Lusaka, Zambia, his widow Miria had moved back into his old house. However, she was away from the city now. As Uganda's former first lady she had decided to stand in the approaching presidential elections, relying on people's tendency to be nostalgic for the irretrievable past to prompt them to vote for the name Obote, which they also associated with the days of their youth. And although not many people had come to her rallies, despite illness and advanced age Miria Kalule Obote was tirelessly touring the country, believing she could convince enough people to let her take power, and thus regain what her husband had won and lost twice over.

For someone as conceited, self-righteous, or even arrogant as Obote was, fate had been extremely kind to him by giving him as many as two chances. It was like having two lives, but he wasted both of them, and clearly saw no reason to be grateful for the distinction he had received. Instead he must have been furious, and probably felt wronged when power was taken from him, though he was incapable of exercising or holding on to it.

Obote's conceit was apparent in everything he said and did. He boasted that he had been "born into a family of rulers," although his father was only a minor Lango chief from the village of Akokoro in the Apac district. His arrogance was evident in his way of dressing, behaving, and speaking. It even showed in the fact that he smoked a pipe. Thrown out of university for taking part in a student strike, he worked as a laborer, salesman, and clerk, until he discovered politics, the miraculous, magic spell that allowed him to gain what he most desired—power. In addition, by coincidence he made this discovery at perhaps the only moment when his wish had a chance of coming true.

Bled dry and exhausted by the great conflicts that in Europe soon came to be called the world wars, Britain, and France too, were hastily saying goodbye to their empires in Africa and Asia. The imperial provinces and colonies were declared independent states; power over them was taken on by presidents and prime ministers who shortly before had only been corporals in the colonial army, post office clerks, court officials, tradesmen, or teachers at village schools.

Coming from the north, Obote decided to gain power in divided Uganda by allying with the ruler of the southern kingdom of Buganda, Kabaka Frederick Mutesa II. The king became president, and Obote was his prime minister. To win over the haughty Bugandans who lived around Kampala, Obote chose himself a wife from their tribe. Obote's marriage to the nobly born Miria Kalule was to be a symbol of Uganda's unity.

The marriage lasted for many years, but the alliance with King Freddie was short-lived. Feeling confident in power, Obote ordered his troops to take the king's palace, Lubiri, by storm. Obote deposed Mutesa and drove him out of the country, then declared himself the new president. In the course of a massacre committed on a clear night in May, his soldiers murdered 2,000 of the Kabaka's courtiers and followers, and the Lubiri palace was handed over to the army as a barracks. The Bugandan king escaped from it via a secret exit, caught a taxi in the street, and told the driver to take him straight to the airport. From there he fled to London, where out of homesickness for his country and his throne he allegedly drank himself to death.

Obote's arrogance soon earned him enemies. He ruled like a chief, convinced he was best at everything and knew better than anyone. He interfered everywhere and wanted to make all the decisions himself, and if anyone disagreed with him he had them locked up. Gifted with charisma, determined and ambitious, like many of the first leaders of independent African countries—Kwame Nkrumah, Julius Nyerere, or Kenneth Kaunda—he saw himself not just in the role of president of little Uganda, but of the entire Dark Continent, united under his control. To start with, he wanted to create one large East African state out of Uganda, Kenya, and Tanzania, and become its leader.

His dictatorial ambitions and friendship with Julius Nyerere, the president of neighboring Tanzania who liked experimenting with socialism, meant that in the British press Obote came to be called a socialist too. In London, where not long before he had been regarded as Uganda's great hope, they began to suspect that, like other socialists in Africa, the Middle East, and Asia, he would want to nationalize the cotton and coffee plantations, the mines and factories.

Condemned and derided abroad, he became increasingly impatient, suspicious, and cruel. Mistrustful of the southern tribes, he now surrounded himself almost exclusively with his kinsmen from the Lango people and compatriots from the north. He also relied more and more on the army, which protected his power, tracking down and crushing anyone who attempted to deprive him of it.

To make sure none of his generals or colonels started to dream of power, he chose as his commander the crude muscleman Idi Amin, who while in the British colonial army had been famous for his loyalty and his powerful biceps. Obote believed that by owing him absolutely everything and being given total license, Amin would guard his throne like a faithful hound.

But Amin himself fell in love with power and the privileges and luxury that came with it. So he kept wanting more and more, and aspiring higher and higher. Finally, just before a trip to Singapore, Obote decided that on his return he would have to get rid of Amin. However, it was ten years before he came back to Uganda. Amin, who had been informed of the president's plans, took advantage of his absence to stage a coup d'état and declare himself the ruler. Before Obote could get back to Africa from faraway Singapore, it was too late. As the road to Kampala was closed to him, he went to Tanzania, to his friend and mentor Julius Nyerere.

Only a decade later, when Tanzanian troops invaded Uganda, ruined and changed by Amin into the African killing fields, could Obote return to his country. And to power, which this time he achieved by falsifying the election results.

Immediately a new war erupted in Uganda, which proved even bloodier than Amin's rule. Death squads massacred entire villages on the slightest suspicion of favoring the guerrillas. From the start, the tribes in the south took action against Obote, but there was increasing rebellion in the government army as well. The Acholi soldiers were not prepared to put up with the government and privileges of the president's Lango kinsmen anymore. Finally they revoked their allegiance and staged a revolt, which the commander of the Ugandan army himself joined. Obote was forced to flee the country again, this time to Zambia.

Fate did not give him a third chance. He lived out his days in exile, in impotent rage, believing to the last that he would succeed in returning once again to Kampala, and that power quite simply belonged to him. Now his widow Miria decided to try and win it, on his behalf as well as her own.

I found the therapy center named after Sister Rachele thanks to a Ugandan army captain whom I met at the hotel bar on my first evening after arriving in Lira. The hotel was chosen for me by a cabdriver I met at the bus station. He assured me I'd have no regrets, just like all the other foreigners, none of whom had ever complained.

The hotel was new and reportedly the best in the city. It was slightly off the beaten track. There were small thatched bungalows tucked beneath palm trees and acacias, temptingly promising peace, quiet, and discretion. The whole place looked more like a seaside resort where you come for a holiday than a roadhouse where you spend the night.

Inside, the hotel was lit with the sort of cozy yellow glow candles usually provide. The reception, bar, and restaurants seemed to be completely empty. Only when my eyes got used to the darkness did human figures loom out of it. The girls at the bar, in miniskirts revealing their thighs or in buttock-hugging pants, attracted the attention of new arrivals with the shining whites of their eyes. Small tables scattered here and there all over the garden, or hidden in the gloom under low-hanging canopies, created an illusion of invisibility. Only the red flares of cigarettes betrayed the movements of the guests sitting at them.

In an open army jacket, the extremely tipsy captain was sitting with two girls quite near the bar when I dropped in for some cigarettes. He was getting ready to leave and was counting out his money to settle the check. As the girls were making him hurry, he had given up on the waiter and come over to the bar. He glanced at me and nodded.

"Girls," he muttered.

"Girls," I agreed.

"You got one here?" he wondered.

"No, I haven't," I said, shaking my head. "I'm looking for a friend here in Lira, a white woman, a Belgian."

"The one with the Aboke girls?"

"Do you know her? Do you know where I can find her?"

His speech was slurred. He told me he had run into her that day in town and that the next day he would take me to see her. He took a hotel room key out of his jacket pocket and tossed it to one of the girls. Stretching, they slowly stood up from their table.

"Just tell me how to find her."

The captain put a handful of crumpled banknotes on the bar and shook his head.

"Tomorrow. Tomorrow I'll take you to her."

I didn't expect to see him again, but in the morning he was waiting for me on a leather armchair in the hotel reception.

◂◦▸

The children's rehabilitation center was located on the edge of the city in several one-story buildings with walls painted orange and flat sky-blue roofs. They were surrounded by a green, neatly trimmed lawn and a high chicken-wire fence. It all looked fresh and new.

The security guard at the gate told me to wait, and made a call to someone. The place was completely deserted and so quiet that I heard the crunch of footsteps on the gravel path leading into the courtyard. I looked up and saw Nora, walking toward me out of an orange-colored building. Only when the girl came right up close did I realize that she just looked like Nora. The same face, voice, laugh, and figure, the same way of styling her hair. She was even wearing a similar dress, thin and light, and she was barefoot, like Nora. For a while I wondered if this might perhaps be one of her younger sisters.

Apart from us there was no one there. The captain drove off without a word as soon as he had brought me to the place. The security guard who had fetched the girl I took for Nora had vanished. Now she was standing in front of me, staring at me in silence, without disguising her amusement. Just like Nora. I asked if she knew the Belgian woman.

"I'm her helper," said Tina—that was her name, Tina.

"I was hoping to see her."

"But she's not here. She moved to Kampala ages ago," she explained. "She decided to go back to journalism."

"What about all this?" I pointed to the buildings. "What's going to happen here?"

She shrugged.

"Go to Kampala. You must go to Kampala."

As she turned back down the gravel path, the wind lifted her dress. She walked further and further away, getting smaller in the dazzling sunlight, until she disappeared among the orange and blue.

❧

"You were in Lira?"

Nora was cross. Back in Gulu, when I told her about my trip, she lost her temper, as if I had broken an agreement or failed to keep a promise.

"You never said you were going there. What did you do that for?"

In her voice, as well as regret, there was a note of blame, as if she had caught me peeking at or secretly reading her journal.

"I only went for one day, there and back."

"Whatever! Why should I care?"

"I'll want to go to Lira again. Will you come with me?"

"When?"

I shrugged.

"I don't know, in a while."

She didn't answer.

As usual we were sitting in the shade, on a wooden bench. We were capable of spending time together without talking, and usually the silence wasn't awkward. But now, though it had never got in our way before, it had suddenly started to be uncomfortable.

"Your Samuel talks about you nonstop and is always asking questions about you. He'll wear me out with it."

I tried to respond to her by smiling, as if I felt guilty for something, or wanted to make up for an offense, but she turned away.

The schoolhouse door burst open, releasing a buzzing, insistent hubbub from inside. Among the children who ran out into the yard I noticed Samuel. He saw us too, sitting in the shade, and came running. I gave him my hand to say hello and he wouldn't let go of it.

"Where were you?" he asked.

And then without a second thought he climbed onto my knees, as he usually climbed onto Nora's.

"I'm going away to Kampala," I said.

"Will you take me with you?" he asked.

"Not now. But maybe another time."

"Are you really going away?" replied Nora, without looking in my direction.

"Yes, I have to go to Kampala. After all, you know the elections are coming up. I'm going to write about it."

"You can just as well write about it from here. People are going to vote here too, aren't they?"

"I know, but I'll write better about those issues from Kampala."

We stopped talking and sat watching the children in the yard. The break between classes had ended, and a sad, heavy silence had fallen in the courtyard again.

"Will you come back?" asked Nora.

"Yes, I think I will."

Before evening fell I dropped in again to say goodbye. Samuel wasn't in the yard. I'd forgotten that the priest was visiting the children that day to pray and sing psalms with them.

"I'll tell him you were here," promised Nora.

She was sitting at the desk in her office, reviewing some official documents.

"Look what I found!" she said.

She handed me the gray cardboard folder containing Samuel's life story, which she had written down.

"May I take it with me?"

"You said you needed it," she replied, nodding. "Give it back when you return."

TWO

AFTER BREAKING LOOSE OF THE vendors at the station, growling and
groaning with effort, the bus shook itself free of baked cassava and
banana sellers, groundnut, orange, and drinks peddlers. It rolled around
a corner, turned laboriously out of the narrow alley, recovered its equi-
librium, and then advanced slowly, trapped in a procession of cars and
trucks all the way down the main street toward the railroad crossing. A
good while passed before it hopped across the tracks and reached the
city limits.

Only there, as the crush on the road eased, could it take a deep breath
full of relief, speed up, and easily overtake those slower and weaker than
itself, whom fortune had not blessed with the happy, carefree sense of
freedom that comes with traveling the world.

Jackson had let me have the window seat, and we had hardly left
town before he fell into a fitful doze, disturbed by the bus bumping
along the potholed, winding road.

That morning, as I left the hotel, the receptionist asked if I was taking
my luggage with me, and whether to keep a room for me.

"I don't think so," I said. "Anyway, it's probably not necessary—you're
not too full here, are you?"

"You never know," he replied.

"In case of need I'll call from Kampala," I said in parting.

It was almost noon, but the air forcing its way into the bus through
the wide-open windows was still bracing, and hadn't yet surrendered
to the heat, which took away brightness and cheerfulness, faith and the

will to live. We passed Palenga, wreathed in blue smoke, as we sped toward the Karuma Falls on the Nile. There the road forks like a lizard's tongue. One road leads east, to Lira. The other continues south, crosses the Nile, and runs all the way to Kampala.

Here the great river still bears the name of the British Queen Victoria. Further on, it plunges into the lake for a while before heading north into Sudan, from which point it is called the Albert Nile, after Prince Albert, Victoria's husband. At the border town of Nimule it changes its name again, to the White Nile, then forces its way on across marshes and deserts before finally flowing into Khartoum, to merge with the Blue Nile and thus form the longest river in the world.

The African river was named after the British royal couple by Sir Samuel White Baker, a traveler and explorer from the London-based Royal Geographical Society. He also named the famous waterfall after his friend Roderick Impey Murchison—there, after squeezing through the rocks, the Nile throws itself off a forty-yard drop, then calmly flows on to Lake Albert. Although the locals named the waterfall Kabalega, even so the foreign name, given by a foreign visitor in honor of foreign rulers, has caught on with them. Just like the name of Lake Victoria, the biggest in all Africa.

"And that's where the problem lies—in the names," said Jackson, roused from slumber. "You give your own names to whatever you find in our country, and you're convinced that once you've named it all, you're also going to understand it all. But we have our own names too, and we look at things in our own way."

◄◦►

Bumping steadily along the uneven road, suddenly the bus made a higher, mightier leap and started to brake hard, until soon it had curbed its own impetus and come to a stop on the hard shoulder. Only then did I hear the agitated, terrified shouts of the passengers in the front seats.

Suddenly shaken from the soothing monotony of the journey, rudely awakened, they had leaped from their seats, and were pushing their way past each other to get to the windows looking onto the road. Clearly excited about something, they were pointing through the open windows. I looked behind me, and thought I saw a dark, writhing stripe cutting across the cracked gray-blue asphalt. But hardly had I turned to show it to Jackson than it disappeared. He was staring through the glass in silence.

"*Njoka*," he said quietly, after a pause.

The passengers piled out of the stationary bus and onto the road. They ran across to the other side of the highway, where the snake run over by the bus had crawled into the tall undergrowth. Unsure what to do, they were staring into the bushes, as if hoping for a sign from in there.

"Do they want to catch it?" I asked Jackson, but he didn't answer, as if he hadn't heard me.

Several men, evidently disheartened, came back to the hard shoulder and smoked in silence. Those who had stayed on the other side of the road were still having an animated discussion about running over the snake as an extremely important event.

"Are we going to stop here for long?" I asked.

Jackson and I were the only passengers who hadn't got out of the bus. Even the driver had switched off the engine and joined the men smoking cigarettes.

"Even if it's dead, they'll never find it in all that scrub. And if it's alive, it could still bite someone and then there'll be trouble," I said, getting fed up with Jackson's silence. "Do you think it could kill?"

He replied that all the snakes round here were deadly poisonous.

"All the more reason to leave it in peace," I said. "Dead or alive. After all, no one's going to take a dead snake to Kampala, even if it's big enough to feed the whole family."

Jackson shuddered and nodded.

The passengers were slowly drifting back. Individuals were gradually leaving the group standing over the ditch and, in no rush, taking their time, were recrossing the empty pavement. Most of the people on the bus were villagers from the Gulu area—women who kept looking around for the countless parcels they were taking to the city, and men with large laborer's hands they didn't know how to occupy as they sat idly in the bus. They were on their way to the big city in the hope of finding work, but also to visit long-lost relatives, bring them gifts from the countryside, and get reacquainted.

⤝⚬⤞

The accident with the snake had roused them from reverie, scattering their dreams and pleasant thoughts. Now they were in no hurry to make the onward journey. They lingered on the hard shoulder, still debating the incident.

"Why are they so bothered about it? It was only a snake."

"In these parts people attach significance to things that to foreigners might seem trivial, strange, or incomprehensible," said Jackson.

Had I already forgotten the story he told me about the Lord's Army guerrillas who drowned crossing the river Atepi?

Fleeing from the Ugandan army, who were hard on their heels, the guerrillas had raced through the bush until their way was barred by a river. Terrified by the rifle shots that were getting nearer, without much thought they jumped into the water. At this point there was a shallow ford and the current was weak, but even so none of the guerrillas had managed to get across to the other side. They were all devoured by the enraged river.

In Acholi-land everyone understood this. Even with the army on their tail, the guerrillas should first have appeased the river for disturbing its peace, made it a sacrifice, placated it, or at least shown it respect. But they had jumped into it with a splash, in their boots, unclean in body and spirit. And they had paid a high price. They had angered the river with their arrogance, or perhaps common folly, typical of children. For although they fought against and were running away from soldiers, the guerrillas were still children.

The Lord's Army officers, adults with experience of life, usually took care to make a sacrifice to any river before crossing it. They also made sure that before entering the water the soldiers took off their boots and washed their feet on the riverbank. But as they didn't trust anyone, least of all capricious, volatile rivers, they actually preferred to avoid them.

They would circumvent rather than cross them. If they pitched camp by a river, they never plunged into the water, but scooped it into buckets for bathing and drinking.

However, once they had finally been surrounded by the Ugandan army in Sudan too, their only hope was to cross the Nile and escape into Congo. Before entering the water, they made a suitable sacrifice to the great river and begged it to let them cross.

After evading the manhunt, the guerrillas attacked, massacred, and robbed the villages on the Congolese side of the river in their usual way, killing the peasants and soldiers from the local army and beheading their officers. But to win victory in war against people, the guerrilla commanders sought the favor of nature. Under threat of the severest punishments the guerrillas were forbidden to hunt elephants or giraffes in Congo's Garamba National Park, and they were also told to protect and care for the white rhinos and okapi living there, the last on earth.

"In the war, poisonous snakes, stinging bees, and even termites fight on the guerrilla side too. So do water and rocks," said Jackson. "But the guerrillas only have to offend them in some way for them to turn against them, and treat them as their worst enemies."

"Are you trying to say these people are worried because the snake might be in alliance with the guerrillas?" I turned my gaze from the road. "And that now the guerrillas will get revenge for the harm done to it?"

He shrugged.

"Maybe not, but it'd be better if it hadn't happened."

On the hard shoulder the agitated passengers were still explaining something to the driver, waving their hands and shouting. The driver was upset, and kept angrily pushing them away as they touched his arms, jostled and prodded him in the back and belly.

"They say something bad has happened and he should be more careful," said Jackson, who was having a lively conversation with an old woman sitting behind us. Clearly excited, she was telling him a story, vigorously gesticulating. Jackson seemed to be worked up too. He kept shaking his head in amazement. When the bus finally got going, interrupting the conversation in mid-sentence, I asked what they were talking about.

The woman had read in the paper that in Karamojong, the sun-scorched land of the herders, large snakes had appeared that no one had ever seen before; by spitting a single gob of poison they could kill up to two dozen people. Strange new snakes had also been found on the savannahs of southern Ethiopia and Somalia. In the woman's view this heralded the imminent end of the world and Judgment Day.

❧

Once it had gathered speed, the bus raced onward briskly and blithely, casting the unpleasant snake incident into oblivion. Outside, dark green trees slipped by, merging and weaving together in motion.

Jackson had dozed off again. The area looked deserted. The road did not pass through any towns or villages, which usually perched comfortably on the hard shoulder. There were bushes all the way to the horizon, with no gray ribbons of smoke rising above them to betray a human settlement. The only living creatures we met were gray monkeys; hearing the roar of the engine, they crowded up to the very edge of the road, almost coming onto the asphalt and under the bus wheels.

They stared at the passengers in a challenging, truculent way and held out their paws for charity thrown from the vehicle, but there was no pleading in their eyes, just a demand. They gathered the fruit and crackers from the road without a second glance at the donors. They took these gifts without thanks or gratitude, as their due tribute. They seemed trusting, confident that no harm could come to them from people.

After all, it was their land, they were the masters here. The Nile, which we had crossed at the Karuma Falls, flows on through jungle-covered hills and savannahs set aside for the largest wildlife reserve in the entire country. Located along the Murchison Falls, between Lakes Kyoga and Albert, it was meant to guarantee safety and peace for elephants, rhinos, hippos, and leopards, and some extra, easy income for people—foreign tourists were happy to pay for the opportunity to spend time among wild animals and nature. In the past, the Acholi chiefs only allowed their subjects to hunt once a year. The penalty for killing a lion, elephant, giraffe, or antelope outside the hunting season was the same as for killing a person.

But the wars that were the curse of Uganda had also affected the nature reserve. Soldiers and guerrillas from numerous armed factions had fled here in the hope of finding a safe place to hide. They fought bloody battles against each other, tracked down the enemy and threw their bodies off the rocks into the waterfalls and rivers.

They also hunted the wild animals whose territory they had invaded. They fired machine guns and cannon at herds of elephants and hippos to get their meat, as well as their tusks, which they sold to Arab smugglers from Juba and Khartoum. The soldiers and guerrillas had killed off all the rhinos and almost all the elephants and hippos, and had robbed and burned down the bungalows and roadhouses built for foreign tourists.

"It all began here," I heard Jackson say. "It was at the Paraa nature reserve that Alice was possessed by spirits and received great power from them."

Preoccupied by my own thoughts, I hadn't noticed he had woken up. Or maybe he was never asleep? He spoke out of the blue, as if reading my mind.

"Here we say that by fighting their wars near the waterfalls on the Nile, people have angered nature. The spirits told Alice to placate it and to restore the proper order of things," he said. "It was at the Paraa nature reserve that Alice formed her alliance with the water, rocks, and wild animals."

"Tell me about the spirits."

"What for? It can't be of any use to you."

◄◦►

In Kampala we parted. From the crowded bus station at the very heart of the city each of us went his own way. Once I was free of the porters, cabdrivers, motorcyclists, beggars, and vendors, stubborn and persistent, tugging at my sleeve and getting in my way, I headed for the downtown area, which was scattered over some green hills.

Jackson, to whom I had said goodbye on the bus, had immediately disappeared from sight in the colorful crowd. He was going to catch a *boda-boda* motorbike rickshaw and get it to take him to a village on Lake Victoria, on the edge of Kampala, where his distant cousin lived. He was going to stay with him. I had reserved a room at the Speke Hotel, said to be the best in town. I expected to find other foreign journalists there, as that was where they usually stayed on trips to Uganda.

I parted ways with Jackson because in Kampala we ceased to need each other. In Acholi-land we stayed at the same hotels and ate together. I paid for his beer, cabs, and tickets. Now it hadn't occurred to me that he could stay at the Speke. Nor did he drop the slightest hint that we could both stay with his relative, though while traveling the Gulu area, we had often spent the night with friends and relatives of his.

In Kampala we no longer suited each other, maybe because he was as foreign here as I was. He lost the advantage of knowing the ropes, and was no longer either host or guide. This gave me a sense of independence and strength. When he vanished in the crowd I felt relief. Suddenly everything that tied us together in Gulu in such an obvious, natural way was gone. Things that had mattered lost their significance in Kampala, former mysteries suddenly paled and stopped enticing me, my questions no longer demanded answers, and my doubts didn't need explaining. The world seen from Gulu blurred and blew away in gusts of warm wind coming off the lake. I knew that along with the rust-colored dust and smell of Gulu, the rest of it would be washed away in the hotel by my first hot shower in days. This thought made me happy.

Large and red as a ripe orange, the sun hung low over the roofs of the downtown tenements and church towers. It seemed to be slowly and cautiously descending from the green lakeside hills that exuded a refreshing coolness, to bring relief to the fishing villages that were scattered along its shores, suffocating in the heat and humidity. A gray patch of shade was moving downward street by street, embracing the city bit by bit. The sun's rays were losing their morning and afternoon brightness, which was almost white, dazzling; now the world was taking on darker tones, going brown, blue, and gray.

The street climbed to the top of a hill—one of several on which the city was spread above the lake. I stopped at a crossroads to adjust my backpack straps, which had loosened during the walk. The cardboard file documenting Samuel's short life protruded from an inner pocket. In the bus on the way to Kampala we hadn't talked about going back to Gulu. Jackson had just said that if I decided not to return, he could take Samuel's documents and give them back to Nora. Either way he would have to go back, so it would be no trouble for him to take Samuel's file.

—◦—

I like the Speke Hotel. When you're staying there, you have the pleasant illusion that you are—and never for a moment cease to be—a real part of the city, a small piece of what's really happening, and not just an observer or witness. It's a rare feeling, because most of the hotels in the world are devoid of personal features, and are designed to be like anonymous, extraterritorial oases—comfortable shelters, but not much different from each other; it is their similarity and lack of individuality that provide a sense of security and a chance to escape. Yet agreeing to be fenced off from the alien world outside and its otherness is written into their price, even though that world is usually the main, but not always the conscious, reason for the journey.

The city entered the Speke at daybreak, along with the first guests, who got up with the damp, gray dawn and came here for breakfast, and it stayed at the hotel until late at night. Reluctant to take its leave, it never did so for long. It would stagger to its feet from the same tables, having spent all day at them, and wobble off at a cheerful pace, leaning on the arms and waists of girls in tight, jazzy dresses who dropped by at night from the Rock Garden Café next door. Then it would vanish into the darkness, tapping the heels of its elegant shoes.

Breakfast was served at small tables set out on the veranda in front of the Nile Avenue entrance. Laid with white cloths at mealtimes, they occupied most of the sidewalk, as if the hundred-year-old hotel, the first and thus the oldest in all Kampala, could push and shove—as if by reason of age and precedence it could demand more space, concessions, and consideration.

Thanks to the proximity of the sidewalk and the street, as you sat in the hotel restaurant you could feel the beat of the city, smell it and sense its mood. Absorbed in their own affairs, passersby came and went right beside the tables like actors onstage, performing an improvised show that was different every day. Newspaper vendors set up their stalls just past the hotel fence, so close you could read the headlines. Even beggars looked in here, only to be instantly chased away by security guards fiercely waving bamboo sticks at them.

The street show continued round the clock, because the hotel is at the heart of the city, next door to banks and offices, major firms and expensive stores. The traffic in the street didn't die down in the evenings either, because that was when the people of Kampala headed into the city at a leisurely pace, as if drunk on freedom, to take their leave of the day in a pleasant way, meet with friends or look for new ones, dine, drink beer or whisky, listen to music and dance. With nightfall came the sound of crickets hidden in the branches of mighty trees towering over the sidewalk. Coyly at first, as time passed they sang ever bolder and louder, until their chirping filled the nocturnal darkness nonstop, drowning the murmur of conversations in the hotel restaurant.

Whenever a downpour fell on the city, cars looking for space outside the hotel came up so close they almost drove onto the veranda. Porters in special uniforms attentively ran up with big black umbrellas to shelter the alighting guests from the rain.

The hotel restaurant on the veranda was always full of people. It seemed everyone in Kampala arranged to meet at the Speke. Foreigners gathered here within the old walls and amid the old furniture to regain the atmosphere of a bygone era, when Uganda was still a British colony. In those days imperial officials used to turn up at the Speke for a glass of Scotch whisky; the British explorer, after whom the hotel is named, discovered the source of the Nile. This was where the local entrepreneurs and traders met to talk business at lavish dinners. The local politicians arranged to meet foreign journalists here to give them interviews, and the foreign journalists invited the local ones here in order to question them, sound out the situation, and investigate the real state of affairs. It was a bit like begging—as shameless as it was humiliating—for charity, for a handout in the form of news, explanation, and advice.

These meetings were an exhausting and embarrassing, but at the same time necessary, game, which was impossible to avoid. Anyone who came strolling along Nile Avenue when one of these conversations between visiting and local journalists was under way would be witness to an unusual transmigration of souls and a magical form of metabolism. The smug look that invariably irritated the locals would gradually disappear from the foreigners' white faces. Masks donned out of vanity, but also to hide weakness, make an impression and gain an advantage, would slowly slip, and the facial expressions—pleasant, but a little superior—would grow humble and come down to earth, no longer challenging, but ingratiating and fawning instead. As the voices grew milder and less confident, so did the words they uttered. Even the shoulders, so buoyant shortly before, would drop and hunch.

All the power that had filled the foreigners would gradually leave them and enter their African guests, whom they had summoned here to the hotel veranda. Hesitant and quiet at the start, suddenly they would sit upright and grow strong; their faces would toughen and their voices acquire force.

Now it would be the foreigners who were leaning over the tables, listening hard to the words of the locals, suddenly spoken sparingly, reluctantly, as a brush-off; they would stare into their faces to be sure not to miss anything, to hear and grasp it all properly—rather than have to ask more questions or request a repetition, for fear of irritating their guest and discouraging him from saying any more. If they interrupted prematurely, in mid-sentence, they would inevitably be cast into the pit of ignorance.

The visitors had to take up this game with the local journalists because they were the only people who really knew anything—who, what, with whom, where, and why. They knew the answers to questions about issues that would have taken the foreigners a long time and a huge effort to understand. These answers were always the stake in the conversations held in the hurly-burly of the hotel veranda. The trick was to find out, at the least cost and in the shortest time, as many as possible of the secrets which the local journalists had spent years on end discovering, and which were often the only meaningful, valuable thing in their lives. So you could understand why they would back off and refuse to give up or share their greatest treasures too easily. Especially with people who by their first word, gesture, or look betrayed that they hadn't a clue about the country they were reporting from. Worse than that—they didn't even think they needed to know anything about it.

So the locals weren't keen to tell all, and would start by trying to dismiss the outsiders with monosyllables, or else intimidate them with an excess of information—not just a rapid stream, but a turbulent river, a flood of details, dates, and foreign-sounding names impossible to remember. But eventually they would give in, and share all the facts they themselves had obtained with such difficulty, quite often exposing themselves to danger in the process.

The richest foreigners, correspondents for the biggest newspapers and press agencies from Nairobi, simply bought all the secrets along with their depositaries, the local journalists, by hiring them for a week, a fortnight, a month, or sometimes for good. They knew they'd return to Kampala and would need those people again. The rest could only play the game with the locals on the veranda of the Speke Hotel. Strategy and tactics.

The locals weren't offended or surprised that the foreigners were always trying to steal their knowledge, only to return to their home country and shamelessly boast of it as their own. Just by turning up at the meetings they were giving them permission to do so; further testimony to this fact were the hotel restaurant bills that would later be presented to the newspaper accountants.

However, the revelations of cornered Ugandan journalists weren't enough for the foreign correspondents. As they listened carefully to what their contacts had to say, they were also on the lookout, casting glances at the neighboring tables, where similar conversations were going on. Without giving themselves away, they were watching other people's faces, pricking up their ears and listening in, catching individual words, names, and dates, and mentally matching them up, seeking hidden connections and meanings.

Then they would suddenly stand up, quickly and loudly say goodbye, glance at their watches, and race upstairs to their hotel rooms to paste together a report out of the shreds, scraps, and snippets they had collected. A forecast of what would happen the next day, a picture of the whole, allowing their readers in faraway countries to imagine and form an opinion about worlds they would never have the chance to see.

◄◦►

On the veranda at the Speke I met with a journalist from the local paper, *New Vision*, Allio Ewaku Emmy. He was older than the other Ugandan journalists who had dropped in at the hotel and were drinking coffee or beer as they waited for their acquaintances from foreign papers to turn up. Emmy was a veteran among them, a legend.

In Kampala everyone praised and recommended him. "Have a meeting with Emmy—he'll explain everything," I was advised at the newspaper offices and radio stations I had been touring all day, in preparation for the fast-approaching presidential elections. "You must meet Emmy—he'll know best."

"Call Emmy, he knows everyone here," said William Pike, editor-in-chief of *New Vision*, whose number I was given by a Polish friend who had assured me I'd learn everything from Pike. In Kampala they said Emmy was simply the best. He had traveled a lot, which meant his accounts had perspective and depth. He had worked for Pike for years and they were old friends. The tall, bearded Pike reminded me of a hunter. Emmy was his tried and tested, faithful tracker dog.

William Pike was British, and had been in charge of the government newspaper, *New Vision*, for twenty years. He had been given the job by President Museveni in recognition of his honesty and courage. They had known each other for decades. As a foreign newspaper correspondent Pike had taken a great risk by slipping through to Luwero, outside Kampala, where Museveni had commanded his rebel army in the jungle, and the government troops, unable to deal with the guerrillas, had inflicted bloody massacres on the local villages.

By going to the guerrilla camps, Pike had exposed himself to two dangers. The government troops might have taken him for a guerrilla spy, and the guerrillas for a plant sent by the authorities. As a white man he could have seemed suspect to both sides. In those days not many foreigners were seen in Uganda. Few people came here—on the contrary, almost everyone was trying to get out of the place. Accustomed to killing with impunity and often drunk, the government soldiers spent their time pillaging and raping, and could have arrested him on any excuse before battering him to death. No one would have gone looking for him, and even if they had, he'd never have been found. Too many people went missing in Uganda in those days.

Pike not only hadn't left Kampala, but had been to see the guerrillas in the forest at Luwero too. It was from his reports that the world learned about the cruelties of the Ugandan tyrants and the crimes committed by their troops and secret police. Also about Museveni, the young rebel, who at the head of a handful of guerrillas was trying to do the impossible. Museveni never forgot what Pike had done, and when he won the war and declared himself president, he offered him the chance to become editor-in-chief of the government paper, *New Vision*.

However, if he was counting on Pike to feel indebted to him and to repay him with faithful service and a servile attitude, he was bitterly mistaken. While remaining on the government budget, *New Vision* did not become a court paper, presenting the thoughtful ruler's daily agenda and a chronicle of his good deeds. It did not hesitate to point out the new government's mistakes, or to severely criticize and reprimand it. Pike took no notice of the presidential officials who tried to tell him what he should write about, and what his journalists should leave alone. He even put down the receiver when he was threatened. Unusual for Africa, *New Vision*'s independence brought it such fame and respect that it became the country's top paper. More people bought it than the opposition *Monitor*, which was hostile to the authorities. The envious grumbled that if Pike were an ordinary black Ugandan, Museveni would have got fed up with his lack of humility long ago and thrown him out. But as it was, they said, he feared the fuss that would be made in the outside world if he fired him. The journalist's white skin and foreign passport guaranteed his security.

Either way, Pike's friendship with the president, familiarity with the dignitaries, and knowledge of all the secrets of Ugandan politics, and also his hospitality, meant that for many years foreign journalists had started their trips to Uganda with a visit to his office or his home.

"The best thing will be if I call Emmy and ask him to meet with you," he said in his room at the newspaper office, where I found him on a Saturday afternoon, and mentioned our mutual acquaintance from years ago. He clearly wasn't keen to talk himself. He gave the impression of being in a hurry to get somewhere, preoccupied by some pressing thoughts.

In Kampala gossip soon reached me that Pike had fallen into disfavor with Museveni, and that the president had finally lost patience with him. Rumors of the journalist's imminent resignation were one of the main themes of the conversations held on the Speke Hotel veranda. It was said that to annoy the Briton, the president was appointing as his successor his own obedient secretary Robert Kabushenga, who had once worked at Pike's paper as a newspaper inserter or bundler at night when he was a student.

The president's anger was prompted by an article published on the front page about how talks between the authorities and Joseph Kony's guerrillas had ended in a total fiasco, and how the army was planning to round up the rebels in the Gulu area, and also in southern Sudan. Museveni was boiling with rage, and in a speech delivered on Independence Day, he threatened that he'd "have to sort out" *New Vision*. That was when the story first went round Kampala that Pike had been summoned to the presidential palace and had angrily resigned. When gossip about this reached the rival *Monitor*, the journalists and editors there couldn't contain their joy.

⁓

When I asked Pike straight out, he replied that it was inappropriate for him to talk about it. Whereas Emmy, who was to give me answers to all my questions and resolve any doubts I had, stated tersely and categorically that the dispute between Museveni and his friend was not about the guerrillas from Gulu, but about the elections; the president had decided to stand as a candidate, despite earlier having more than once given assurance that he wouldn't run again.

It started with the fact that, with Pike in charge, the paper had not supported Museveni's courtiers, when on their master's orders they had started insisting on the need for an amendment to the constitution, which unambiguously limited the presidential terms of office to two. Museveni was already in the twentieth year of his rule. First he had reigned for ten years as victor in the civil war, conqueror of those wicked, bloody tyrants Amin and Obote. Then, however, wishing to disassociate himself from the old African despots whom he had publicly condemned, he had announced elections and had won them twice. In the process he had reached the nonextendible limit for a president's time in office that he himself had introduced.

But now, clearly unable to cope with losing power, he had decided to change the rules that he personally had established. Until now he had always insisted that political parties are the source of all evil, the cause of all the misfortunes that had befallen Uganda. It was they, he explained, who had caused the divisions between people and prompted them to split into us and them, friends and enemies; incapable of achieving reconciliation, they had incited wars and killed people.

On assuming power, he had immediately banned the activities of all political parties as the embodiment of pure evil. They could exist, but they weren't allowed to hold rallies, congresses, or demonstrations, and above all to take part in elections. Their candidates were allowed to enter electoral lists, but only by first name and surname, without any reference to party allegiance, color, or program. Every five years he held a special national plebiscite in which his subjects voted for whether they wanted the political parties to return or preferred to make do without them. Not wanting to infuriate their ruler, but also genuinely agreeing with him, each time his subjects had declared themselves to be against political parties.

And now all of a sudden Museveni had changed his mind and started saying the complete opposite—that political parties were necessary, that they must be introduced, and for this purpose the constitution should be amended. Now he was encouraging something he used to regard as the worst possible sin, nothing less than a crime. It looked as if he was trying to put his compatriots to the test in a cunning way, using a ruse to discover what they really thought. Only later did it turn out that he wanted not just to add a paragraph about political parties to the constitution, but—having once got permission to introduce amendments—he was also planning to delete the regulation limiting presidential terms of office, and thus the length of his own reign. Consent to the activity of political parties was just going to be a concession, in exchange for which Museveni aimed to guarantee himself the top job for life.

Pike's newspaper had said this straight out, reminding the president that he was not only breaking his own promise, but that through this faithless act he was changing from a revolutionary into a common ruler who no longer regarded power as a service, but as a war trophy, or a reward he justly deserved. And so he would really be no different from those whom he had accused of being blinded by power, calling them despots, a disgrace, and the curse of Africa.

Only two or three years earlier Museveni had announced that if his subjects so wished, he would hand over power and resign his post without regret. Now, as demonstrators marched along the streets of Kampala, all the way to Nakasero Hill, where the presidential palace stood, shouting at the top of their voices "*Agende!*" meaning "He must go!" he seemed not to remember or understand a thing. "I should simply go? Leave all this?" he said, with a note of genuine surprise. "I fought, I risked my life for you to be free. And now you're telling me I should simply go away and tend my cows? You don't just shoo away a freedom fighter like a common pilferer out of the henhouse!"

He went to South Africa to ask the advice of Nelson Mandela, whom he regarded as his mentor. Mandela, the most famous political prisoner of the late twentieth century, had gained his freedom and become the first black president of his country. Promoting the need to forgive old wrongs and drop the desire for revenge, he had given up power after five years in government. In Africa something like that has rarely been

seen. Only the greatest, most eminent and invincible warriors, dream-
ers, and poets—Mandela, Julius Nyerere, or Léopold Senghor—were
able to give up something that others regarded as the most valuable
prize of all, the elixir of life.

The model of the good, righteous African ruler, whom many people
saw as Mandela's political heir, Museveni said he had decided not to
give up power yet. "Why is that?" asked Mandela. Museveni replied
that his subjects still needed him and still loved him. "Listen to me,
my son," answered Mandela, "the best time to leave and hand over
power is while the people still love you. For when they start to hate you,
you won't just be giving up power, you'll be afraid of them." "It's true,"
admitted Museveni, "but I still have so much to do, there are so many
things I haven't had time to complete." Mandela thought for a bit, and
then said: "How long have you been in power, Yoweri? Almost twenty
years? If you haven't managed to finish something in twenty years, you
won't do it in forty either. I'm already ninety and I still have so much
to do."

But now Museveni seemed more willing to listen to the words of the
Libyan leader, Colonel Muammar al-Gaddafi, who had ruled his country for almost forty years. This man encouraged him to stay in power,
and endorsed his plans. "Yoweri Kaguta Museveni is a revolutionary
who brought about revolution in Uganda. And revolutionaries are not
cans of Coca-Cola, they don't have sell-by dates," he said, when he
stopped in Kampala for a visit while traveling across Africa in a convoy
of cars. "Real revolutionaries do not resign or retire. You cannot muzzle
them with elections, because they didn't gain power as a result of them.
People who have been raised to the top by revolution should be allowed
to stay there to the end of their days."

Museveni's meetings with Mandela and al-Gaddafi, including the
words said at them, were reported by both papers, the opposition *Monitor* and the government's *New Vision*. Museveni demanded that Pike
should fire three journalists who had written critical articles about him.
Pike refused to do it. And so he had to leave.

"It's not like him. When did he change? What's got into him?"

We were sitting at the back of the veranda, smoking. The day had started off cloudy and gloomy. Fine rain had been lashing down since morning, driving the pedestrians and street vendors off the sidewalks.

"Who has changed? The president?" Emmy remarked across the table. "No, I don't think he has changed particularly."

For quite a while now, in fact from the very start of our meeting, he had seemed bored and absent. If not for Pike's intercession, I'm sure he wouldn't have accepted my invitation to the hotel, or even have answered my call.

"But he used to be different," I said, trying to keep the conversation going.

I wanted to find out who Museveni really was—the leader of whom it was said that instead of Uganda's savior he had become its latest curse. I hadn't the faintest chance of meeting him, all the more since he had already left Kampala in advance of the elections and hidden himself away among the acacias at his beloved farm, Rwakitura, in the west of the country, where he kept a herd of more than 1,500 head of long-horned cattle of the Watusi breed. "My cows are waiting for me," he would say, whenever he decided to leave the capital. It was said of Museveni that he kept photographs of his beloved, priceless cows in the family album, alongside pictures of his four children.

Apart from Pike, who hadn't time for conversations with foreign journalists, the only person who could tell me about Museveni was Emmy. He knew him just as well, and had done for just as long as Pike. In fact he knew everyone . . . But each question I asked, each remark was more forced and shallow, betraying my ignorance. Instead of encouraging Emmy to reveal confidences, or draw him into conversation, I kept alienating him more and more; with each passing moment he was getting closer to ending the meeting as soon as possible.

"Maybe he has changed, maybe not. In my view he was always like that," he said. "At first we saw him as an angel, which he never was. And now he's regarded as virtually the devil incarnate, but he's not that either."

◂◦▸

That evening, as I reviewed newspaper clippings about Museveni spread all over the table, I felt someone's gaze on me. I turned to look, but there was no one in the room. Through the wide-open door, I could hear music from the Rock Garden Café nightclub just across the wall, scraps of conversation, laughter, and the song of the cicadas hidden in the trees.

I had the door open to ward off the loneliness that crept in here with the falling darkness. For fear of it, the people living in the upstairs rooms preferred to sit until late at night on the noisy, lively hotel veranda, to put off the moment when the door would crash shut behind them and they'd be left all alone in total silence.

I had chosen rooms in a wing on the ground floor, beside the wall separating the hotel from the nightclub. They gave an illusion of familiarity and security that wasn't apparent in the isolated rooms upstairs, even the ones adjoining the corridor. You only had to leave the door open and let in the noises coming from the street or across the wall, the smell, or even the heavy night air, steeped in the humidity of the incipient rainy season, to drive away loneliness and the bitter, stifling feeling of confusion, pointlessness, and universal doubt.

The sensation that someone was looking at me, which had distracted me from my notes and clippings, had eased a bit. However, I could still feel that gaze quite distinctly. Outside night was falling, pitch-black, stuffy, and cloudy. The impenetrable darkness echoed with noises. Somewhere I once read that darkness separates people, and thus intensifies the desire to be together. Maybe that was what made the guests from the upstairs rooms sit on the veranda until late at night, and told me not to close the door.

Attracted by the stream of light, sometimes girls from the bar looked in here. Newly hired young waiters who couldn't find their own rooms in the dark occasionally stopped to ask the way, but would feel too shy to speak; they'd stand petrified in the doorway, and try to catch my attention with an imploring stare.

As I stood up, I caught my thigh on an open drawer. And there was Samuel looking out of it, gazing at me from a black-and-white photo. I knew that expression, but this time it seemed even more serious and adult than usual, totally unsuited to his boyish face.

Since arriving in Kampala, I had stopped thinking about Gulu. I had left the town, its affairs, and its inhabitants on the far side of the Karuma Falls, on the other bank of the great river.

In wealthy, carefree Kampala, the war in Acholi-land, the spirits and phantoms there seemed nonthreatening and so far away as to be unreal. It was impossible to believe they were part of the same world. They didn't fit in with this one, and were just as surprising as the beggars who came at dawn to the downtown area, perched comfortably on the hills. Tattered and torn, dirty and gray, they didn't fit in with the rich hotels established in colonial tenements, or the clean, bright glass skyscrapers housing banks and airline companies.

The beggars came from Kireka, the part of town known as the "Acholi district," which was on a hill across the railroad tracks. More than 10,000 war refugees and runaways were said to live there, in shacks made of cardboard, plywood, tin, and plastic sheeting. No one knew exactly how many of them there were, because no one from the city ever went there, nor was anyone concerned about them. They were alien, from another world. The most disturbing and incomprehensible thing about them was the look in their eyes—full of despair and fear, subservient and beseeching. Only the older residents of Kampala recognized something about them that, though long since forgotten, was still horribly familiar. The days when fear and despair had been part of daily life in Kampala too were not in fact quite so remote.

◄◦►

As I gazed at Samuel's photograph, for a while he seemed like a stranger. Without the picture I couldn't have said what he looked like, what his eyes and mouth were like, the shape of his head, or the tone of his skin.

I also confirmed to my surprise that I couldn't remember Jackson's face, the look in his eyes, or his movements. Was he tall or small? Thin or well-built? I could relate in detail what he had done and said, but not what he was like physically. I could remember his words, but not his voice. I could remember the cold beer we drank at Franklin's Inn, the smell of the food coming from the kitchen in the yard, the relief brought by the shadow of the dying day—everything that had an effect on the senses, size, color, smell, sound, and touch.

But Jackson was stuck in the middle of it all like a phantom, with no face, shape, or any physical properties whatsoever. Or perhaps I had taken them away from him myself, reducing him to the role of an object, a useful device. He didn't interest me as a person—he was just necessary to me to understand what I was dealing with. Although we had spent such a lot of time together and talked to each other so much, I knew very little about him. I didn't know what he wanted in life, what he dreamed of, or what he feared. I had never asked him. And as he hadn't been asked, he didn't say. Maybe he really was an apparition? A spirit, so many of which were flying about in Acholi-land?

Nora told me about herself, even if I didn't ask. She also listened to my stories with curiosity, and was interested in them. I could remember her and see her clearly, as if she were standing here next to me, close enough to touch. I could hear her voice and feel the sun-warmed skin on her arm.

What about Samuel? I had never thought about what would happen to him in the future; I only really knew about his past. That was what concerned me. Why couldn't I remember his face?

Peering into the drawer at the cardboard folder lying in it, I ran my eyes over a page in Nora's handwriting, where Samuel was describing how he had been given a gun. It happened soon after the incident on the square at the guerrilla village in Sudan, when he had seen Joseph Kony, leader of the Lord's Army, in a white robe like a priest's cassock. He couldn't refuse to accept the gun, just as he couldn't refuse to travel back into Uganda with his unit.

One night they had raided a village called Siriri, where everyone was fast asleep. They attacked by night, because in the daytime there were sentries placed around the villages and camps, and if they spotted guerrillas in the bush, they sounded the alarm with loud whistles. In Siriri they had managed to surprise almost all the residents. Only a few had escaped into the undergrowth beyond the village. The guerrillas had driven the villagers out of their round thatched huts and gathered them on the main square. They separated the children from the adults. The

older guerrillas began questioning the peasants about soldiers—where
they were stationed, how many of them there were, when they called in
at the village, and which of the locals reported to them. Meanwhile the
younger rebels, including Samuel, looted the huts, taking money, food,
clothes, hens, and even cooking pots. Once they had plundered each
hut, they set fire to its thatched roof.

The flames shooting into the sky made the square as bright as day.
When they had finished their interrogation, the older guerrillas started
killing the villagers. The commanders forbade them from shooting
unnecessarily, to save bullets, and also because the noise of shots could
alert the army. The peasants were tied up and made to lie on the ground,
as the guerrillas unhurriedly murdered them one by one—men, women,
old people, and also small children who weren't fit to be prisoners. They
killed them with machetes, axes, hoes, and large knives, usually used as
agricultural tools. None of the villagers put up resistance or fought for
their lives. Terror and a sense of doom had taken away their capacity
for any kind of action.

As they left the brightly burning village, they cut down the mango
trees growing on its edges. They always did that, to prevent the trees
from bearing any more fruit, which could have saved the inhabitants
from dying of hunger.

They never, or almost never, attacked army posts. They only raided
Acholi villages, whose inhabitants refused to believe in the power of
Joseph Kony, which was seen as a betrayal deserving a terrible punishment. So, on the orders of their superiors, the guerrillas killed the
villagers in extremely cruel ways. They butchered and burned them
alive, forced the prisoners to commit cannibalism and infanticide. They
raped and tortured, cut off people's lips, gouged out their eyes, and
chopped off their hands and feet. They left behind bloodied corpses
and gutted houses. And also the wrappers from cookies and candy they
stole from the village stores, which instantly changed them back into
children unable to resist sweets. With every murder the more senior
guerrillas kept telling the younger ones: "Now you have nowhere to go
home to. There's no way back for you."

At first Samuel was horrified by the savage cruelty of the boys who had been guerrillas for several years. They outdid each other in horror, basking in it, as if they could find the meaning of life in this nightmare, or some pleasure. But he too never refused to kill. Gradually he became just like the guerrillas who had kidnapped him from his village and robbed him of his old life. Now he too was kidnapping other children, shooting at soldiers, attacking villages, looting, and murdering.

Those of the guerrillas who stood out for their obedience and cruelty were promoted and became officers. The older ones were given wives as a reward, and the younger ones were better treated—they weren't beaten, had subordinates to do things for them, and received better food, and even medicines. The girls who bore the commanders children didn't have to fight. But no one cared about the ordinary soldiers, not even when they were killed. Samuel remembered how they had lost a battle against Dinka warriors in Sudan, after which his commander Opiro Anaka had looked upon dozens of dead guerrillas, then just shrugged his shoulders and said: "That's nothing. Uganda is full of children."

I closed the drawer.

The table was covered in newspaper clippings about President Museveni. Without thinking I started to put them in order, first according to length, from shortest to longest. After a while, however, I decided to sort them by date, from newest to oldest. The oldest one was from a British illustrated magazine which called the Ugandan president Africa's great hope.

◄•►

No other Ugandan president had ruled the country for as long. In fact few leaders in the whole of Africa could boast of such a long reign. And Museveni was still in power and had no intention of resigning. On the contrary, with each year he tightened his grip and extended his influence. It was said that Uganda alone wasn't enough for him, but that he was thinking of a large, mighty empire stretching into the heart of Africa, on the shores of its great lakes, from the jungle-bound river Congo to the Sudanese marshes on the Nile. And even further, all the way to the ocean.

Hadn't he sent his troops to the wars in neighboring Sudan, Congo, and Rwanda, and hadn't he tried to put his friends on the thrones of those countries, after helping them to form guerrilla armies and incite armed uprisings? He didn't even hide his ambitions and plans. "I do not regard Congolese or Rwandan affairs as foreign," he would say, urging the presidents of Kenya, Tanzania, Rwanda, and Burundi to agree to unite their countries into one mighty state, an African superpower. "We only have to agree to this and we would be a second Persia, a state with vast territory and one hundred million inhabitants," insisted the Ugandan, who to the irritation of the haughty Kenyans regarded himself as best suited to the role of hegemon of this empire on Lake Victoria.

The readers of one of the local papers had voted him "Greatest Ugandan of the Twentieth Century," though at the time there were still a few years left until the end of it. Out of more than seventy candidates suggested by the paper, Museveni had gained the most votes. Far behind the president, in second and third place were John Paul Ofwono, the tallest man in Uganda, at a height of seven foot six and a half inches, and Kabaka Ronald Muwenda Mutebi, ruler of Buganda, the biggest of the local kingdoms.

I had met King Ronnie, as his subjects called him, years ago in Mbabane, capital of the southern African kingdom of Swaziland. The Bugandan Kabaka had come to attend the birthday party of Swazi King Mswati III, an annual event to which the other African monarchs were regularly invited.

The host was a ruler in the full sense of the word, the last real king in Africa who not only reigned but ruled, not only led his subjects but regarded himself as their guardian and master. The party was held at a soccer stadium; from first light warriors had been coming down from the hills in feather headdresses, leopard and buffalo skins, carrying spears and shields. On the field, military and school bands were playing marches and jazz standards, and women in colored calico dresses were performing whirling tribal dances. The most distinguished guests were arriving in limousines, which drove up to a podium where the birthday boy was sitting with the Queen Mother.

The Bugandan Kabaka got out of his car with a worried look on his face. He stopped hesitantly before the red carpet spread on the grass, as it usually is for world leaders and heads of state. He seemed to be trying his best to avoid setting foot on it. A Ugandan journalist who was watching this scene explained to me that Museveni allowed Ronnie to be king on condition that he didn't behave like a king. Otherwise he would not only take away his crown but dissolve the whole kingdom of Buganda. The Kabaka was afraid that if he stepped onto the red carpet, Museveni would regard it as a breach of the rules.

He couldn't yet sense or decipher the moods of Africa. He had only recently returned to Uganda from Britain, where he was educated and had spent his entire life. He was a small child when soldiers stormed the palace of his father Mutesa II, who apart from being Kabaka of Buganda was also president of the country. His prime minister, Milton Obote, had no intention of sharing power with the Bugandan king, so he had incited the army against him, deposed him and driven him out of the country.

Only Museveni, who had triggered off and won a civil war, had agreed to resurrect Buganda and the other Ugandan kingdoms, Toro, Bunyoro, Busoga, Ankole, and Rwenzururu, which had been banned by the power-mad Obote. He had also allowed Ronnie, heir to the throne, to return from exile to the palace on the hill. But the president had imposed a condition—the kings were not to meddle in running the country or get involved in politics at all. They could not have their own police, courts, or prisons, as they had in the past, and they weren't allowed to collect taxes or duties from their subjects. They would only be allowed to make sure the old customs and rituals were preserved— their role was to see that the young people were brought up to respect their traditions and ancestors, and were guarded against the temptations of modern life.

Moreover, he had only permitted the revival of the Ankole kingdom to win the support of his own compatriots. Museveni came from the Hima people, herders and warriors from the Ankole kingdom in the west of the country, between Lakes Victoria and Edward. The Hima are cousins of the Tutsi, who rule the neighboring kingdoms, and also the modern states derived from them, Rwanda and Burundi.

Although he was from the proud Hima, Museveni had never been a monarchist. When Obote deposed the Kabaka-president and abolished the Ugandan kingdoms, Museveni was studying political science at university in Dar es-Salaam, Tanzania, whose president Julius Nyerere was a pioneer and teacher of ascetic African socialism. In those days the academy in Dar es-Salaam was a hotbed of young revolutionaries from all over Africa, who idolized their Tanzanian master, or *Mwalimu*, and were only too eager to get their hands on a diploma, and if necessary, a rifle too, before returning to their own countries to oust the old order and introduce a new one in its place.

During his studies in Dar es-Salaam, as a member of the revolutionary fraternity, the young Museveni underwent military training in neighboring Mozambique, where black rebels had raised an armed revolt against the white colonizers from Portugal.

After returning from revolutionary academy in Dar es-Salaam he enlisted in President Obote's secret police, but he didn't keep the job for long. It was less than a year before Ugandan army commander Idi Amin Dada staged his coup d'état and deposed Obote. Museveni escaped to Tanzania, where with the help of his *Mwalimu* Julius Nyerere he founded his first guerrilla movement. He was then twenty-seven years old.

—o—

Amin and Nyerere genuinely loathed each other. The *Mwalimu* in Dar es-Salaam, a visionary, a worldly man of great culture, was outraged by the Ugandan's crudeness and ignorance, and regarded it as a disgrace and a profanity that someone incapable of passing an exam to become an army officer should have the audacity to strive for power and call himself president. Meanwhile Amin regarded the Tanzanian leader as the embodiment of everything he despised. He disdained the conceit and arrogance of the chosen few who succeeded in graduating from learned academies, their doubts and philosophizing, incomprehensible to ordinary people, their physical weakness and fear of violence.

"I wish to assure you that I admire and love you greatly," wrote Amin to Nyerere in a letter which before sending he showed to all the journalists in Kampala. "If you were a woman, in spite of your gray hair I would regard you as worthy of becoming my wife. However, you are a man, in view of which this eventuality does not arise." When the Tanzanian failed to respond to this taunt, Amin called him a coward and a whore.

The world was truly outraged at Amin's cruelties, but more often laughed at his eccentricities and buffoonery. Only Nyerere took action against the tyrant. He supported the Ugandan rebels who escaped from Amin to Tanzania and formed a guerrilla force in exile. The infuriated Amin challenged his neighbor to settle the argument like a man, in the boxing ring, without involving others.

Amin was a giant, almost six foot six inches tall, and weighed more than 220 pounds. Everything he achieved in life he owed to his physical strength. Serving in the British colonial army, he had stood out as an excellent rugby player, and was also a heavyweight boxing champion. He had won all his fights and left the ring undefeated, to take on command of independent Uganda's army. Knowing his advantage over Nyerere, who was small and slight, and looked like a dwarf next to him, Amin promised he would only fight him with one hand, his left, weaker one, and would have the right one tied behind his back.

Until finally, impudent, bumptious, and convinced of his own might and invincibility, Amin made the greatest mistake in his life —he sent troops across the border and invaded Tanzania.

By all accounts the boundary war erupted by mistake. Regarding himself as the hero and chief of all Africa, Amin was planning to lead African troops into Pretoria and Cape Town, to release his South African brothers from the slavery and oppression imposed by descendants of the European settlers who called themselves Africa's white tribe. With this aim, as field marshal and commander-in-chief, he was conducting exercises on Lake Victoria, during which the Ugandan airmen, gunners, and infantry were training for the liberation of South Africa.

And it was during maneuvers on Lake Victoria that the unfortunate error was made, fraught with consequences. At some point one of the units came under fire from its own artillery. Having staged a coup and usurped power himself, Amin did not trust his own generals, and even on exercises refused to provide them with radio communications, in case they should happen to form a conspiracy. Unable to inform the artillery batteries that they were firing on their own troops, the Ugandan soldiers who were under fire fled across the border, accidentally invading Tanzania.

War broke out. Amin's soldiers set about robbing, murdering, and raping, but were defeated and driven back by the Tanzanians. The Tanzanian army, supported by Museveni's Ugandan guerrillas, crossed the border and headed straight for Kampala. Seeing no way out, Amin secretly fled the capital, never to return again.

In Kampala a new government was formed, in which Museveni, as the guerrilla commander, became minister of war. Elections for a new president were announced too, in which Museveni decided to take part. However, he was beaten hollow, all the more since Obote, who had returned from exile to regain power, had no qualms about cheating, and his supporters falsified the election results.

When Obote declared himself winner of the election and thus the new president, Museveni refused to swear allegiance to him, and returned to the bush to found a new guerrilla force. This time, however, he did not flee to Tanzania, nor did he ask anyone for protection and help. He fought his new war just outside Kampala, in the vicinity of a town called Sambwe, where he holed up in the forest with his most inseparable and loyal friend, his half-brother Caleb Akandwanaho, who in the guerrillas assumed the name Salim Saleh. "At the start there were barely thirty-five of us and we only had twenty-seven guns," said Museveni, recalling those days without hiding his emotion.

The rebels were up against an army of 100,000, whom they were fighting at the very gates of the capital. It looked as if the soldiers would easily beat the guerrillas, track them down and catch them in the forest and villages, torture them to death and wipe them out entirely. But far from it—Museveni and his comrades often gave them the slip, avoided the traps set for them, survived the ambushes uninjured and exposed various tricks and plots. The generals called Museveni a snake and threatened to rip out his deadly poisonous fangs and crush his head. News of the elusive, audacious rebels soon ran round the towns and villages all over the unfortunate country, oppressed by wars and tyrants, and bullied by cruel government troops who got away with their crimes scot-free. More and more volunteers kept joining the guerrillas in the forest near Luwero, some to get revenge, others in search of adventure, and to gain a victory they were increasingly confident of winning.

After five years of fighting, the guerrillas defeated the government troops, who scattered and dispersed. Just like Amin before him, Obote fled the country. The rebels entered the capital, which the soldiers had abandoned. Museveni appointed his guerrilla commanders as ministers and provincial governors, and soon after declared himself the new president. Never before in Africa had anyone brought off such a splendid and unexpected victory.

⚬

The leafy town of Luwero, bisected by the asphalt highway from Gulu to Kampala, seemed to have forgotten the days when its small fields, banana groves, and mango trees were regarded as a sinister land of death, where people were killed by the thousand, for no reason, and in extreme agony. Presidents changed, but the nightmare continued, and Uganda never stopped flowing with blood, as if it had been sacrificed to the god of war and evil.

In Kampala it was said that in the triangle marked by the towns of Luwero, Mubende, and Mpigi the ground was strewn with human bones. Soldiers hunted guerrillas, guerrillas hunted soldiers, soldiers murdered each other, while everyone murdered peasants from the local villages. There were so many corpses that no one could keep up with the burials, and they neglected the proper funeral rites and ceremonies. The soldiers just abandoned the victims' bodies in gutted villages, on vegetable plots, in savannahs and forests—the kingdom of wild animals; often they submerged them in Lake Victoria or threw them into the Nile from helicopters.

As a result, a vast number of ghosts of all these war victims had appeared in the green hills of Luwero. Not given a proper send-off, not having received the due sacrifice, their spirits hadn't made their way to the land of the dead, but were still in the world of the living, seeking solace, and also retribution. They were getting revenge by bringing down plagues and misfortunes on their murderers. They also went into the service of evil witches, the only creatures capable of appeasing them. These witches then sent them among people to cause all manner of harm to those on whom they cast their spells.

On the right bank of the Nile, in Acholi-land, people believed the neglect of funeral rites disrupted the natural order and led to an unusual multitude of evil spirits thirsting for revenge; to their minds, this was the cause of all the disasters which had befallen their land, and the rest of Uganda too.

From Luwero the spirits wandered into the world, using unsuspecting people as their guides. They would imperceptibly enter soldiers from the routed government army, who in fear of revenge and punishment, were trying to make their way home unnoticed. Tainted with death and the harm they had done, they were defenseless against the spirits, who found them easy prey.

Many Acholi had served in the government troops in Luwero, including Jackson's father and his uncle Vincent Otti.

◄○►

As we passed Luwero on the way to Kampala, Jackson said that whenever he came this way he thought of his father, and tried to imagine him as a killer, a master of life and death, drunk on power. Luckily he could hardly remember him. He was a small boy when his father came home from the war to his native village of Atiak. His mother told him that he came back possessed. At night he would spring awake and shout in a strange, incomprehensible language. He became violent and full of anger. He would disappear for days on end, without telling anyone either where he was going or when he'd be back. His mother told the children to keep well away from him.

Until finally he hanged himself on the branch of a mango tree just outside the village.

"He must have had something on his conscience," said Jackson, staring through the bus window at the roadside market stalls flashing by. "Considering how he died."

He could remember his father being cut down from the tree.

In Acholi-land people are afraid of suicides. Taking one's own life is regarded as proof of possession, and anyone who does is even more dangerous after death than in life, because the spirit that got inside him will now try to get out and find a new victim. So no one is allowed to touch a hanged man while he is being buried or while funeral rites are being held for him.

And so rather than taking the body of Jackson's father down from the tree, his sons dug a pit underneath the branch where he was hanging, which was to serve as his grave. Once it was ready, they fetched an old woman from the village who, if only in view of her great age, was regarded as highly resistant to spirits and spells. It wasn't easy to persuade her to cut the rope by which his father was hanging. The Acholi believed that whoever cut a hanged man's noose would soon die too. Finally they had managed to win the old woman over with two clay jugs of *kwete* beer, one of which she drank on the spot in a single swig; then, muttering to herself, she clambered up the tree and hacked through the rope with a machete.

The corpse tumbled to the ground, but did not fall straight into the grave dug for it. Its legs bent at the knees, its bare feet stuck out of the shallow pit in the red sand. The old woman scrambled down the tree but refused further assistance; clutching her second jug of beer, she tramped back to the village. With no one to help them now, the relatives decided that Jackson would push his father's legs into the grave. As a five-year-old boy he was the most innocent, and by that token also more resistant to evil forces. One of his uncles cut a long pole from a bush and showed him how to use it.

Only once he had shoved the bare feet into the pit did they fill in the grave and press it flat. And that was all—there were no funeral rites for the hanged man, nor was there any mourning. That evening the men cut down and uprooted the mango tree, and burned it for charcoal, which was shared out among all the villagers. Only the dead man's relatives were excluded; they weren't allowed so much as a stick of it.

That night his father came to Jackson in a dream. The next morning, when he told his mother about it, she seized him by the hand, raced at top speed to the market, and bought a black hen. Then, still dragging him after her, she ran to the nearby home of the old woman who had cut his father down from the tree. She was called the *ajwaka*. She knew how to cure illnesses, and it was also said of her that she could hear and understand spirits, and they talked to her if they needed something from people.

They didn't go into the hut where she lived, but stopped outside the open door, where his mother called to her. The woman told Jackson to describe once again what had happened in his dream. She listened carefully, without saying a single word in reply, and then massaged his head with her hands. Her wrinkled, bony fingers were warm, and their touch was nice and gentle. In a voice trembling with anxiety, Jackson's mother asked if his father's spirit could have got into the boy. Jackson didn't know how the old woman replied, because on her instruction his mother had sent him a short way off, and he couldn't hear what they were talking about from that distance. Then they went home without any rush, and his mother seemed calmer. The black hen they had bought at the market remained in the old woman's yard.

In Acholi-land in those days there were lots of people like Jackson's father, who came back from the war near Luwero and couldn't get a grip on themselves again. Terrified by their own transformation, they fell seriously ill and died. Some took their own lives, others vanished without trace. No one knew what happened to the spirits that had possessed them, changed them, and driven them to madness or death.

There were also men like Jackson's beloved uncle Vincent Otti, who without ever taking the uniform off their backs went straight into the forest to join the guerrillas. A vast number of these people appeared after the war too. They took their spirits with them—it was the spirits that controlled their future destiny, thoughts, and deeds.

The number of corpses kept rising, and with them the army of spirits grew and gained strength. The spirits spread about the whole country and would eventually have taken over the entire world of men, making them into their lackeys, if not for a warrior who issued them a challenge.

He had decided to wage one last war on them and their servants. He was determined to win it, to stop all the devastation and destruction, and put an end to the killing. Then the spirits would stop multiplying, and there would be time to bury the bodies with due ceremony.

The name of this warrior was Yoweri Kaguta Museveni. He must have allied with some powerful forces, for not only had he won the war and declared himself the country's new leader, but he had also conquered the evil spirits. He had brought peace to the lands of Buganda, Ankole, Bunyoro, and Toro, and had prevented more killing. The spirits had stopped multiplying, and people were slowly starting to cope with burials and funerals again.

Only on the other bank of the Nile, in Acholi-land, had the spirits proved even stronger than Museveni. They weren't afraid of him and wouldn't give up their weapons, so the war was still going on there as before. Elsewhere, purged and free of spirits, people were going home to their villages and families, and returning to their old incarnations as farmers, shepherds, fishermen, masons, and carpenters.

In Acholi-land things were different, and nothing had gone back to normal. One day, when Jackson's uncle, Vincent Otti, returned to his native village of Atiak, he told his men to set it on fire and kill all its inhabitants, his own neighbors and kin.

◄◦►

Kampala was getting ready for the elections like a girl preparing for her first ball. Plastered in yellow posters advertising the ruling party, the city was waiting for the appointed day impatiently, but trustfully, with faith in a happy outcome, like a hopeful person looking forward to his dreams coming true, in anticipation of the kind of adventure he only knows from stories, which makes it all the more enticing.

Full of concern and gravity, the faces of candidates for ministers and deputies peered at the public from the city's walls. The candidates in yellow colors boasted of their experience and promised to be caring and responsible. From much smaller, poorer posters in other colors, their rivals promised change. The election campaign was gradually reaching its end. The last rallies, gatherings, and social evenings had been convened, and the party activists were now appearing in the final pre-election broadcasts and debates on radio and television. In the morning papers well-known journalists and scholars from the local university were predicting the election result and forecasting what it would mean for Uganda. For the first time the citizens were getting real, full freedom to choose their next ruler. If only for this reason unusual events were expected.

New Vision, the newspaper regarded as favorable to the government, recalled a story from some years earlier, when by way of experiment President Museveni had allowed the citizens of Kampala to elect their own mayor. As if to defy the president, from a large number of candidates, Kampala had chosen the very one whom Museveni considered the least suitable.

Nasser Ntege Sebaggala was a devout Muslim, and since making the pilgrimage to Mecca had gained the right to add the honorific title *al hajji* to his surname. He was a businessman, and had made his fortune in the days when as leader Idi Amin had expelled 100,000 Indians from the country, descendants of poor workers whom the British had drafted in long ago to help construct the railroad from Mombasa to Kisumu on Lake Victoria.

Many of these new immigrants had then settled in Africa, and thanks to their entrepreneurship and diligence, instead of workers they had become doctors, teachers, traders, bankers, and the owners of factories, cotton, sugarcane, tea, and coffee plantations. Hating them for their wealth, education, and superiority, the natives regarded them as ruthless usurers and bloodsuckers. So when to win favor with his compatriots, Amin told the Indians to get out—he claimed to have done it on the orders of the Supreme Being, who came to him in a dream—the Ugandans danced in the streets with joy.

Amin had divided the Indians' property among his courtiers, soldiers, and friends. But not knowing how to run banks, stores, factories, workshops, or plantations, they had squandered them or sold them off, reducing the entire economy to ruin. In this formerly affluent country, terrible poverty prevailed, though some people had made money out of it. So indeed, by taking advantage of the lack of competition and the empty stores, the bold, enterprising Sebaggala had made his fortune, opening several fashionable clothing boutiques in Kampala and a foreign exchange bureau.

Former students at Makerere University can still remember how he used to drive up to the university yard in a golden car, dressed from head to toe in gold or orange, to charm the prettiest girls with his wealth, extravagance, and flamboyance. The students envied him his fortune, but despised his vulgarity and lack of education.

When he announced that he was standing for election as mayor of Kampala, the capital's elite whooped with laughter. Museveni had ruled that important official posts could only be held by people qualified with at least a high school diploma. Sebaggala had not even finished grade school; he was self-educated and could barely stammer along in English, though that was the official language in Uganda. Thus his candidacy was regarded as just more madness, another eccentric idea from the capital's rich man.

However, Sebaggala's decision to become mayor was not a joke, but was designed to take power away from Museveni, whom he regarded as an enemy. The president had not only returned their stolen property to the Indians, and thus increased competition for the local rich, but by reviving the country's economy he had also deprived them of the convenient, idle privilege of the monopolist and the opportunity to get rich easily on contraband or trade in controlled deficit goods.

When Sebaggala defeated the candidates supported by Museveni and won the election, the city was speechless with amazement. All the mockery and ridicule of Sebaggala's manners and lack of education had come to nothing. Most Kampalans had left school even earlier than he had, so he was more familiar to them than all the smart guys with diplomas. Anyone who had some reason to be dissatisfied with the president voted for Sebaggala—not just people who had benefited from the unexpected promotion afforded them by Amin, which Museveni's new rules had now doomed, but also some of the president's former comrades and supporters, who were now accusing him of betraying the revolution and of having dictatorial ambitions.

But before the new mayor took office, it came to light that he had faked the certificates from correspondence courses he claimed to have completed at colleges in Great Britain. A trip he made to America led to an even bigger scandal when he tried to cash some fake traveler's checks at an airport, was arrested and given a prison sentence. Finally pardoned and released, he came home to Uganda, where a crowd of several thousand people was waiting for him at Entebbe airport; they greeted him like a folk hero, and even admired him for trying to rob the rich on the other side of the ocean.

Museveni realized that Sebaggala would bring shame on Uganda and took away his post as mayor. In vain, because the new elections that immediately had to be announced were won by a loyal friend of Sebaggala, who meanwhile declared that he would run in the next presidential elections. This time he was totally crushed, but during the campaign he toured the country, predicting that his fight against Museveni would end the same way as the duel between David and Goliath. "And you all know how it ended," he would swagger.

The episode with Sebaggala had put Museveni's patience to the test, and for a long time had discouraged him from the idea of holding elections for deputies, mayors, councilors, or senators, and above all for president. Indeed, he had only agreed to the elections in order to be able to stand in them an infinite number of times himself, and stay in power until death.

Museveni was sure he was right. As a rule, however, big cities don't like their leaders, and are just waiting for the chance to settle scores with them. Whereas leaders aren't fond of their ungrateful capitals. This time too there was a hint of potential surprise in the air in Kampala. A good friend of the president, his old comrade-in-arms and confidant, was trying to deprive him of his kingdom, with the support of his wife, who was Museveni's former girlfriend from the days when he was still fighting as a guerrilla. This woman had never forgotten or forgiven him for dropping her.

The first time I came to Kampala, the city was only just back on its feet after years of indigence, collapse, lawlessness, and war. It was impoverished, sad and gray, unsure of itself and weak. It only took a few years to recover and regain its former flowery beauty.

Winston Churchill was enchanted by Kampala and called it the pearl of Africa. Spread over green hills above the vast blue lake, it had seduced the British conquerors, explorers, and settlers. It was one of the few cities in all Africa that weren't founded by foreigners, but which had existed and flourished before they got here.

It was the capital of the kingdom of Buganda, whose rulers had chosen Mengo and Rubaga hills as the sites for their courts and palaces. In time the city grew, occupying more hills and moving down from them, ever closer to the shores of the lake. On one of the hills the British soldiers pitched camp and later erected a fort; they had come here under the command of African conqueror Lord Frederick John Dealtry Lugard, veteran of wars in Afghanistan, Sudan, and Burma.

The newcomers from the distant British Isles were amazed by the wealth and power of Buganda, the biggest and strongest of the local kingdoms. Before subjugating Buganda, they sought agreement with it. In the first place they preferred to conquer the only slightly weaker and less splendid kingdoms of Ankole and Toro, and above all valiant Bunyoro, which had resisted the British until its population was almost entirely annihilated. The fall of Bunyoro pleased only its rival Buganda, which, too self-confident, easily let itself be cheated by the perfidious British and agreed to accept their protectorate in exchange for a promise of authority over other, adjoining kingdoms. The Kabaka of Buganda regarded himself as an ally and equal of the monarchs in London. His officials and soldiers served as lackeys for the British, conquering the lands around the lake and collecting tributes from their residents. Out of Buganda and the rest of the conquered monarchies the British created the protectorate of Uganda, and years later when it declared independence, they gave back Kampala to be its capital. They had grown fond of the city and had built Makerere, the first university in the whole of East Africa here, opened Mulago, the best hospital in the area (a gift from the British queen), and brought in the railroad.

Kampala had everything needed to claim the title of number one metropolis, not just in the whole of East Africa, but at the heart of the continent too. But just as Uganda seemed set for a bright future, suddenly all the plagues on earth descended on the country, rapidly changing it from cheerful and carefree to gloomy and dismal, a land full of danger.

-◦-

The first seven of many lean years came with the reign of Idi Amin Dada.

Perhaps no leader did as much harm to Africa's reputation as Amin. He was the personification of horror, known as the curse and disgrace of Africa. Milton Obote said that Amin was the most terrible monster ever to emerge from the womb of an African mother. For many years after he fled Africa, those who were ill-disposed to the continent would cite him as an example of the allegedly innate barbarity of the Africans.

Those who knew him claim that he exuded menace and goodwill in equal measure. He always stood out from the crowd—for his height, weight, strength, booming voice, noisy laughter, jabbering speech, insatiable lust, shrewdness, and brutality. People said his mother was a witch who knew how to cure people, but could also cast spells on them; moreover she was from the Lugbara tribe, which produced many powerful wizards. The popular explanation was that as the son of a witch, Amin was bound to be different from ordinary mortals.

His eccentricities and outbursts of cruelty were explained by fits of a shameful disease he had caught from one of his numerous lovers, and also by the fact that he had never known his father, who had left the family in a rage, convinced Idi was not his son, but a bastard sired by the Bugandan king, Kabaka Daudi Chwa. Amin's mother had been summoned to the palace to treat the Kabaka's family. She was also meant to provide advice from the spirits who entered into her and told her how to prepare healing concoctions and herbs.

Abandoned by his father and brought up by his mother the witch, Amin grew into a giant and strongman, but in his heart and soul he remained a child—a large, cruel child, tetchy and irascible, going from one extreme to the other, from amusement and delight to dejection and rage. These mood swings and racing thoughts made him unpredictable.

"Amin's temperament is unstable and unreliable. One day he emits an extremely warm and friendly aura, but soon after his face assumes a terrible, grim expression. One moment he is convulsed with laughter, honestly amused like a child, but the next moment he flies into a rage," the London *Observer* wrote of him. "His strange disposition is reflected in his political decisions."

Only in the British colonial army, where he served loyally, was he ever successfully restrained. Men like him, strong and ruthless, but eager and obedient, were readily signed up. Later on, when the British colonies became independent states, they were promoted and entrusted with power, in the belief that after being such submissive servants and adjutants, they would do what they were told as free, independent people too. Thus from being a bold bullyboy sergeant, Idi Amin Dada was elevated to the role of commander-in-chief of the Ugandan army.

But once he was a general, he seized power and declared himself president. He did it out of fear for his own skin, when he realized he was in extreme danger of losing everything. In any case, he always acted that way, driven by instinct, and in time morbid suspicion too. He killed and ordered killings not out of madness or a savage bloodlust, but as a result of brutal calculation. He killed in the conviction that otherwise he would be killed himself. He got rid of his enemies the way a person removes obstacles in his path—without hesitation, doubt, or scruples.

In the case of Amin, power took a natural, primitive form, as pure and real as could be, totally unadorned, with no epaulets, embellishments, gold braid, court ceremonial, or liturgy of fine words. Amin didn't pretend he needed power to carry out a revolution, or that he had assumed it to serve others. In his hands power meant nothing but supremacy, or precedence. It was a privilege which allowed him to command others, to do and to have at the drop of a hat everything other people could never hope to get, but could only imagine in their dreams. It gave him total freedom to indulge his whims, even the wildest, most deeply hidden ones. Once he had power, Amin could do anything that came into his head, demand any item, take or confiscate it from someone else without having to reckon with anyone—without fear or sense of shame.

When I asked William Pike about Amin, he said it was that unceremonious attitude to power that the foreign journalists and diplomats who visited Kampala in those days found so fascinating. While others regarded power as the holy of holies, placed on an altar, Amin had made it into his whore, which prompted both admiration and alarm, delight and disgust. All the more since Amin was quite capable of looking them straight in the eye and suddenly saying: "I know what you are like. I am exactly the same as you."

If he really was the same as others, then anyone could have become an Amin. Anyone could take possession of power and make it his slave girl. I thought of Nora, who said that if Amin had stood for election and run for power, she would have voted for him. I took this to be her latest form of provocation, but she just shrugged.

"That's exactly what I'd have done. Nowadays it's easy to dump everything that's bad on Amin," she said indignantly, "but it was only thanks to him we stopped being slaves. At least he didn't pretend to be anyone—he wasn't ashamed of who he really was, or what he wanted most of all."

Thanks to the power that fell into his hands, he turned everything upside down—the old order, set customs, existing hierarchies, and codes of good and bad conduct. With a single command he was able to promote a corporal to general, and appoint an illiterate peasant to an official post at a ministry. In a single moment he could make a rich man into a homeless beggar. Wasn't that just what he did with the Indians, when he told them to get out of Uganda? And by giving away their factories, banks, and plantations to ordinary storekeepers, accountants, and constables he had also changed those people's destinies forever. Knowledge, education, experience, tradition, and social position, all of which had formerly determined status, now lost their significance. Henceforth only Amin was to promote and demote, which made his power almost supernatural. He sealed human fates and made life-and-death decisions. He played with his power and flaunted it, especially in front of foreigners, like a child having fun. And like a child, he loved applause.

"He used to watch journalists, trying to tell if he was making an impression on them, to sense if they were interested in what he had to say, whether it amused them. He put a lot of effort into that," said Pike. "People were outraged by the crimes he committed, but they also used to laugh at his eccentricities and escapades. It meant all the foreign correspondents liked him—there was always something to have a laugh about. Their Ugandan friends just occasionally asked the foreign correspondents not to write anything about Amin that could anger him. When he was in a good mood, he sang and danced with people, but when he was enraged there were no limits to his blind cruelty."

He declared himself the conqueror of the British Empire and King of Scotland, Field Marshal and President for life, the greatest and finest world leader. He insisted on being addressed as the lord of all living creatures on earth and of all the fish in the seas. He awarded himself military decorations for valor during the Second World War, and also called himself doctor of philosophy, though he admitted that he had never read a single book in his life. "I know more than all the doctors of philosophy put together, because as a soldier I know how to act," he would say. "I am a man of action."

As a man of action, he volunteered to join a war to retake Palestine from Israel. He also boasted that he would challenge the boxing champion Muhammad Ali to a fistfight. "But on condition the fight takes place in Tripoli, my brother Muammar Gaddafi will be the referee, Ayatollah Khomeini will be the announcer, and Yasser Arafat will agree to be my second," he would say, roaring with laughter at his own jokes.

He also declared that the UN headquarters should be moved to Uganda, which in his view was right at the heart of Africa and the entire world. At UN conferences in New York he spoke in his native dialect, Kakwa, claiming that English—of which he had a poor command—was the language of imperialists.

He was always writing letters to other world leaders. To the UN secretary-general he wrote that "Hitler was right to send six million Jews to the gas chambers because, as everyone knows, the Jews do harm to others." He accused the Zambian president Kenneth Kaunda of licking the boots of the imperialists and being their puppet, and he advised U.S. President Nixon to fire his secretary of state Henry Kissinger, whom Amin regarded as "a spy and a killer." "Altogether it would be a good thing if someone with black skin were finally elected as president of America," wrote Amin. "Henry, that guy who's running Uganda is some kind of a monkey," complained Nixon on the phone to Kissinger.

But his favorite, most frequent addressee was the British queen, whom he had visited on one of his first official trips as president. On this occasion the queen took him for a ride in a carriage, entertained him to dinner at Buckingham Palace, and showed him Scotland and the sea, in which the guest from Uganda had insisted on bathing. On returning to Africa, Amin had thanked her for her hospitality with the promise that if the British were ever dying of hunger, he would have them sent bananas, which were in surplus in Uganda. Another time he threatened to incite the Scots, the Irish, and the Welsh against her, as they were being exploited by the Crown. On another occasion he sent her a telegram saying: "My dear Liz! If you want to know what it's like to have a real man, come to Kampala straightaway!"

He loved to shock, horrify, amaze, and amuse. He did his best to monopolize attention and wielded it jealously, like the jester, the star of the show. He used to show off his harmonica playing to the foreign journalists. Once, during a reception given in honor of some foreign diplomats, he said he had tasted human flesh. Another time he told how his Kakwa kinsmen sacrifice human beings, drink their blood and eat their livers, in order to possess their earthly might and win the favor of the spirits. Some people said it was these spirits from his homeland that made him so different, that they could get inside him, and that when they possessed him, they made him change from a clown receiving and entertaining guests into an *nduli*, a monster who gave orders for them to be murdered in a cruel way.

It was said that when he suspected one of his wives of being unfaithful, he had her killed and quartered; also that he conferred with witches who told him to sacrifice one of his sons to the spirits, so that he could live and rule eternally. Or at least to find out the hour of his own death. Indeed, he used to boast of it, often repeating: "I know when I'm going to die." Thanks to this he emerged intact from numerous assassination attempts that were made on him. Although several of his adjutants, drivers, and bodyguard were killed in them, nothing ever happened to Amin, not a scratch.

Professor Frederick Gwedekko, whom I had met a few years earlier at Makerere University, maintained that there wasn't much truth in all this. The three-year-old Moses, whom Amin was supposed to have killed as a sacrifice to the spirits, had gone to school in Paris and got an academic diploma there. And the beautiful, intelligent Kay Adroa, daughter of a pastor, had been betrayed and neglected by the lustful Amin, and then found herself a lover, Dr. Peter Mbalu Mukasa from the capital's Mulago hospital. When she found out she was pregnant, fearing Amin's anger, she insisted that Mbalu Mukasa abort the child himself. During the operation the doctor lost his nerve and was unable to stem a hemorrhage, so drop by drop, Kay's life had drained away. Out of his mind with despair and fear, the doctor had decided to get rid of his lover's body, and it was he who cut off her arms and legs to make it easier to hide and burn the remains. But he couldn't face up to such a great tragedy. He went home and took poison, after first poisoning his wife and five children. "All this could be checked, but people preferred to believe Amin had committed murder," said Professor Gwedekko. "It was too good a fit with the image of Amin that everyone had created for themselves. So Amin was the way they wanted to see him, not the way he really was."

I found Professor Gwedekko's statement about Amin among my notes, on a yellowed scrap of paper torn from a newspaper. I decided to go to Makerere University, find the professor, and talk to him about the presidential election that was be so significant for Uganda.

⤙⚬⤚

As I traveled about Kampala, I kept an eye out for things and places to help me imagine what it was like when Amin was alive and in power. It was a small city in those days, where almost everybody knew each other and nothing was far away. I was told that Amin had set up jails and torture chambers in the cellars of apartment buildings in the downtown area. Apparently while strolling about the city, you could hear the screams and groans of the torture victims coming through windows left open because of the heat. A Western journalist Amin had imprisoned recalled that in his dungeon during the day he could hear children's voices from a nearby school, and in the evenings, when the fun began at the local bars, the sounds of music and girls laughing.

On the first day I found the Congress Palace, which Amin had built at the heart of the city to receive and dazzle the presidents invited for a summit of the Organization of African Unity. As the host, he was then chairman of the organization, and in this role he was received by the pope at the Vatican. Later, in the cellars of the empty, redundant palace Amin had a prison and a torture chamber established. He used to go there along a secret underground tunnel dug all the way from the presidential palace on Nakasero Hill.

The Congress Palace turned out to be useless because it didn't offer me any clues or fire my imagination. It was ordinary, just as all Kampala was ordinary, though charming, with its hills and houses plunged in greenery, noisy bazaars, and little streets climbing steeply. I couldn't find any trace of the former threat in them, and this effort to travel in time was just as fruitless and futile as all the previous attempts I had made to summon up the spirits of the past, as I wandered aimlessly around Kigali, Kisangani, Lubumbashi, Bunia, Soweto and Juba, Teheran, Saigon, or Phnom Penh. Or Gulu.

The passage of time had changed these places where dramatic events, bloody coups, unimaginable revolutions, and assassinations had once occurred. They seemed to bear no relation to recent history, to have no connection with it anymore, no memories of it, as if the nightmare-scarred past had ceased to exist as the pages were torn from the calendar.

People who visited Kampala in those days or who knew it from that era recalled that whenever Amin's soldiers drove up in their trucks, markets, streets, and entire villages emptied in a flash. The citizens of the enslaved country lived in a state of terror. They went to sleep worrying that they might they be woken in the middle of the night by rifle butts banging on the door. When they came out in the morning, they looked about apprehensively for fear of tripping over the corpses of people executed in the night, left lying in the gutter. They set off from home with rolls of banknotes stuffed into their pockets to pay off Amin's wild, drunken soldiers, who made their thieving easier by blocking the streets with checkpoints—barriers made of barbed wire and sandbags.

On occasion Amin actually sent for people he had already executed. He was quite unaware of the extent of the crimes committed during his rule. In a Kampala bookstore I bought a book by Henry Kyemba, a former friend of Amin who had been his minister of health. Once he had finally conquered his own paralyzing fear, he had fled from Uganda and written his memoirs in exile in London. "Not even Amin knows how many people have been killed under his regime. He does not know how many he himself has ordered to be killed," wrote Kyemba. "The country is full of corpses."

Eventually defeated and deposed by the rebels, Amin fled first to Libya, from where he went to Baghdad, and finally settled in the Saudi city of Jeddah on the Red Sea coast. To the end of his life he solemnly believed that his compatriots had happy memories of him, and that if only they were free to choose, they would want him to return to power.

He gave only one interview in exile. "I live here at peace with God and with myself," he said in a conversation with a journalist from *New Vision*. "And I am a happier man than when I was president of Uganda."

He had grown very fat. His almost bestial appetite had always been a source of amazement, but the gluttony to which he succumbed in exile changed him out of all recognition. Once a giant and strongman, he was transformed into a vast, shapeless hulk, weighing almost a quarter of a ton, more like an ogre than a human being. He didn't fit into any clothes, so when he went to the mosque for prayers, or for rare walks along the seafront, he donned loose, flowing Arab robes.

He lived to a great age and died in his sleep. In keeping with Islamic ritual, he was buried on the day of his death, before nightfall. His grave is in Jeddah, because the Saudi king would not agree to Amin's wishes to be buried in Mecca, Islam's holiest site. Not many people attended the funeral, and when news of his death reached Kampala, *New Vision* replaced the leading article on its front page with a quotation from the Book of Isaiah in large type:

You also have become weak, as we are; you have become like us. All your pomp has been brought down to the grave, along with the noise of your harps; maggots are spread out beneath you and worms cover you.

But the demons he had awoken when he took the helm of government in Kampala did not die down or go away with him. Amin was evil, but what came after him proved even worse. Wracked by lawlessness and violence, Uganda continued to be a bloodbath, doomed to horrific destruction, cursed with an apocalypse. In Kampala the rats began to drive out the population—at one point there were four times as many rats as people.

◄◦►

The office of Professor Gwedekko, lecturer in political science at the university, was locked. At the reception they told me he had gone to London, and that in his absence the junior lecturer, Dr. Phinneas, was taking his classes. He was just finishing a lecture, so I decided to wait for him. I had nothing better to do anyway, and for my report I needed some preelection opinions from the mouths of academics who could be regarded as authorities.

The elections had started to feel a terribly long time away. One just like another, the days were passing more and more slowly and seemed to be getting longer. Each morning I bought the daily papers, the *Monitor* and *New Vision*, read them over breakfast on the hotel veranda, and made notes in my room. Then I headed into town for conversations with politicians, journalists, and academics. In the evenings I sorted out my new notes, reviewed the old ones, made calls to book my next appointments, and worked on the report I was planning to send to my editor.

"Are you here to see me?" I heard.

I was expecting Dr. Phinneas to be a young man who, after gaining his diploma at this respected college, had taken a job as assistant to the famous professor, in order to boost the progress of his academic career. But here stood a tiny, gray-haired, shriveled Chinese man in a dark suit and vest, with a black bow tie. He was older than Professor Gwedekko, and he looked much older.

"You wanted to see me?" he asked again. "Was it you who asked for me at the reception?"

I said I wanted to talk to him about the elections and Museveni's chances of victory. And then I asked about Amin—whether it was true that he was a cannibal who demanded the heads of people killed on his orders to be cut off and brought to his palace. In an extremely serious tone, choosing his words carefully, Dr. Phinneas replied that there had in fact been occasions when Amin had visited the hospital mortuary, where bodies were taken from the city; then he had dismissed the doctors and his own retinue, and remained alone with the dead. Some said he touched them and spoke to them. Dr. Phinneas did not think this behavior resulted either from Amin's madness or from his penchant for barbarity and horror. Wishing to avoid the vengeance of the spirits of the people whose killing he had ordered, the president was there to perform a ritual—to come to terms with them, appease them, and say farewell.

Pike told me that not long before my arrival in Kampala an American production company was making a movie about Amin in the city. Whenever the actor playing the dictator appeared in the streets dressed as him, people went crazy, shouting, cheering, clapping, and greeting him, as if Amin had risen from the dead. I was reminded of a minister from one of the African countries who once said that if Africa could elect a king for itself, the people would choose Amin, as if they had forgotten what he did and forgiven him everything. "Unfortunately," confirmed Dr. Phinneas, "people forget all too easily."

"Children are forgiven," I said, adding that a friend of mine had called Amin a large, cruel child. "I get the general impression that in Uganda the children often take the place of the adults."

I also told him I had come from Gulu, where children fight in the guerrilla army, and as they say of Amin that he never stopped being a child in the body of an adult, then surely Joseph Kony, the guerrilla leader, is a child too.

It was supposed to be a joke, a way of breaking the ice, but Dr. Phinneas pretended not to have noticed.

"No, it's out of the question," he said, with a solemn look on his face. "Joseph Kony definitely isn't a child."

"Have you ever heard of Ching Po, the Chinese spirit who serves him and who enters him from time to time?" I asked.

"As far as I know it isn't a Chinese spirit, but a Korean one."

◄◦►

Ching Po was just one of many spirits that entered into Joseph Kony, spoke through him, and used him as a medium to communicate with the living. By making his human shape available to them, Joseph Kony, as it were, resurrected people who had died long ago. For them he was a sort of welcoming haven, a home where the door is always wide open to vagabonds. Anyone could enter and stop for a moment or two—or settle in for longer.

Some spirits, the more timid, awkward ones, entered Kony's body merely to pass on important news from the world of the dead or to complain of wrongs they had suffered. Others, predatory and ungrateful, immediately started to tyrannize him, turning their host into a servant. "When they enter me, they tell me what I am to do, they give me orders," Kony told a British journalist, the first foreigner from outside Africa to whom he agreed to give an audience at his hideout in the bush. "How many of them are there? How many spirits speak through you?" asked the journalist. "I don't know how many, but there are very many of them and they all speak to me," replied Kony. "They come as a dream and tell me everything. They predict what is going to happen. They come and say: 'You, Mr. Joseph, tell your people that the enemy is planning to come and attack them.' But they also come and tell me what herbs I must use to prepare medicine to cure my people of illnesses and wounds."

Sometimes the spirits possessed Kony individually, in turn, introducing themselves by name. But at other times they all entered him at once, pushing past each other and shouting in unison, without keeping order or exercising good manners. Witnesses to this sort of possession said that when it happened Kony's voice changed out of all recognition, his body shook as if in convulsions, and his face was weirdly contorted, assuming new, entirely different features. At these moments no one knew who was speaking through Kony's mouth, who was controlling his body, or who he actually was.

Ching Po told Kony how to command the guerrilla army and how to obtain rifles and vehicles for them. During the battles he decided whether the shots they fired would strike the enemy, and also whether the hostile bullets would only hit those guerrillas who had committed sins and not been absolved of them before the fight. He also made sure that once the battle was over, all the rifles and bullets were locked away in armories, and that guards were posted outside them.

According to some accounts, Ching Po came to Acholi-land all the way from Korea, brought there by some Korean artillerymen who had trained the Ugandan army years ago at the barracks in Gulu. Those who maintained that Ching Po was a Chinese spirit claimed that he was named after the hero of one of the cheap adventure movies originally from America, Taiwan, or Hong Kong which were brought to the Nile area by the owners of Gulu movie theaters and had been extremely popular there. One of the spirits that haunted Joseph Kony was even called Bruce Lee.

Ching Po was a mild, protective spirit, who never argued with others. The guerrillas liked him because when he entered Kony, he made him kind, or even loving. The guerrillas also liked the Congolese spirit Franco, whom out of respect they called *Mzee*, which in Swahili means an elder. Franco was responsible for supplying the guerrilla army; he was a calm spirit, even-tempered, good-humored, friendly, and fond of a joke. The guerrillas were sorry he entered Kony so rarely. It was the same with the female spirits from Sudan and Acholi-land who took care of healing and medicines. Whenever they entered him, Kony became caring, spoke in a shrill voice like a woman, and even behaved like a woman.

But the guerrillas' greatest fear was a Congolese spirit who made Kony become cruel and bad. Piece of Evil, as this spirit was known, was the most important and most powerful of them all. When he entered Kony, there was usually an order to kill. At those times no one was allowed to get in his way or look straight into his bloodshot eyes. I read about this in the stories Nora had recorded, told by children who had been abducted on Kony's orders, and had eventually run away from his camp.

"Everyone knows Joseph Kony serves the spirits, and that he is almost always possessed by one of them. However, no one ever knows if a good spirit will enter him or a bad one," I read in a story by Nancy, a little girl whom Kony had chosen for himself as a wife and kept at his home, waiting for her to grow into a woman and bear him children. "When a good spirit entered him, he was nice, and played with us, made jokes and was someone you felt you could love. But at any moment a different spirit could possess him, a bad one, and then he became a completely different person, and it was terrifying to look at him. One minute he'd be laughing and playing, the next threatening to have us all killed."

Piece of Evil was the worst, most frightening spirit. He spoke haughtily and imperiously. He told Kony the orders he was to give the guerrillas, and he was a cruel, malevolent, and vengeful commander. He liked leading his people into temptation, luring them with the most shameful, deeply hidden desires and longings. He was always putting them to the test, and when they let him down, he inflicted the cruelest punishments on them. "Kill! Kill them all! You must kill them all!" he ordered Kony, who summoned his guerrillas and sent them on their way. "Let no one from Kitgum survive," he called after the departing soldiers.

In one of the Ugandan newspapers I read that Joseph Kony is a man of many faces and many varied, often contradictory personalities. I remembered being told the same thing about Amin, who was also capable of being an engaging, genial joker, seconds later to change into a cruel, ruthless beast, hateful and insatiable in his hatred. Foreigners, and also some of the Kampalan doctors called it a split personality, a handicap, or mental illness. In Acholi-land this affliction was explained by an extreme susceptibility to spirits, and it was regarded as a gift and a distinction, rather than a curse.

◄◦►

Each morning as I headed into the city, I was struck by how much it had changed, and how little time it had needed to assume a new incarnation. From an impoverished, frenzied city, Kampala had been transformed into a happy metropolis, strong, attractive, enjoying life and wanting to make the most of it.

They say it's easy to destroy something that has taken long years to develop. Perhaps the reason why Kampala had such a magnetic, almost magical charm for me was that every day it reminded me that it is in fact possible to recover from a fall, and that in favorable circumstances rising from the ruins doesn't have to take an eternity.

Uganda might have looked like a hopeless case. After almost two decades of the tyrannical regimes of Obote and Amin, civil wars, massacres, lawlessness and bankruptcy, plague and famine, and one and a half million corpses, it had come to be known as a doomed country, whose citizens' only aspiration was to break free, to run as far away as possible and forget the place as quickly as they could. However, it only took about ten or fewer years for them to come back to it, and to think of Kampala as a city where dreams can come true and life can be truly appealing.

This was achieved by Museveni, Uganda's first good ruler, the best thing to have happened to this unlucky nation. For once, everyone in Kampala was in agreement. As soon as he took power, like a good wizard he had altered life in an instant.

He had started with himself, changing from a die-hard young revolutionary into a ruler who no longer wanted to turn the world upside down but improve it gradually, step by step. He renounced his youthful revolutionary approach quite easily; having inherited a ruined state, he needed money and advice to rebuild it as rapidly as possible. Meanwhile, only rich bankers from the Western world could offer him help, but they were enemies to all form of revolution, believers in the need for moderation. They favored the view that the leader of a country should interfere as little as possible, and should recognize that anything is permissible, as long as it hasn't been banned.

Museveni was the first ruler on the African Great Lakes to start governing in just this way. He was capable of adapting. He did what the Western bankers and leaders wanted him to, and said exactly what they wanted to hear. He surprised everyone, most of all his own compatriots and other brothers all over Africa, whose vices he mercilessly pointed out to them—above all their tendency to sentimentalize their fate and cast the blame for their own failures on others. "We like to complain about the whites, but have we ever wondered why only Africans let themselves be made into slaves? Why didn't we put up resistance?" Whenever he posed such questions at summits of African presidents, he caused his colleagues some embarrassment. "It was our own greed and quarrelsome nature that ruined us. That's why we were defeated and conquered. We ourselves are to blame. It was our chiefs, waging fratricidal wars, who took people prisoner to sell them to slave traders from Europe. It was those black traitors who bear the blame for slavery. They are still a huge problem for Africa—there are still plenty of them among us." Before him, only Mandela had ever spoken like that when, after almost thirty years in jail, full of bitterness and anger, he scolded the African presidents, saying: "What have you done with our freedom?!"

The West was generous to Museveni with praise, loans, and advice. He was acclaimed as the model of the good African leader—strict, but honest and fair. And so he was. Compared with some of the other presidents, he seemed a virtual ascetic. He didn't drink alcohol or smoke tobacco, he didn't live in the lap of luxury, but liked to be seen as a simple man.

Self-confident, relaxed, free of the pathological arrogance and suspicion of his predecessors, he wasn't afraid of the people—on the contrary, he made an effort to convince them a president is just as ordinary as a trader at the local market, or a fisherman on Lake Victoria. One time the helicopter bringing him back to Kampala from his country residence had broken down and been forced to land outside the city. Museveni had walked to the road, stopped a cab, and told the astonished driver: "To the presidential palace, please."

He paraded his fondness for cattle, but was rather disdainful about the classical music his wife was so fond of. "Beethoven, Mozart...what can I say? Listening to that stuff makes me feel sick," he once said. Even when wearing a suit for an official ceremony, he would put on the sort of hat most people take on safari, though he must have known he looked comical in it.

He used to say he had no close friends, but just "colleagues at work," and would ask not to be called a politician. "Please don't insult me," he told a foreign journalist. "I prefer to be called a warrior, a rebel. Politicians have a very bad reputation here in Africa."

To another one he admitted that although he is a Christian, he is not guided by the principle of turning the other cheek in response to a blow. "I don't turn the other cheek," he said. "If someone kills someone else deliberately, he deserves to die too. Here we kill people like that."

Delighted by Museveni, the rich West provided loans, donations, and advice which enabled Uganda to flourish just as quickly as it had declined, and once again it became the lovely, lush garden of Africa.

In the plundered, neglected, abandoned downtown area, skyscrapers shot up out of the ruins, weeds, and garbage heaps. Everywhere stores, offices, and enterprises were opened. The freedom to get rich, as well as the peace and safety Museveni had brought, meant that Kampala's recently empty bazaars were soon filled with a wide variety of goods. Not long ago everything had been in short supply, and only the privileged few had had access to deficit items. Suddenly there was plenty of everything within easy reach. The lines disappeared that had even been common outside banks—in those days you had to do your share of standing in line, just to withdraw your own savings.

No longer afraid of robbers or drunken soldiers at roadside checkpoints, buses and convoys of trucks set off boldly into the country. Once again farmers began transporting fruit and vegetables to markets in the capital, where they sold them at a profit. They no longer had to hand them over to corrupt officials for almost nothing. The defunct coffee and tea plantations were revived. Traders imported soap, salt, sugar, and clothing from abroad, and soon after perfumes, expensive cars, and electronic goods. Museveni was also the first African leader to declare war on AIDS: in Uganda they have succeeded in curbing the lethal epidemic.

From a synonym for disaster, Uganda was transformed into a synonym for success. Its capital, provincial Kampala, became a construction site and suddenly began to grow. Each new skyscraper was taller than the one before. The citizens started to enjoy a rising standard of living and increasing success. They ate better, dressed better, sent their children to ever better schools and could afford education at the most acclaimed foreign colleges. All of a sudden the Ugandan capital was competing with the Kenyan capital, Nairobi, for precedence as the regional metropolis.

However, what amazed and pleased the Ugandans most of all was that they had stopped living in fear. Museveni had restored their former, almost forgotten sense of security. They stopped fearing tomorrow, and whether it would come at all. Once again they could make plans for the future. They reveled in this feeling. They were no longer afraid of each other, no longer feared for themselves, or had to fear their own leader— this one didn't fill them with terror, the way Amin had.

And yet they didn't feel grateful. They regarded the freedoms, rights, and privileges they were now enjoying thanks to Museveni as something to which they were simply entitled. They soon forgot the past, and the evil that had dominated and pervaded their world.

There are probably no worse ingrates than the beneficiaries of changes introduced by good, progressive rulers to free their countries from centuries of backwardness, lawlessness, and tyranny.

Some rulers think a revolution, even a cruel and bloody one that destroys the old order, is the best way to change things. Others who are more patient, or maybe just more cowardly, choose the path of gradual reform, which, without destroying the old world, little by little transforms, modernizes, and perfects it. Both these approaches usually end in failure. Once they have clashed with the world's annoying inability to change, the ardent revolutionaries turn into new tyrants; whereas by being slow and cautious, the reformers alienate their impatient, increasingly disenchanted supporters. And the first people to throw accusations of betrayal in a new leader's face are usually those who owe him the most—the traders and entrepreneurs who are making money, the young officers who come from poor families, but whom he has promoted, or the students and graduates of foreign colleges, who have only been sent to them in the first place thanks to the goodness and generosity of the state.

Having been far away at their foreign academies, they come home with their heads stuffed with ideas about even more daring and rapid changes. They become more aware of their own country's backward-ness, its parochialism and the huge gulf separating it from more modern, richer ones. They cast the blame for all the deficiencies and wrongs—which is all they seem to see around them—at the rulers, thanks to whom they were able to go abroad and gain an education at all. They don't feel any gratitude toward them, but just anger, because in their view the old rulers have stopped halfway, and are standing in the path of progress—they have become an obstacle, an anachronism.

So the young people want to change everything as fast as possible and catch up with the outside world. But to make changes, first you have to gain power, or at least have some influence on it. However, the only political tools available are the same old ones as before. No ruler, especially a reformer, will start a general overhaul of the state by dis-mantling the political structure, a move that could threaten his own control. Without exercising power—says the reformer-ruler—I won't be able to change anything.

But by adopting the old rules of the power game, by joining the old political parties and accepting their customs and values, the young rev-olutionaries are forced into the old order. Then they lose their impetus and shrink to fit the old forms. They also lose time, and the older they get, the more they sink into resignation and discouragement.

The young rebels who are dissatisfied with everything face a dra-matic choice. If they want to change the course of the river, they have to dive into it; only then—without letting themselves be carried away by the current—can they try to influence its flow, though under no illu-sions that they will succeed in diverting it. But if they don't enter the water, all they can do is stand on the riverbank and watch it go by.

⋘⋙

I left a visit to the main opposition headquarters to the end. This was to be the topic of my final report before election day. Museveni's rival, Kizza Besigye, was touring the country soliciting votes, and wasn't plan-ning to return to the capital before the election result was announced. However, he had left his trusted people in Kampala to take care of his affairs in the city and run his campaign. On voting day they were going to monitor the elections to make sure they were honest.

The office of the opposition Forum for Democratic Change was in a small one-story house on the road to Entebbe International Airport. Deo, the cabdriver I arranged to meet every time I went on a trip, was waiting for me in a small square by the church tower of Christ the King, not far from my hotel. By meeting him there I saved him from the protective hotel security guards, who made sure guests at the Speke were only driven about the city by their cousins and friends.

"They'll take you for your last penny," ranted Deo, promising every time that he charged honestly and cost less.

Deo was a Bugandan and came from Kampala. He was planning to vote for the opposition. He had met many of its leaders, and knew when and where they were going to hold election rallies or antigovernment demonstrations. As he drove around the city from dawn to dusk picking up customers, he listened to the radio, and had promised that as soon as something important or unusual happened, he would call me and wait for me at our usual meeting place. This time I saw him from some way off—he was standing next to his red Toyota, making angry gestures at some children begging outside the church to keep away from his car.

The downtown area was full of beggars. They crept along the sidewalks and lurked in the shadows outside banks, offices, hotels, and restaurants. Chased away by the security guards, they ran straight into the road, under the wheels of fast-moving cars which braked with a squeal of tires. But in an instant more of them would come running from all directions, and cluster like a swarm of locusts around the immobilized traffic, begging for alms.

Deo reckoned the beggars in Kampala were refugees from the Karamojong, a tribe of herders renowned for their warlike spirit. There had been a drought in their lands for some years; in order to survive the men went on plundering raids, attacking the territory of the neighboring Teso, Acholi, and Lango peoples, and even parts of Sudan, Ethiopia, and Kenya. Meanwhile they sent the women and children to Kampala out of concern for their safety, and also to earn some extra pennies begging.

"They bring shame on the city," muttered Deo. "But it'll be over soon.

They said on the radio the police are going to drive the beggars off the streets. By fall they're not going to be here anymore."

In the fall the Queen of England was due to make an official visit to Kampala. By then Museveni also wanted to deal with the opposition, which in the run-up to the elections was accusing him of all sorts of crimes and villainy. He was charged with having lost the patience for which he was once so famous, and with having ceased to tolerate not just his opponents, but even those who hardly disagreed with him. Apparently he had started interfering in everything, wanting to make all decisions himself. As a result, every success was his success, but every failure, every mistake was also charged to his account.

He had become touchy and was easily offended. He called anyone who opposed him an enemy, and branded them traitors. One after another his old friends and comrades-in-arms from the days of rebellion were moving away from him. They were accusing him of being too fond of power, and of believing too firmly in his own infallibility and in the idea that he would rule forever. They said he didn't trust other, well-meaning people, but was so eager for applause that he surrounded himself exclusively with compatriots from the Hima tribe and yes-men aiming to make a career for themselves through flattery. He was outraged when the newspapers wrote about corruption and theft, not just in the government agencies under his control, but even among his beloved troops.

In his days as a guerrilla, government minister Amama Mbabazi had been nicknamed Kariaburo, "he who feeds on millet." Now the papers were printing caricatures of him and distorting his nickname into Kariasausage, "he who feeds on sausage." Another of the guerrilla veterans, James Kazini, had earned himself the rank of general, an impressive fortune, and a small paunch by exploiting his record as an old warrior and his kinship with the president's wife. Now he was busy buying up hotels and nightclubs. When the Ugandan army invaded neighboring Congo, he had declared himself consul of Kisangani and had pillaged the local gold mines. Even hunting down the Lord's Army was exploited by the Ugandan army to cut down teak—highly valued worldwide for making furniture, yachts, and ships—and transport it

from Sudan to Uganda. Even Museveni's favorite stepbrother, his closest confidant, Salim Saleh, was accused of smuggling and plunder in
the Congolese war. "I don't believe it," said Museveni, shaking his head.
"People who joined the guerrillas simply aren't capable of selling themselves for bribes."

His old friends, of whom he had fewer and fewer left, warned him
that he was changing, and that just a little longer and he would squander
his life's hard-won achievements, everything he held most sacred. They
said he would become exactly the sort of person he had sworn not to
be—a typical African despot, regarding the state and its citizens as his
property.

Museveni said goodbye to his old comrades with no regret, but
rather in anger. "People do not understand me, they don't understand
my intentions, my plans," he once told a British journalist. "I'm used to
that by now. First of all, when I was a guerrilla, they called me a rebel, a
troublemaker, evil personified. Later on, once the results of my government had shown them who I really am, they started praising me to the
skies. So if nowadays they are denying me respect and faith again, and
are complaining that I am leading my country toward a precipice, I see
that as just the latest misunderstanding. People do not get it, and will
only judge me fairly once they see the fruits of my actions."

I thought of William Pike, who in telling me about Museveni had
mentioned that although he had proved a genius and a visionary, he
had already ruled for such a long time that his power, the state, and his
personal life had all merged together.

I cut an article out of the *Monitor* in which Museveni's former friend
and lover, Winnie Byanyima, spoke about him. "Museveni is a progressive person and ruler, no question. He instinctively senses what needs
to be changed and improved in the country, and how to do it," she told
the journalist. "But he is incapable of seeing or accepting the fact that
other people, even when they agree with him to the last word, might
have even better ideas, and that by joining forces with them, he could
achieve even more. Museveni is so sure of himself and has so little faith
in others. He isn't capable of being a team player. He always wants to
instruct and to lead. If only he understood that he is a wonderful player,

the best, but he is only one of many who play on the team. But he sees himself as a virtual messiah, who is going to lead Uganda to the promised land. What's more, having won the guerrilla war, he thinks it best to solve all sorts of problems in the same, military way. He doesn't believe in diplomacy or politics. The longer he governs, the more he is convinced that he is always right. The vast power that he possesses renders him more and more cut off from reality. He quickly forgets about his own mistakes and defeats, and only remembers when he has been successful. Those who do not agree with him, who point the finger at him, he calls traitors. That is typical of all leaders who spend too long in power."

Winnie, poor little Winnie . . . Museveni called her a low-down traitor too.

She had a crush on him as a little girl, when he was still studying in Kampala and he used to come to their house to thank her father Boniface, a respected member of parliament, for the money he gave him to pay his tuition fees at school. She fell madly in love with him when he declared war on everyone and everything, went to hide in the jungle, and instigated an armed uprising.

Winnie dropped her studies and her comfortable life in Kampala for him, and went into the bush to join the guerrillas. For five years she was his comrade-in-arms, his lover, housekeeper, and caregiver. She knew all along that he had a wife, called Janet, but she must have believed he would send Janet away, and spend the rest of his life with her, Winnie. But when he won the guerrilla war and moved into the presidential palace on Nakasero Hill in the capital, he threw her out and had his legitimate wife brought to Kampala.

Winnie spent a long time suffering because of her broken heart and humiliation. But once the pain was gone, she swore vengeance against Museveni. First she became the member of parliament for Mbarara, and in every speech she made, she pointed out the president's mistakes, failures, and lies. Then she married Dr. Kizza Besigye, Museveni's personal physician from the guerrilla war era, his close friend and trusted confidant. Pike had no doubt that having married Besigye, Winnie incited her husband against the president to pay him back for the wrongs he had done her. And although all three of them vowed in unison that it wasn't about settling personal scores, few people in Uganda believed in these assurances.

After marrying Winnie, Dr. Besigye—promoted by Museveni to the rank of colonel and various ministerial posts—suddenly sent a long letter to the press. In it he accused the president of betraying the ideals and aims of the revolution he had once led. He called on Museveni to step down before he changed from a good leader into a tyrant like Amin and Obote. So when Museveni announced new presidential elections that he intended to win again and extend his reign, Dr. Besigye cast him a challenge and stood for election too.

Those elections, several years ago, had already revealed the disturbing change that had come over the Ugandan leader. He could not bear the fact that someone, especially a subordinate, was questioning his competence and precedence. He never even considered answering the charges, and refused to take part in a television debate with Besigye, regarding his rival as not worth the effort.

But he did shower him with terrible insults, calling him a traitor and a coward. He also accused him of secretly conspiring with the Ugandan rebels hiding in Rwanda, Congo, and Sudan to form them into an insurrectionary army, attack Kampala at its head, and seize power. He even claimed that Besigye was in cahoots with Joseph Kony, and that he had sent his adviser James Opoka into the bush to persuade Kony to form an alliance. However, before he had managed to do that, the savage rebels had murdered him.

Museveni had won those elections and, fearing for his life, the defeated Besigye had immediately fled the country—first across the border into Rwanda, and from there to South Africa. But the joy of victory was spoiled for Museveni by knowing that one in four of the population had voted for his rival.

Now Besigye was back, and was trying to take power away from him again. This time Museveni's police, informers, and officials had charged Besigye with keeping an unregistered gun at home. Once again he had been accused of treason and terrorism, and was suspected of planning to conduct an armed coup. On top of that, the case against him from years ago for allegedly having raped a mentally handicapped teenager called Joanita, the daughter of a friend, was dredged up again. Besigye admitted having had intercourse with the girl, but swore it happened with her consent. He also denied that she had fallen pregnant by him, that he had forced her to get rid of the child, and that he had infected her with HIV. Either way, he was stuck in prison for weeks on end, so Winnie had to stand in for him, fighting for votes at election rallies. He had only been released shortly before the election took place.

The further away from downtown Kampala, the more opposition posters appeared on roadside walls, viaducts, advertising pillars, and streetlamps; Kizza Besigye looked out from them with a stern, determined expression. "Time for change! Choose change!" urged the captions on the opposition posters.

What sort of change? Change to what?

Although Kizza Besigye came from the same tribe as Museveni, the Ankole, he had much darker skin, and the serious pose chosen for the photograph had caused some anxiety. "He desires power too much and too openly for me to be able to trust him," William Pike said of him.

The road out of town to Entebbe ran steeply down from the green, flowery hills toward the lake. After gathering speed at the top, below the church towers and skyscrapers, and after crossing some broad avenues that bisected it at right angles, it went into narrow, ever messier and more crowded back streets, losing momentum. Until finally it ran at the same slow speed as the motorized rickshaws, cyclists, and pedestrians squeezing their way among the stalls set up on the hard shoulder. Quiet and expansive, the shady bungalows of Nakasero looked from afar onto this teeming tangle, quivering with noise, heat, and odors, full of workshops, bars, small stores and kiosks, market stalls, churches, mosques, and Hindu temples.

The opposition headquarters was in an ordinary suburban villa— only the large number of party posters and flags made it look different from the rest. Final preparations for the elections were under way. Young people, with cell phones to their ears, were pacing the courtyard, corridors, and rooms, trying to shout over each other, giving orders and advice, and asking for news. In the vestibule there was a young boy in a cotton shirt sitting at a table with a large notebook lying open on it.

Until recently he had been one of the most important people at this office. He had been entrusted with the job of making sure anyone who came into the building wrote their name in the book. Each visitor had to fill in boxes with their first and last names, arrival time and purpose of visit, the names of the people they had come to see, departure time and signature on leaving. But on the last day before the elections no one was bothering to complete the formalities anymore, so no one was registering their name in the visitors' book.

The receptionist was called Ronald. Out of boredom, or maybe spite at being ignored today, he identified the party leaders for me in the bustling crowd.

"That man is called Samuel Akaki—he is from the youth organization—and that's Suleiman Kiggundu—he's responsible for the election campaign in Kampala," he said, pointing. "That one is Livingston Kiizito, a very important man. Off you go, go on, have them talk to you."

Suleiman Kiggundu assured me that his party and its leader Kizza Besigye would carry off a triumphant victory in the elections, because all Uganda had had enough of Museveni's tyrannical, criminal regime. He said that the whole world had seen through him, and everyone had turned their back on Museveni, who had proved to be just as cruel a dictator as Amin and Obote.

"He has brought the country to ruin, people are starving, and the land is flowing with the blood of the innocent," he said, as fast and as smoothly as if he had uttered this statement hundreds of times, until finally he had it down pat.

I wanted to test this claim, but the only way to do it was to interrupt him with another question and abruptly change the subject. But that proved quite impossible—Suleiman Kiggundu went on and on talking, faster and faster, as cell phones nagged him, jangling impatiently in the pockets of his white shirt and pants.

"That's who Museveni is! He is so afraid of our leader that he had him thrown into the worst prison in Luzira, along with the common criminals," Kiggundu speechified, furtively checking to see who was calling. "But what's it all for? To kill him! They tried to poison him in jail, but our lawyers advised him not to eat anything that was not brought from the city."

Suddenly his eyes lit up, as if he had remembered something. Out of a drawer he swiftly drew a brochure printed in tiny letters, and scribbled a row of figures on it in ballpoint pen.

"This is our program—you'll find everything you need in here," he said, offering his hand for a farewell shake. "And that's my phone number. Call me, because only I will know the truth about how the elections are run and who really wins them!"

As I talked with Samuel Akaki, I was barely listening to what he was saying. I was overcome with fatigue. The sky above the city had taken on a shade of weary red and dark blue. It occurred to me that darkness would fall before I got back to the downtown area. And as I had to leave straight after the election, I had to find Jackson to give him the folder containing Samuel's story, which I still hadn't had time to read right through. I planned to do it that evening.

◂•▸

Once I had opened the folder and found the bit where Samuel described the night attack on a Ugandan village, the evening news came on TV. The foreign channels were still featuring the Ugandan elections, but they had stopped being the major topic of the day. On the BBC News they were only mentioned at the end, in the part including odd facts from around the world.

Although it was being heralded as a sensation, after only a few days in Kampala it was clear the election would not bring any surprises. Museveni had the victory in his grasp. He didn't even have to cheat. If not for the army of journalists who had come here, lured by rumors of a political crisis in a country that conjured up the grimmest associations, not a word would have been said about these elections. But as the editors had sent their best, though now bored and disappointed, special correspondents and war reporters to Kampala, like it or not, they would have to find space for their reports.

On the eve of the elections the local television wasn't allowed to issue any news that could influence voting decisions. While watching the Ugandan TV newscast, I caught myself looking out for news from

Gulu. Since I had arrived in Kampala, neither Gulu, Acholi-land, or the war there had been mentioned once. There wasn't much about them in the papers either. Generally I got the impression no one in Kampala knew what was happening on the other side of the Nile, and no one was interested either.

That evening the name Gulu only showed up in the weather forecast, which said it would rain.

The rainy season suited the Lord's Army guerrillas—that was when they left their hideouts in the inaccessible Imatong Mountains on the Sudanese side of the border and headed into Uganda, in search of plunder and to kidnap children from the villages. During the dry season the trees and grass wilted in the sun and failed to provide shelter, making it easier for the soldiers to pursue the guerrillas in armored cars which could race across the scorched, rock-hard wasteland. In the rainy season the savannahs and field roads became boggy, immobilizing the army columns, while trees and bushes revived by the drizzle hid the guerrillas from helicopter pilots.

But the Lord's Army didn't only fight Ugandan soldiers or just attack Ugandan villages. Hostile to Museveni, the regime in Sudan had been helping Joseph Kony, giving his people shelter. In exchange the Ugandan guerrillas had had to fight against Dinka warriors who were rebelling against the authorities in Khartoum.

Compared with the children in Kony's army, the Dinka—regarded as the tallest people in all Africa—were real giants. They were also superb soldiers, but they couldn't face up to Kony's guerrillas, and lost battle after battle against them.

The small guerrillas from the Lord's Army fought standing, running along and shooting straight ahead. On penalty of death, they were not allowed to fall to the ground, crawl along, or hide. They were only permitted to take amulets made of pebbles into battle, which they tied around their necks, believing they would protect them from enemy bullets. Even though their commanders forbade it, calling it superstition, some of them also fixed bunches of special grasses to their rifle barrels, which was supposed to make them invincible.

Because of their height, the giant Dinka were an easy target. They had to hide in trenches, from which they could hardly see the attacking enemy. The Lord's Army guerrillas could not even think of running away. To reach Uganda, first they would have to get across Dinka territory. They were so afraid of the Dinka that Kony didn't even have to post armed guards around the guerrilla camps.

However, it wasn't fighting the Dinka or the Ugandan army, but diseases, hunger, and above all maddening thirst that were the worst problems for the guerrillas. They had devastated almost all the villages in Acholi-land, so now they had to make longer and longer journeys in search of food: to the land of the Karamojong, on the left bank of the Nile, to the national park above Murchison Falls, and even further, to Garamba in Congo and the province of Bahr el-Jabel in Sudan. Moreover, the Sudanese government had finally come to terms with Museveni, and now not only denied the rebels help and hospitality, but allowed the Ugandan army to venture after them on the Sudanese side of the border.

Samuel described how he was always hungry and always on the move. They lived on anything fit to eat—wild fruits, roots, bark, even lizards and insects. Wherever they appeared, the whole area was instantly vacated. At news of the guerrillas, people ran off with all their belongings and never came back. It was getting harder and harder to find a village, or even an abandoned vegetable patch, worth raiding. The only thing worse than hunger was thirst.

And they were always on their way somewhere, walking all the time. Plagued by diseases, exhausted by hunger, incessantly hunted and attacked by Ugandan helicopters and infantry, the guerrillas kept marching from dawn to dusk. They made short stops, usually at noon, when the sun was unbearably hot. At that time of day the commanders would gather around transistor radios to listen to the national and world news. But they never shared their knowledge with the children, who, after being kidnapped from their villages, knew nothing but what they saw and experienced. They weren't even allowed to talk to each other, because the commanders viewed it as an attempt at conspiring to escape, and immediately killed anyone suspected of such a plan. They also killed anyone weak or sick, who couldn't keep pace and was holding up the march.

After dark they would set off again, to look for something to eat, a waterhole, or an appointed meeting place to join up with other units and attack a village, or ambush a late bus. Constantly changing location was the only way to avoid pursuit, but only the strongest could survive this endless journey.

Samuel had been taken prisoner for the second time during a battle on the banks of the river Aswa, where calamus and papyrus grew. Government helicopters had tracked them down at dawn as they were crossing the river, which marks the border between the Gulu and Kitgum districts. A bullet from a high-caliber machine gun had almost torn off Samuel's leg. Wounded, he lay in the tall grass all day. Finally, at dusk some soldiers from a patrol had found him.

The doctors at the military hospital in Gulu had saved his leg, then sent him to the center, where children like him were treated and healed. There he had met Nora, the first person to whom he had told everything he had seen and endured.

It was coming up to midnight when I decided to call Jackson. It was late, but Kampala wasn't in the habit of going to bed that early. And yet his phone was silent.

✧

The day fixed for the elections overslept and got up late, looking gray. For ages it couldn't gain full consciousness and get itself going. From dawn, dark clouds swollen with rain hung low over the city, and fog wreathed the villas perched on the dark green hills.

Although it was a Thursday, Kampala was as deserted as on a Sunday. The stores and offices were closed, the shutters were down, and the iron grilles were locked and chained. Security guards in waterproof capes streaming with moisture were sitting on steps and window ledges, or lurking in gateways, smoking in silence. Except that there was none of the singing and prayers that usually came pouring from wide-open church doors and windows on a Sunday, merging into a single cry, filling the city with thanks for life and pleas for mercy.

It was obvious a storm was brewing, or at least some torrential rain was coming, which would rinse the weary, heat-choked air, breathing

freshness into it and a new interest in life. Days like this induce indo-
lence, provide an excuse not to leave the house and not to take on any
obligations or make any effort—thanks to the imminent downpour,
they'll be doomed to failure anyway.

Deo called and said he would come to fetch me from our usual meeting place at noon. To prove he had already been to vote, he showed
me his finger marked with purple ink that would remain indelible for
several days. I knew he had voted for Besigye, though he appreciated
Museveni's merits and regarded him as a better leader than his rival.

"He's held power for too long," he kept saying, however. "He should
hand it over now."

We set off for the city, almost without exchanging a word. The polling stations had been set up at offices and schools, but also in the open
air, in streets, markets, and parks. The role of screens to guarantee voting privacy was being performed by large bowls made of colored plastic,
the kind in which village women do their laundry. Now, bending at the
waist like them, the voters were hiding their voting cards inside the
bowls, putting a cross by their chosen candidate's name and dropping
the completed cards into some transparent urns.

Outside the market in Katimba, near the bus station, an agitated
crowd of people were waving their fists and swearing at some policemen, who were guarding a closed iron gate. They were only letting
people go through to the polling station set up among the empty market stalls if they had documents entitling them to vote in Kampala.

Lots of people were being turned away because their names weren't
on the electoral roll.

"You should have reregistered in advance. Now, if you want to vote,
you must go home, to your villages, because that's where you're registered," the officials were explaining.

At some point, among the people trying to vote in Katimba I noticed
Dr. Suleiman Kiggundu, the man I had met the day before at the opposition headquarters. He assured me that the opposition victory was
close and a certainty, although Museveni was trying to hold on to power
through various forms of fraud, like this one—excluding the names of
opposition supporters from the register.

"But if they're registered in their villages . . ." I said.

"But they work in Kampala! These are poor people, they live from hand to mouth because of Museveni! Have they really got to give up their hard earned shillings to pay for bus tickets? They should be allowed to vote where they work!" Kiggundu gave me a look of amazement and disapproval. "How can you fail to see the point? Aren't you wondering why only people who wanted to vote for the opposition have had problems finding their names on the electoral roll?"

As we drove off, Deo said the opposition leaders were to blame for all the confusion, because they hadn't told their supporters to reregister before the elections so they could vote in Kampala.

"It suits Museveni fine, because the countryside has always voted for him," he added. "Those country people don't understand a thing."

The rural voters, who represented the majority of the population, were still grateful to the president for peace and quiet, order and predictability. Moreover, in Africa all the ruling presidents or premiers can always count on the support of the countryside, where people have an almost religious respect for authority.

The violent storm that had been expected all day broke early in the evening. The officials, voters, and bystanders fled under umbrellas and roofs. Only some wet marabou storks remained outside, huge birds which, like loyal sentries, never left their posts on the streetlamps, even during a downpour.

The evening newscast announced that according to preliminary estimates Museveni had not only won the elections, but had gained more than half the votes, which was what he required to declare himself the victor without the need for a runoff. However, as one of the commentators taking part in the program noted, with each election the president had won a disturbingly smaller share of the votes. Ten years ago, three-quarters of the citizens had voted for him, and five years ago two-thirds. Now it was only slightly over half. The voters had also rejected as many as seventeen ministers from his cabinet in these elections, one-quarter of the government.

From a map posted in the television studio it appeared that Museveni had lost in the capital. As if to spite him, the Kampalan citizens

had elected *al hajji* Nasser Sebaggala as mayor. The people in Acholi-
land, in Gulu and Kitgum, hadn't voted for Museveni either. The TV
program mentioned that before the elections the president had threatened, as if in jest, that when the time came for him to share out money
between the country's provinces, he would do his best to remember
which ones had voted for him, and which had chosen his rival.

◂•▸

Now it only remained for the official results to be announced. That
day I was planning to call at a travel agency in one of the nearby glass
towers to check the flight connections from Europe and reserve a ticket
home. I wanted to do it straight after lunch at the hotel restaurant, to
which I had invited Allio Ewaku Emmy, the man who knew everything
and everyone.

I was going to thank him for his help, but also to ask what he thought
of the elections, to give me his prognosis for the future and to clarify
the prospects. My editors were expecting my final report from Kampala
to say what significance President Museveni's victory had for Uganda
and for all Africa, and whether the elections proved that an era of civil
liberties had dawned here too, or maybe quite the opposite—that day
would never come. I was to write whether the Ugandan elections were
a turning point, a milestone, or just a crossroads where Africa was at a
standstill, worried and full of doubts which way to go.

"Definitely write about that. And don't forget to say at least something
about Amin," the duty editor had insisted the night before. "People
remember him and want to read about him."

Straight after breakfast I set about writing. But I soon got stuck, hope-
lessly log-jammed in a tangle of words and sentences, which seemed to
me banal and stupid, less and less true by the moment. "In the first free
elections for almost half a century..." "In the country that produced the
bloody tyrant Idi Amin..." "... the African killing fields..."

So what significance did the Ugandan elections have? They were
not a breakthrough, they hadn't brought any dramatic or even excit-
ing decisions. They were neither a step backward nor a leap forward,

nor were they proof of desperate courage, progress, or madness. They hadn't brought Uganda to the edge of a precipice, nor had they steered it onto the road toward a bright future. Meanwhile Amin had absolutely nothing to do with it. I thought I should ask Emmy or Pike if their duty editor would remind a Ugandan journalist sent to Germany to report on elections to the Bundestag to be sure to mention Adolf Hitler. Does anyone in Uganda remember him? Is that what people want to read about?

We try to guess the readers' and viewers' tastes, and tailor our reports to suit them. Instead of being eyewitnesses to events and messengers bringing news, are we becoming a new kind of traveling salesman or court jester?

⊸⊙⊱

At noon I gave up. I decided to wait and see what Emmy would say. He was due at any moment. I locked the room and went to the hotel restaurant on the veranda. Hardly anyone was there, and the waiters were only just laying the tables for lunch. Suddenly I stopped in my tracks—there at a table by the entrance to the reception sat Jackson, drinking a bottle of beer.

"I didn't want to disturb you," he said, smiling broadly.

"What are you doing here?" I asked, and felt joy, a strange relief, and a restored sense of security.

"Having a beer," he snorted with laughter. "I think it's the third one by now. You'll find out for sure, because I've been telling the waiters to put them on your bill."

A newspaper lay open on the table, pinned down by an ashtray.

"Have you seen?" He jabbed a finger at the paper.

For several days all the local papers had been covering this story. Just before the elections, the police in Kampala had arrested an evangelical pastor from America. During a search of his home the detectives had found four machine guns and six clips of ammunition hidden in the bedroom.

The Reverend Peter Waldron was from Wyoming, and had been

in Uganda for four years. He worked as a consultant at the Ministry of Health, held prayer meetings on Sundays, and wrote articles and took photos for newspapers. Apparently he had even been thinking of founding a political party which would set itself the aim of introducing just and truly god-fearing laws and morals in Uganda.

Those who knew him admitted he was more like an athlete than a priest. Although he was approaching sixty, a young man might have envied him his muscular arms and thighs and tough guy's physique. Apparently before becoming a pastor, he had served in the U.S. Army.

"They say he was just pretending to be a pastor and journalist, but he was really a CIA spy," I heard Emmy's voice above me. As I focused on the newspaper article I hadn't noticed him approaching. I introduced Jackson to him.

"He's a journalist too, he works for a radio station," I said.

Jackson stood up to shake Emmy's hand.

"I've been reading your articles for years," he said.

Cup chinked against beer bottle with an uneasy clunk.

Emmy seemed tired of the admiration he prompted. He only took an interest in Jackson when I said he was from Gulu.

Emmy ordered himself coffee. When I asked what he thought about the case, he said all the evidence implied that Waldron had been planning an expedition into the Garamba jungle in Congo, where Joseph Kony had been hiding lately, to catch him, then hand him over to the European tribunal and collect the reward that was on his head—over one and a half million dollars. The Ugandan government had offered a reward for Kony too, but because of budget difficulties it was only worth about ten thousand dollars.

The rewards offered by the superpowers, international tribunals, and organizations for catching or killing the most dangerous criminals and rebels on the wanted list had brought out whole regiments of "headhunters," knights errant, adventure seekers, and swaggerers; confident of their own exceptional talents, lucky star, and ability to earn some easy money, they had gone hunting.

Pastor Waldron was not alone; some over-the-hill commandos from Great Britain and South Africa had hit on a similar idea, and had banded together for a military expedition to capture Charles Taylor, the former tyrant of Liberia then living in Nigeria, kidnap him, and hand him over to the international tribunal.

In Afghanistan a retired U.S. commando called Jonathan "Jack" Idema had been determined to win millions of dollars for the head of Osama bin Laden. He had set up a private jail in Kabul where he held and tortured prisoners to get information enabling him to track down the Saudi outlaw. When the matter came to light, the Afghan military police arrested Idema, and a Kabul court sentenced him to ten years in prison.

To capture Kony, the Reverend Waldron had planned to hire a group of guerrillas from the Congolese Revolutionary Movement, who to escape their own state army were hiding in Uganda. The pastor had already recruited the rebel leader, Dido Manyiroha, to help him, promising to split the reward for Kony with him, and so far had given him an advance payment of twenty thousand dollars.

The plot had failed when two couriers, who were smuggling weapons into Uganda for the Congolese expedition, arrived in Kampala and then panicked. Convinced they were being followed by a man who seemed to them suspicious, they took out their pistols and started shooting. The crowd in the street took them for common bandits. Someone called the police, and the rest set off in pursuit of the armed Congolese. Terrified and completely out of control, they ran at top speed to the house where Pastor Waldron lived. There the crowd, baying for blood by now, caught up with them and beat them unconscious. Then the police decided to search the pastor's home.

"In the process a scandal erupted, because it came to light that guerrillas from Congo were still hiding in Uganda just as before, even though President Museveni and President Kabila of Congo had sworn not to support rebels anymore," said Emmy. "Now, if the Congolese decide to take revenge, they'll start helping Kony, just as the Sudanese government did."

"I once talked with a commanding officer from the Lord's Army," Jackson butted in. "He said Kony had predicted to them that just as Judas agreed to betray Jesus for thirty pieces of silver, there'd be people who would have designs on his life once they were promised a reward for it."

At first he listened to Emmy's stories with interest, but he gradually seemed more and more absent, lost in his own thoughts.

"Ginaro, I remember," he said. "That's what the officer was called. Ginaro."

Emmy cast him a look but didn't say anything. He tore a page from a notepad and started drawing a diagram, using solid lines to mark state borders, military fronts, and the routes of troop movements, and dotted ones to show strategic alliances—who was with whom and against whom. Almost all the dotted lines met in the Sudanese capital, Khartoum. Emmy was just back from a long tour of Congo, Sudan, and the Central African Republic, and said he had seen few reasons for hope, but plenty for concern.

"Sudan is a threat to all its neighbors," explained Emmy, who had begun his career as a journalist reporting on the war in southern Sudan.

For years the Christian black Africans there had been rebelling against the governments of Muslim Arabs from the north. Uganda was one of the Sudanese insurgents' most loyal allies. In retaliation, Sudan had started to back Kony and his Lord's Army.

In this part of Africa, as they vied for precedence and influence, each country was making every effort to harm the neighbors and support their enemies. Kampala supported the insurgents in Sudan, and the Khartoum regime was helping the guerrillas in Uganda. Sudan had also armed the guerrillas in Chad, whose government in its turn was sending guns to the rebels in the Central African Republic. This country was hiding rebels from Congo, and the Congolese government was giving shelter to just about all the outlaws from the entire Great Lakes area. Ethiopia was trying to hurt Eritrea and Somalia, while Somalia wanted to make life hard for Kenya. Everyone was fighting and betraying everybody else, and they were all plotting against each other, singly and in alliances, which were only held together by hostility and a common enemy.

Yet in recent months almost all the countries in this part of Africa had been accusing Sudan in unison. Uganda blamed it for having torpedoed the peace talks it had tried to hold with Kony's envoys. Chad and the Central African Republic were accusing it of supporting local rebels, saying that Sudanese troops had been making armed forays across the border too. The southern Sudanese authorities also had grudges against Khartoum; after a war lasting half a century they had finally won themselves the right to autonomy, even to break away from the rest of the country and declare independence. The government in Juba, their proclaimed capital—formerly a remote backwater, the country's southernmost garrison town—had now complained that Khartoum was sabotaging their postwar reconstruction by trying to turn the local Nuer and Dinka tribes against each other, to incite fratricidal war between them and thwart the secession of the south.

Taking its model from the south, the black Africans of Darfur, situated in the west of the country on the border with Chad, had also triggered an armed uprising against the Arabs in Khartoum. By declaring itself an independent state, southern Sudan could assure the Darfur rebels—supported by Chad, of course—that an armed struggle not only makes sense, but is the one effective tool for getting your own way. If Darfur tried to gain independence, the province of Kordofan, rich in crude oil, would immediately follow in its footsteps.

As I pored over the crisscrossed map, I tried to memorize and understand it all, scribbling down on a paper napkin the complicated, similar-sounding names of all the various guerrilla factions and their embattled commanders. Anything to keep up with Emmy, and not put him off with my ignorance or a request to repeat or explain something more clearly.

"All this connects up," he continued, drawing the next dotted line. "There's no coincidence."

To pay back Chad for supporting the Darfur rebellion, and also with the aim of suppressing it, the Sudanese government had been trying to make sure the war covered as much terrain as possible and threatened everyone. It had incited the Chadian guerrillas to storm Ndjamena, and they had almost captured the presidential palace. The Darfur war had also spilled over into the neighboring Central African Republic, which was known mainly for the regime of its bloody tyrant, self-declared

Emperor Jean-Bédel Bokassa. The president of this poor, weak country kept the entire state army in the capital and forbade them from crossing the city limits, in case someone tried to take it in their absence. Rebels from Darfur had easily conquered the entire northeastern part of the country along the borders with Sudan and Chad, as well as some territory on the border with Congo.

"For years we have been calling this region the Wild West. No authority has ever reached it, and only a variety of bandits have ever had control of it. It includes the borderland marshes, the nearby Garamba jungle in Congo, and the floodplains on the western bank of the Nile in Sudan. There are no roads, phones, or electricity there, but lots of dense forest, and the grass on the savannahs is three yards high. It's the perfect hiding place," said Emmy. "By helping the rebels in almost all the neighboring countries, the Khartoum government has caused this terrain to pass into the possession of all manner of insurgents, warlords, deserters, and other outlaws. Sudan protects them to be able to use them later on against its neighbors."

According to Emmy, it was in these savannahs that Joseph Kony and his juvenile army were hiding.

"He's not in any danger there, but he couldn't stay in the Imatong Mountains in Sudan any longer. The Sudanese have not only promised not to support Kony anymore, but on top of that they've allowed the Ugandan army to make expeditions across the Sudanese border in pursuit of him. Now that he's lurking in the Congolese jungle, or in the savannahs of the Central African Republic, no one can accuse Sudan of supporting him. But whenever they want, the Sudanese government can summon him in an instant and send him to the war in southern Sudan or in Darfur."

Emmy was convinced Khartoum would never agree to the secession of the south, even if it had to start a new war. And it might need Kony's guerrillas for that. So he didn't believe the rumors that the Lord's Army was a wreck, decimated by disease, starving, and quarrelling among themselves, ready to surrender and conclude peace with Museveni.

"It's just a game," said Emmy, shaking his head. "My informers, and they're reliable people, say Kony's men have already been seen in Chad, and that they fought on the side of the local guerrillas. They're getting guns from Sudan again."

"Lakwena . . . When Lakwena enters him, Kony can read other people's minds," put in Jackson from across the table, moving an ashtray so the waiter had somewhere to put the next bottle of beer—his fourth or fifth. As I listened to Emmy, I had lost count. "So it's impossible to cheat him or hide anything from him."

"Is everything okay?" I asked.

"Couldn't be better," he replied, smiling broadly, then turned to Emmy and said: "It's funny to hear someone else explain it all. At home in Gulu I've been telling him about it. And now I'm just sitting here listening."

"Did you tell him about Lakwena?" asked Emmy.

"Only a little. Somehow it didn't come up," he said, nodding. "Thanks to Lakwena, Kony knows everything. And it's impossible to catch Kony, or deceive him or hide anything from him. It's impossible to escape from him. If he wanted, he could easily track down the runaways from his guerrilla army and punish them as an example. He's also capable of predicting future battles and ambushes. And everything that's going to happen. He never gets it wrong."

"But I'm told this magical power of his is plain old espionage intelligence provided by the Sudanese," said Emmy.

"No, no . . . it's not the Sudanese, it's Lakwena . . ." Jackson protested. "Oho! It's not so easy to trick Kony! They say he can even change into an old woman, a lion, or any wild animal. That's why he'll never be caught or killed. Unless Lakwena himself demands it of him."

Emmy was starting to take his leave, saying it was time for him to go. I asked if I could keep the page on which he had drawn the diagram of alliances and wars. He nodded. He left the hotel veranda and turned toward the traffic circle. I watched him ward off the children of a beggar woman who pitched camp and set up her checkpoint next to the newsboy each morning. Once he had vanished around the corner, I realized I hadn't asked him about the elections.

"I forgot," I said to myself.

"So it would seem," agreed Jackson, smiling and wiping drops of beer from his lips. "All because of Lakwena."

He said he had come to visit me, and to ask if I fancied going on a trip with him tomorrow, to the village on the lake where his cousin lived. Then we could go to the school where the girl who had run away from a guerrilla camp was a student—the one he had already told me about in Gulu.

I nodded, still bothered that I hadn't asked Emmy about the significance of the elections.

"But I think Kony may have lost his power, so perhaps he isn't invincible anymore," Jackson suddenly said.

"What?"

"I said Lakwena may have abandoned Kony," he repeated. "Kony and his people have crossed to the west bank of the Nile. If he didn't appease the river in advance and has offended it in some way, Lakwena could have got angry with him, the way he did with Alice. He dropped her when she crossed the river without winning it over first. She thought she was so powerful she didn't have to do that. She had stopped listening to Lakwena so he abandoned her, and without him she meant nothing."

"Is that why she was defeated?"

He nodded.

"And then what? Kony took him over?"

He shook his head.

"You can't take Lakwena over or tame him. It's he who chooses who he wants to possess. He entered into Kony, and before that he possessed Severino, Alice's father."

"And what if he gets angry with Kony now?"

"That's the whole problem. He has gone across the river, and if he has angered Lakwena, he will drop him. And choose someone new instead of him. But no one knows who."

"He could choose anyone?"

"Anyone he singles out for himself."

⟜⟡⟞

Jackson stayed for ages. By the time he left it was getting dark. I escorted him to the bus station, from where he would travel to the village on the lake. I went back to the hotel on foot to postpone the moment when I would have to sit down, write, and send in my report on the elections.

As usual, night fell suddenly, as if someone had blown out the day in a single puff. The streetlamps brightened the darkness with a warm yellow glow. Under a wide canopy of trees, at night the downtown avenues looked like murky tunnels. Bats flitted among the branches spreading above the sun-baked asphalt, calling or warning each other with loud squeaks. The street was empty, deserted.

On the way to the bus station Jackson told me that Kony had killed his uncle, Vincent Otti. Apparently they had fallen out at a camp in the jungle. Kony had suspected Otti of trying to make the soldiers rebel against him, lay down their weapons, and surrender. So he had him imprisoned and then shot. He didn't trust anyone, not even those whom, like Otti, he had appointed his deputies. Or maybe he trusted them least of all. Otti had become Kony's deputy in place of another commander, whom Kony had also eliminated.

Tired and lost in thought, I turned into the street where the hotel stood. Gentle music was coming from the Rock Garden Café nightclub. Suddenly I heard a loud thud, as if something had dropped straight out of the sky onto the sidewalk, but I couldn't see anything. Only when I took a few cautious steps did I notice a big, bloodstained rat lying on the ground.

I looked up and saw a marabou stork staring at me from a streetlamp. The large gray birds seemed to nest on every lamp, tree, and post in this city. By day, perching on top of them, they gazed down at the cars crawling past below. In the evenings they glided in circles above the city with their wings spread wide, like sinister scarecrows.

The marabou gazed down at me from the top of the lamppost. He must have dropped the rat, prey from his evening hunt. However, it looked just as if he had spat it out at my feet on purpose. It occurred to me that it must mean something, and I should tell Jackson about it. And also ask him about the enraged river that had betrayed the possessed Alice for not having shown it due respect and consideration.

⋘

I didn't write any more about the elections. It was too late to send the report.

I ordered an Indian takeout dinner to be delivered to my room.

Jackson's unexpected visit had disrupted my day, but it had also brought relief. Now I didn't have to decide anything—the next day we were going on a trip to the village by the lake, then to the school. The decision to leave was postponed.

In my notes I found a page torn from a British newspaper with the first interview Joseph Kony ever gave to a foreign journalist, Sam Farmar. I'd been thinking about it ever since the lunchtime conversation had moved from the elections to the Lord's Army.

"You are the first journalist who has come to see me in the bush. So here I am, you can see me for yourself. I am a human being like you. I have eyes, I have a brain, I wear clothes also."

"How do you present yourself? Can you tell me who you really are?"

"I am a military person who is fighting in Uganda. I am a freedom fighter, fighting for freedom in Uganda. But I am not a terrorist."

"But the methods you're using to achieve your aims are horrific. Thousands of people have been killed, and you've made thousands of children into guerrilla fighters. You are accused of some terrible crimes. Do you know that your guerrillas cut people's hands and feet off, they cut off their lips and ears?"

"That's only what they say about me, but it is not true. That is propaganda spread by Museveni."

"But I've seen photographs of people whose lips have been cut off with knives."

"That is Museveni's propaganda. Let me tell you the truth. Yes, things like that are happening in Uganda. But it is Museveni and his people who attack the villages, murder the people, and cut off their lips, then they put the blame on my guerrillas. It is slander. I cannot cut the ear of my brother. I cannot put out the eye of my brother. I cannot kill my own brother. What you have been told is not true."

"Are you saying the Lord's Army has never committed any of these crimes? It has never committed any rapes, abductions, or mutilations?"

"Yes, that is so."

"You've never done any of those things?"

"No, we have never done that. We have never abducted anyone, or forced anyone to do anything. It is true that among us there are many young people who joined us when we were fighting. But they came as volunteers. Do you think war is a good thing for children? I can tell you it is not. I have no child soldiers. I don't have acres of maize here, of onion, of cabbages. I don't have food. If I abducted children like that, here in the bush, what do they eat? That is Museveni's lies."

"Has God told you to fight this war?"

"No, no, no. It's not like that. God didn't tell me to fight this war."

Yet in another interview, for a Sudanese newspaper, he said something else. "God came to me in a dream and told me to fight for people to start living according to His commandments," he said. "So I went to Talanga forest on the border between Uganda and Sudan. There I prayed for sixty days for God to give me faith and strength to liberate the people of Uganda from sin."

I went back to the British journalist's conversation with Kony.

"So what are you really fighting for?"

"For freedom. For total freedom. I am fighting for a just cause."

"Is it true you are also fighting for the people of Uganda to live according to God's commandments?"

"Yes, we are fighting for that too. Is that bad? And that commandment was not given by Joseph Kony. No, that commandment was given by God."

"Do you feel guilty?"

"I am not guilty, I am not guilty, I am not guilty . . . People do not know me because they have only seen a little of me. So they believe the lies my enemies tell about me. I am not a criminal, I do not kill people. If I am a killer, why do you meet me? I am just the same sort of man as you. I am like others, I am just the same as you."

I was reminded of Idi Amin, who said the same thing, striking terror. I am just like you.

Suddenly the phone jangled. I recognized Jackson's voice. He said that tomorrow he would wait for me outside the main post office. He also asked how long I was planning to stay in Uganda and when I'd be back. I replied that I didn't know yet. But when he talked about returning, to my great surprise my first thought was of going back to Gulu.

◀◦▶

Jackson's cousin was called Hobart Senoga and he was a fisherman. He lived in the village of Kasenyi on Lake Victoria. He said that until recently he'd have called it a fishing village, because everyone there used to live by fishing—until recently.

"A year ago, here, where we're standing, the water came up to our shoulders," he said, watching his sons unload fish from their boat, which had just come in from the night catch. "But now? You can see for yourself. There used to be fish swimming here, and now there are goats grazing."

Lake Victoria, the biggest in Africa and one of the biggest in the world, had been drying up. Following the recent dry season the water level was the lowest for a hundred years. In the course of a year it had come down by almost five feet.

Several years earlier the local fishermen, farmers, and herders had noticed that the water in the lake was going down, but none of the authorities in the nearest countries, neither in Kampala, nor in Nairobi, nor in Dar es-Salaam, were concerned about it. Just as they weren't concerned about the increasingly meager, less and less frequent rainfall, or the wasteful felling of the surrounding forests, which retained water and stopped the fields and pastures from turning into desert.

But when rocks that used to be underwater had started looming above the surface of the lake, and the passenger ferries could no longer sail into the ports, the Ugandan government had finally recognized the evaporation of the lake as a disastrous threat to the country's future development. (Nowadays there are carriers at the Ugandan port of Luziro who wait for travelers arriving from Kenya or Tanzania and transport them, first in boats, then on their own shoulders, from the ferries to the shore.)

The falling level of water in the lake and in the reservoirs for the hydropower stations on the White Nile had forced the authorities to introduce electricity rationing. In most districts of Kampala it was now switched on every other day. At nightfall, half the city was plunged into darkness lit only by the flames of bonfires, candles, and oil lamps. The lights were only on without interruption in hotels and restaurants whose owners could afford their own generators.

For a long time the Ugandan government insisted that the only reason for the problems—which were temporary, of course—with the electricity and the evaporation of Lake Victoria was the terrible drought that had affected the whole of eastern and central Africa that year, threatening millions of people from Somalia to Zanzibar with famine. However, the foreign experts who came from Nairobi to investigate the causes of Lake Victoria's evaporation decided that the drought was only half the reason for the disaster. Equally to blame, in their view, was the Ugandan government, which for the needs of the hydropower stations, and also the president's beloved factories and steelworks, had drained more and more water from the lake and from the White Nile. As it grew and became richer, Kampala was sucking it up like an ogre whose thirst is never satisfied. As a parting shot the foreign specialists warned that Lake Chad, which used to be one of the world's biggest lakes, had dried up in just the same way; if people didn't start treating lakes and rivers with more care, they would soon become stinking bogs, and the green pastures, savannahs, and forests would change into lifeless deserts.

Hobart Senago the fisherman reckoned things were bad, and getting worse.

Only a year ago he used to sail out onto the lake in the evening to set his nets, come home for the night, and go back out at dawn to bring in the catch and sell the fish to traders from the market in Kampala, who waited on the beach for the fishermen to come in. Now Hobart Senago sailed out in his boat and stayed on the lake all night.

"The lake is escaping, and the fish are escaping with it," he sighed heavily. "Now we have to go much, much further to catch them. We need motorboats and fuel, and that costs money. We can't afford to come back for the night anymore."

But even long trips by motorboat couldn't guarantee a rich catch.

"Once we used to sail out to our familiar fishing grounds. We knew where to find the fish. Now we're fishing in unfamiliar waters. Sometimes the catch is a success, but sometimes we come back empty-handed."

He stopped talking, and only when silence fell did I realize that he alone had been speaking, with no one interrupting him to ask questions. Embarrassed, or maybe disappointed by my lack of response, he had walked a few steps away. Now he was leaning over, helping his sons to sort the fish, putting aside the ones fit for sale, and choosing some to take home for dinner. He threw the rest of the catch—tiny little fish, broken mussels, slimy crabs, and seaweed—onto the dirty gray sand behind him.

The entire length and breadth of the shore, the intense, silent ritual of inspecting, sorting, valuing, and selling the catch was under way. There were some tawny yellow dogs impatiently hovering around the fishermen, their wives and children, and also the dealers from Kampala. Casting ingratiating looks, the dogs were begging for permission to start the feast. On the alert to defend their position at any cost, they kept glancing suspiciously at the seagulls and terns perched on poles sticking out of the sea, and at the pelicans circling overhead. Only the puppies were fooling around, jumping on crabs as they scuttled across the stinking, litter-strewn beach.

"Why did you bring me here?" I asked Jackson. "I should be writing my report on the elections."

"Haven't you written it yet?" he said in surprise. He gazed at the lake, stretching away to the horizon. "I thought you'd like it here and you'd be interested."

"In an evaporating lake?" I said, shrugging. "It's not the end of the world yet."

"But here they say this could be the beginning of the end of the world."

◄◦►

The end of the millennium was supposed to herald an apocalypse.

It was predicted by a self-appointed prophet, Bishop Joseph Kibwetere, an excommunicated Catholic priest who, along with several other clerics and nuns who had been expelled from the Church community, had founded his own one. He called it the Movement for the Restoration of the Ten Commandments of God. He told his followers, whose numbers grew by the week, that he had overheard a conversation between the Virgin Mary and Jesus Christ. Apparently, Mary had said that if people didn't finally start dutifully observing the Lord's Commandments, God would send an apocalypse down on them. Kibwetere insisted that he had even heard the date of the end of the world—the last day of 1999. After that date, time was going to end.

In preparation for Judgment Day and eternal salvation, the prophet's followers came from all over the country to his church, near the town of Kanungu at the foot of the Mountains of the Moon, on the border with Congo. Warned by the priests against contact with sinners, they kept well away from the local country folk. They didn't talk to each other much either, but communicated through signs instead, to avoid committing blasphemy or wounding their loved ones with a cross word. As they said goodbye to their earthly life, the prophet's followers killed their herds, sold off all their belongings, and handed the money over to the leaders of the sect. For a week before the predicted end of the world, they held a farewell feast lasting seven days. They roasted several oxen and bought up supplies of Coca-Cola from the entire district.

But the end of the world didn't happen. Time did not come to a halt. The prophet explained to his surprised followers that evidently he had misheard, and the apocalypse would come in a year from now. Not all of them believed him. More and more of them demanded that the prophet and his priests should return the money they had entrusted to them when the end of the world was approaching. According to the Ugandan police, it was the growing number of grievances and increasing doubt that prompted the prophet to announce that the world would end on March 17, without waiting for the year 2000 to be over. On that day the Virgin Mary was going to manifest herself to members of the sect, and take them in a wooden ark to heaven, where they would live forever after, naked, carefree, and happy, like Adam and Eve before they committed sin. Only they would be saved. Everyone else on earth would be exterminated.

On the morning of the appointed day, five hundred of the believers dressed up in specially made black, green and white robes, and shut themselves in a wooden temple erected by the prophet, singing psalms. Soon after, the church was in flames, and all the people inside it were burned alive. At first the police suspected a mass suicide, but they changed their minds when their investigations revealed that before the fire had engulfed the temple, its doors and windows had been nailed shut. Among the maize and sugarcane patches in the surrounding hills, the police also discovered some mass graves containing almost five hundred more bodies. They had no wounds, so it was clear they had either been suffocated or poisoned.

The inhabitants of the local villages were horrified. They believed that fire causes total annihilation—it destroys not only the human body, but also the soul. That was why they burned convicted witches and people who were possessed by evil spirits on pyres. They did not feel sorry for the prophet's followers who had died in the temple on the hill. They were shocked by the idea that by spending years living next door to the servants of evil they had been unwittingly exposed to a deadly danger.

To cap it all, no one knew if the prophet Kibwetere had gone up in flames with his followers or not. His corpse was never identified, but one of his priests was later seen in Rwanda and in Kenya. Warrants were issued for his arrest, as for a common criminal.

Doctors from Kampala confirmed that they had treated Kibwetere for some severe psychoses. But as in the case of Alice of the Holy Spirit, ordinary people believed the unfortunate Kibwetere must have been possessed by a spirit. Credonia Mwerinde, a onetime streetwalker who had joined the prophet and become his confidante and lover, claimed that the spirits of the Virgin Mary and the Archangel Michael entered her too—it was they who told her one night to renounce sin and listen to the prophet Kibwetere.

For ordinary Ugandans, another portent of the end of the world were the major floods affecting the country increasingly often. When the biggest flood yet struck Acholi-land, various prophets immediately appeared in Gulu and Kitgum, proclaiming it to be the deluge, which would be followed by the end of the world.

The flood really was extremely dangerous. Half a million people were made homeless, the government had declared a state of emergency, and reassigned money previously budgeted for other needs to aid for the flood victims. Pastureland, manioc, sorghum, and groundnut fields were all submerged. Although they had managed to bring in the harvest just before the deluge, the water had carried most of it away. Everything they had been able to save was wasted, because they couldn't get it to market. Falling incessantly for two months, the torrential rains had turned roads used by trucks, tractors, and bikes into rapid, dangerous streams. Now they could only be traveled by boat. Some people had to wade through several miles of water to escape from their villages.

Additionally, the floods came after a long and destructive drought, which gave the prophets of doom another argument to support their credo that the end of the world was nigh. Francis Opwonya from Gulu claimed to be one of these prophets, sent by God to bring people eighteen new commandments and to help them prepare for Judgment Day. He preached God's prediction that five signs would herald the end of the world. First an AIDS epidemic would erupt, then a famine, and then an earthquake, followed by floods and finally hailstorms. When the prophet's fame spread beyond Gulu, the police arrested him on charges of organizing illegal gatherings, disturbing public order, and abusing officers of the law.

Prophets proclaiming the end of the world have often appeared when a mysterious, lethal epidemic has erupted, decimating whole villages and districts. The people here have a particular fear of diseases that have come across from Congo, which they regard as a sinister country full of horror and magic spells. The epidemic caused by the deadly Ebola virus was known as the Congolese plague; it killed its victims extremely nastily and quickly, with no chance of survival.

The sufferers died in dreadful convulsions, insane with fever, pain, and terror, as the lifeblood flowed out of them through every bodily orifice. Usually the virus killed them so rapidly that there wasn't time for them to infect anyone else. But in the year 2000—when according to the prophet Kibwetere the world would end—when the Ebola virus affected Acholi-land and five other districts bordering Congo in the west of the country, it killed more slowly and insidiously, causing people to infect each other.

The first people to fall victim to it were the villagers in a small place called Kikyo, at the foot of the Ruwenzori Mountains. Initially it was thought they had died of malaria, which was common in the area. But when the relatives and neighbors who had helped wash and bury the bodies started to die too, doctors were called in from Kampala. They confirmed that the Ebola virus—first discovered in an extinct village on the banks of the river Ebola—had evidently crept across the Congolese border again. They were sure of this when they learned that the first people to die of it had roasted and eaten a goat which had been bitten by a wild animal, most probably a monkey.

The scientists think the killer virus had been living in remote parts of the jungle for years, killing wild animals, mainly monkeys. It only started attacking people when they invaded its terrain while hunting game and felling trees to build homesteads and farm plots in their place. It couldn't kill bats, but was carried by them.

The researchers discovered to their alarm that once it started to attack people, the virus grew more dangerous and deadly, constantly changing, adapting, and perfecting itself. It still caused inevitable death, but no longer destroyed its victims so quickly. Just like the killer virus that triggers AIDS, it let those whom it infected live awhile, long enough to pass the disease on to others.

Panic had erupted in the town of Bundibugyo when people infected with the Ebola virus started arriving there from the neighboring villages. The local people kept them at a distance, like lepers. All it took was a handshake to fall sick with the incurable illness too. It was its extreme power and virulence that made it so terrifying. People saw it as a punishment from God, a curse on them.

I remembered that Nora had lived in Bundibugyo for some time. However, she had never said a word about what life had been like there during the epidemic.

To prevent the disease from spreading, the army put up checkpoints on the roads. No one was allowed in or out of the town. Convinced the authorities had condemned them to death, the townsfolk slipped away through the woods—anything to escape from the cursed town. Even the local doctors and nurses ran away; for them treating the patients meant a death sentence.

President Museveni made a statement on television, advising his compatriots not to greet each other by shaking hands, at least for a while. During mass the Catholic priests stopped giving the congregation communion by hand.

Doctors who came from Kampala, equipped with protective overalls, told people not to conduct the usual burials for their dead relatives, but as soon as they died to pack them into special bags and bury them in the ground like that. Islamic clerics exempted Muslims from their duty to wash corpses. "It's true that the Koran tells us to wash the bodies of the dead before burying them, but it even more strictly forbids us to take our own lives," declared the holy *hajji* Nsereko Mutumba in Kampala. "And washing the bodies of people who have died of the Ebola virus is tantamount to taking one's own life."

The unfortunate citizens of Bundibugyo were at a total loss. By not washing the dead bodies and not completing the funeral rites, they might indeed be protecting themselves against the killer virus, but they were exposing themselves to the anger of the spirits—not properly dispatched to the afterlife, they would remain in the world of the living and take revenge for the injury done to them. The plague epidemic that erupted in Acholi-land almost at the same time as the Ebola virus attack was seen as proof of this. It was mainly women who fell ill with the plague, which was carried by fleas. According to village custom the men took the beds for themselves, forcing the women to sleep on clay floors.

"When human life consists of nothing but suffering, worry, and endless labor, it's easy to persuade people that they can only expect real peace and justice after the end of the world, which they should look forward to with joy," said Father Patrick from Bishop Kihangire Secondary School in Kampala.

We went there from the fishing village on the lake to see Eve. That was the name of the girl abducted by Kony's guerrillas, who had spent almost five years with them. Made into a soldier, she had killed and kidnapped other children. Then she had been given to one of the commanders as a wife, and had borne him a daughter. But two years ago she had escaped from the guerrilla camp with her child. She had ended up at the same center in Gulu where Samuel was now living.

After completing her therapy she had nowhere to go. Her parents had been killed in the war, and her more distant relatives refused to acknowledge an unmarried girl with a child. They regarded her as a shameful burden. They were afraid of her and didn't believe the life she had led in the guerrillas was now behind her. So from Gulu she had been sent to Bishop Kihangire school in Kampala, which was known for accepting children released from the Lord's Army. Christine, a colleague of Nora's who had been Eve's caregiver in Gulu, had told me the girl was doing very well in Kampala. She was popular, she was a model student, she was going to university and wanted to become a teacher.

Eve's story interested me because Samuel had no one either, and it wasn't clear where he would go when his therapy ended and he was discharged from the center.

Father Patrick taught algebra at Bishop Kihangire school. He was also the grade teacher for Eve's class.

"It is Satan who sends false prophets into the world to give people illusory hope that kills instead of giving strength for life. They promise salvation here and now. They refer to the Bible and Christ, but there isn't a word about the Cross in what they say."

◄◦►

Eve was dead.

She had died of pneumonia a month ago. She had fought the illness for a long time, but the killer AIDS virus had been patiently and cold-bloodedly destroying her, hollowing her out from the inside and taking away her immunity. Until finally, weak and defenseless, she couldn't resist it any longer.

She had contracted the virus at the guerrilla camp from the commander to whom she was given as a wife. He must have caught it from his previous wife, who had died in the bush. Eve had passed the virus on to her daughter, giving her life and death all at once.

"We knew she had the virus, but she was so strong and brave, she had so much confidence and hope … We thought she'd manage to break free of the nightmare and find her old place in life," said Father Patrick. "She'd been through so much, endured so much. Others had lost, they hadn't coped, but she had remained so unchanged! Even when she was forced to do harm, like everyone in the guerrillas, in her soul she had never yielded to evil. For us she was proof that a person can overcome anything."

But the invisible virus was alive inside her, lying in wait, and when it launched its lightning attack, giving no chance for defense, it was too late to save her. Eve had finished her high school studies and was planning to continue them at Makerere University, where there was already a place on a teaching course waiting for her.

"It looked as if she had the worst behind her," sighed the priest heavily, staring at the cold marble floor. "It's the work of Satan. He knows how to hit where it hurts the most."

I had already heard people in Gulu say that Kony was the servant of Satan, if not the devil himself. The priest at the Blessed Virgin Mary church had said it, and also that Kony confused people by telling them good was evil, and evil was good.

"It's the work of Satan," repeated Father Patrick. "All this unfinished business—death sentences passed but not carried out, postponed, but not revoked. Maybe it'd be better if they were killed in the guerrillas. If they never came back."

With his open-necked shirt untucked and his long, ruffled hair, he didn't look like a clergyman, nor did he look suited to the stark teacher's study, which was just like a parish office.

"You think you've already saved them, you've won, you've beaten evil," he continued. "But it's quite untrue. They're not free or healed at all. There's still a sort of curse hanging over them. Satan could have killed them, finished the job, but that's not enough for him, so he sends them among us. They come back among people, and seem no different from the rest of us, but the truth is they can't return to normal. They're doomed, dangerous. Or they die, like Eve, just as hope is dawning. And a small part of us dies with them, those of us who believed evil could be beaten. Maybe that is our cross to bear throughout life."

"Unfinished business?" I wondered.

"It's the work of Satan," he repeated. "To my mind business once started should be taken to its conclusion. Otherwise better not take it on at all, because it slips out of control, lives its own life, and becomes unpredictable. The loose ends of it can be picked up by others and taken in the wrong direction."

⤚⊙⤙

"Where to now?" asked Jackson in the car.

"I have no idea," I replied. "I must think."

Unfinished business. I had so much of it.

It included almost every journey, every story, every acquaintance. The evidence was drawers full of old business cards, ageing notebooks with addresses and phone numbers scribbled in them, first names and surnames. Each one represented a promise not kept, a broken word, a betrayal. Unfinished business.

I got the impression that for all these people, our meeting was the start of an acquaintance. But for me it was the end as well. I eagerly wrote down the names, addresses, and phone numbers of all the guides and interpreters who helped me, all the people I interviewed and the heroes of my stories. I promised them I'd be in touch, I wouldn't forget, I'd visit. As I was saying it, I kind of believed it myself. Or maybe, fearing everything that's irrevocable or unchangeable, I just wanted to believe it.

But I had never gone back, because even when I did return to a place again, it was never the same. Journalists' stories don't usually have a continuation, and their heroes only live for a while. They appear once, and then disappear. I don't know what happened to most of them, and I've never tried to find out. I have just finished the story and gone to look for a new one.

So I don't know how Dr. Mumbin from Kabul is getting on. He was my guide to the Panjshir Valley on a journey that ended with a horseback ride across the Hindukush. I don't know how Said Hamzat is doing, my host and guardian angel in Chechnya. What happened to Jayne from the burned-down house in the suburbs of Eldoret? She went on writing for weeks after I left Kenya. Messy, abandoned friendships, business started and interrupted, then forgotten, littered the routes of all my journeys.

In a way, the journalist's profession has betrayal encoded into it. It demands gaining people's trust and extracting confidences from them, purely in order to publicize and reveal them, all for a sense of a job well done, for satisfaction, applause, and prizes. The only, and adequate, justification for this abuse of other people's trust is to find out the truth.

As I talked to Samuel, or rather listened to his tales, I also felt like an intruder, stealing his innermost secrets by deceit.

And Nora . . .

⤞

"Where are we going?" This time Deo the driver asked me.

I didn't answer. There was a long pause before I turned to Jackson and said:

"Did you know her?"

"Who? Eve?" He made a face. "I don't remember her from Gulu. I know her husband."

"You know him? That guerrilla commander?"

"Yes, who else? She never had any other husband."

"How did you get to know him?"

"The usual way, in Gulu. You know him too."

"I do?"

"I've seen you both at breakfast in the hotel a few times, so I thought you knew each other."

In Gulu I had gone down to breakfast late, when the waiters were starting to clear away the buffet. I remembered a small, slight man whom I had seen several times. He wore a dark suit, which was shabby but clean, and he had a shaved head. He was polite, and always bowed first. We had exchanged a few perfunctory courtesies.

He only ever put fruit on his plate and then poured yogurt over it. He never ordered eggs and bacon from the chef, or even toast. He said he had to watch his diet, mind his liver. I couldn't tell what he did for a living, or guess his age. Maybe he took great care of himself, or he may just as well have aged prematurely.

After the meal he'd go back to his room upstairs. I never saw him again for the rest of the day.

"But he lives at the hotel," I said in surprise.

"Where should he live? They keep guerrilla officers who are taken prisoner or who surrender at the hotel or in the barracks. I thought you knew who he was."

"Were all the guests I lived with at the hotel guerrillas?"

"Maybe not all, but most of them. Not many people come and stay in Gulu these days. People prefer to avoid the place."

Silence fell. We were still sitting in the car outside the school. I thought of the men who had frightened Samuel so much when I took him to lunch at the hotel.

"Do you think they'd be willing to talk to me?"

"Why shouldn't they?" he asked cheerfully.

"It's a pity I didn't know that."

"Nothing's lost. You can still do it," he said, shrugging.

"What else could I have done in Gulu?"

"That I don't know," he said, laughing.

I thought that if I went back to Gulu for a few days I could find out what was going to happen to Samuel. At least this part of his fate would be settled while I was there. I could also return his folder to Nora.

Jackson was going back to Gulu the next day, on the afternoon bus, which got there before nightfall. If Nora was on duty, I could still go and see her that day. But I'd have to make it by dusk, because the security guards had orders not to let anyone into the center later than that.

I should make it by dusk. I told Jackson I had decided to go back to Gulu with him.

"What about the elections?" he asked. "They haven't announced the results yet."

"I can write about it in Gulu."

"In that case you never really had to leave the place."

Slowly, in no hurry, we climbed the alleyways up to the downtown area. Deo asked if he should come and drive me from the hotel to the bus station, but I said no. I felt relief. Suddenly all my doubts and dejection were gone.

"I'm glad I'm going back to Gulu," I told Jackson. "I still have a bit of business I should take care of there."

He nodded, and after a pause he said:

"Severino. Alice of the Holy Spirit's father."

"What about him?"

"He lives in Gulu too. We could find him."

I agreed. There was another long silence.

"Though they do say he's completely crazy," said Jackson.

"Maybe it's the spirits?" I replied. "Maybe Lakwena is back and never leaves him alone now?"

Jackson gave me a look but didn't reply.

THREE

I FAILED TO GET THERE BY DUSK. As night fell, we were only just crossing the bridge over the Nile beyond the Karuma Falls.

Despite the growing darkness, life at the crossroads leading to Gulu and Lira was in full swing. The vendors were shouting away, touting their wares and trying to tempt travelers. The small flames of oil lamps and lightbulbs swaying on the gentle breeze were twinkling, and generators were whirring softly, giving off an acrid smell of gasoline.

The colorful buses, with the names of the transport companies "Nile" and "Gateway" written on their sides in large letters, pushed their way through the market, trying to find the road ahead in the yellow beams of their headlamps. Some of them turned off to Lira, others to Gulu, yet others to Arua.

"Just think, not so long ago, in order to get from Gulu to the Karuma Falls the buses used to gather in convoys and only set off with a military escort," said Jackson, staring through the window at the small lights flashing by in the darkness. "And traveling at night was out of the question."

Doomed to wander the wilderness endlessly, the Lord's Army guerrillas used to lie in wait along the main highways to rob incautious travelers. The blackened skeletons of burned-out buses and big trucks pushed onto the hard shoulder marked the trail of their old ambushes. However, once the Ugandan army had driven the guerrillas out of the border area, and the local Sudanese rebels had made peace with the government in Khartoum and set up their own regime in Juba, new life had entered the neighboring towns and villages.

Cautiously at first, still fearfully, but gradually more and more boldly, people had started making journeys, to visit friends and relatives they hadn't seen for ages, do some shopping, or see to some business. Once they were home from the first trip safely, they were soon off on another one. And then another. Until eventually they forgot all the things that had happened in the past, and that had determined their lives until so recently. Once again goods appeared at the markets and in the stores—items they had almost forgotten existed, and others they only knew about from hearsay, which were now being imported from Kampala, or even from Congo and Kenya.

"How quickly it all changes," sighed Jackson. "Take Gulu, for example. Only a couple of years ago the whole town consisted of just four streets, two bars, and one hotel. There was nothing around it but the Lwal forest, where the guerrillas were on the rampage. And now? You can hardly believe it."

The bus skipped over the railroad tracks marking the borders of the city and, braking gently, rolled slowly toward the bus station located in the marketplace. The sky was almost black, starless, heralding the start of the rainy season, so loved by the guerrillas and so hated by the citizens of Gulu, who kept watch in the darkness for warning signs—the glow of handheld flashlights dancing in the gloom, as the guerrillas used them to find their way.

The seasonal rains always affected life in Acholi-land. They turned deserts into green fields and cultivated plots into stinking bogs. The swollen rivers overturned weak bridges, washed away roads, and cut off remote villages from the rest of the world. In the rainy season the muddy ground immobilized army columns and prevented pursuit, while trees and bushes revived by the rain hid the guerrillas from helicopters.

Changes were expected to come with the start of the rainy season—big ones, unfamiliar and disturbing. There was nothing in particular to herald them, yet they were anticipated. Maybe because the rainy season itself, so volatile, irritable, and angry, took away all sense of certainty and made it hard to see ahead. It even surprised people by not bringing the changes they expected, such as every time a cloudy, sultry night was suddenly followed by a hot, white morning, as if a curtain had gone up.

Night had already settled on Gulu for good, and though some of the lights were still on, it was long past the hour when the town was full of the children who arrived at dusk from the whole area. Silence reigned, broken only by frogs croaking in rain-filled puddles and ditches.

As we passed the center where Samuel lived, I noticed that all the lights were out. Even if she was on duty that night, Nora must have gone to bed by now. The driver switched off the engine, as if trying not to wake the children sleeping under the arcades, and almost noiselessly rolled the bus into the litter-strewn, deserted bus station, where the wind was tossing some torn newspapers.

"Yet in Kampala they still say Gulu is possessed by demons. They think we're all possessed here," said Jackson when the bus stopped and the driver switched on the inside lights to let the passengers sort out their luggage.

❧

At the Acholi Inn Hotel there was a party going on to celebrate Museveni's win in the elections. Although the official results hadn't yet been announced, the president's victory was undoubted.

The hotel courtyard, covered in rust-colored gravel that crunched underfoot, was packed with cars. Among expensive vehicles, clean and shiny, there were some dusty, well-used vans plastered in yellow and green posters, which I had seen in town before the elections. They had toured the streets slowly, as if trying to find their way, while some old loudspeakers fixed to the roof called on the citizens to vote for President Museveni on election day, as the only candidate who could restore peace and plenty to Acholi-land. "He and he alone can do it! No one else!" screeched the voice from the car roof. Sometimes a jaunty song came out of the loudspeaker, *The Man in the Color Yellow*, which was his election anthem. The president really did dress in colors that were quite close to yellow, as he wore beige shirts and khaki pants.

The same song was now booming out of the banqueting hall at the Acholi Inn. I could already hear it from the bridge, where I parted from Jackson, and walked the rest of the way to the hotel alone. It was such a black, impenetrable night that I had to scrape my shoes along the asphalt to avoid going off the road and falling into a rain-filled ditch.

As the receptionist was entering my details in the hotel register, I asked about the man I had met in the restaurant at breakfast, the guerrilla officer.

"Yes, that's him." He nodded, without looking up. "He's staying here."

"What's his room number?"

"I'm not allowed to say," he replied politely. "And you're out of luck, because he left for Kampala on the morning bus today."

"What about the others? I'm told there are other guerrillas living here too."

"They are former guerrillas, sir. They have surrendered and given up the bush," he corrected me. "Yes, it's true. They do live at our hotel."

"Which rooms are they in? I suppose you're not allowed to say that either?"

He smiled and shook his head.

"Maybe I'll meet them at the party."

"I don't think so." He handed back my passport and gave me a room key. "Welcome to Gulu. Welcome back."

⟿

The party to celebrate the election victory was being held on the lawn. In the small courtyard between the restaurant and the bar there was a band playing on a stage made of fresh planks. The musicians were wearing yellow shirts with a picture of the president on them. The waiters were in snow-white shirts, circulating among the guests with trays full of frosted beer bottles and glasses of whisky and gin.

The town's most important officials and officers from the local garrison were all at the party. Busy talking, they seemed not to hear the loud music. Below the stage, their wives were whirling about on the dance floor in colorful, shimmering dresses with fanciful bows tied at the shoulder. They burst into loud, happy laughter every time the musicians launched into a new song. Setting their broad hips and arms in hypnotic motion, they dropped their heads, as if ashamed of their own uninhibited desire for fun.

I ordered coffee at the bar. Apart from the military and the town hall notables, I couldn't see any of the locals. The people of Gulu never hid the fact that they didn't support the president, and always voted for whoever was running against him.

In the first elections that Museveni had allowed after entering Kampala at the head of his rebel army, the Acholi had voted almost to a man for Paul Ssemogerere, though he was a Bugandan, not a popular tribe in this part of the country. Although he won in every other region, Museveni gained less than a tenth of the votes in Gulu and Kitgum.

Five years later the Acholi voted for the opposition candidate again, Kizza Besigye, and Museveni had another humiliating defeat. In the elections that had just ended, history had repeated itself. Museveni had been victorious throughout the country, but in the north the Acholi had voted for Besigye again.

The locals couldn't bear the president and blamed him for all the injuries and misfortunes that had befallen them—wars, massacres, looting, poverty, and even the epidemics, floods, and droughts. "Museveni wants our destruction," they would say. "He wants revenge on us for old wrongs the Acholi soldiers did to his compatriots. He wants us all to die, and then he can take our lands for himself and his people."

Meanwhile, Museveni's opponents promised that as soon as they beat him, they would immediately negotiate with Kony and his Lord's Army, put an end to the war, and restore order and prosperity. Kony himself had also sent messengers to the Acholi villages before each election to explain to them that if they voted for Museveni's enemies, the guerrillas would willingly surrender. Jackson told me that before the last elections Kony's spies in Gulu and the area had reminded the Acholi that the Lord's Army leader was expecting great changes after the vote.

The Acholi understood the message well—they were to vote for Museveni's enemies, otherwise they'd be regarded as his supporters, and would pay a high price for it. When Museveni beat Kizza Besigye five years earlier, the guerrillas had started attacking, robbing, and burning villages soon after the elections. Now Museveni had won again, so people were expecting the worst.

❦

To tell the truth, Museveni too had been promising the Acholi an end to the war and threatening that they'd bitterly regret it if they didn't vote for him. After losing in Gulu in the last election, he had warned that he wouldn't listen to the citizens' complaints, take care of their needs, or provide money for new roads, hospitals, or schools because they had turned away from him. "You should have thought of that earlier," he reproached them.

He usually threatened never to negotiate with Kony, but to defeat him, crush him like a treacherous snake. Once, however, he had surprised everyone by making a personal trip to Odek, Kony's native village, and informing the rebel's kinsmen that he no longer felt any anger toward him. "I was angry with him, but my advisers have persuaded me that I should show him mercy," he declared to the people of Odek. "So tell him to come home and stop hurting people. Also tell him that you make your own choice about who is going to govern you." Museveni even promised that if Kony surrendered, and they chose him as a member of parliament in the next elections, as president he would make him a minister in his government. However, Kony wanted to be president himself, so he hadn't accepted Museveni's offer.

Usually, however, Museveni cursed Kony and his guerrillas, shaking his fist at them. "Now they'll get what they deserve! This time they can't count on mercy!" he threatened before the elections. "Before the next dry season is over there won't be any rebels left in the north of Uganda, or anything to disturb the peace."

Once, when addressing some journalists, he predicted that in less than seven months his army would kill or catch Kony. He added that he was even ready to bet a million shillings, then worth about a thousand dollars. A journalist from Kampala took him up on the bet. In the *Monitor* newspaper I read that this journalist was called Tamale Mirundi, and that when he won, the president's office paid him the money in two installments of half a million Ugandan shillings each.

◀◦▶

So Museveni had proved helpless. Yet as a former guerrilla leader, a victor, he should have known how to fight and conquer rebels in the bush. And what had he done? Incapable of beating Kony, he had been forced to ask a foreign tribunal to declare him and his top commanders to be criminals and outlaws. The judges in The Hague had listened to his request and had issued arrest warrants, demanding that Kony be prosecuted anywhere on earth. Now wherever he set foot, he could be arrested and brought before the tribunal in Holland.

By doing this, Museveni had deprived himself of the right to deal with Kony in his own way. He could no longer apply either his own punishment or forgiveness. By surrendering Kony's fate to foreign judges and bounty hunters, he had not only shown weakness, but had openly demonstrated it to the whole world.

Even more than they hated him, the Acholi people loathed Museveni's soldiers. Continuous civil war for years on end, repeated looting and rape had led the northern Ugandans to regard the soldiers as oppressors rather than defenders.

After a tour of the northern garrisons, Museveni himself despondently admitted that the units stationed there lacked discipline; the soldiers were lazy, and too keen on drink. The officers took their subordinates' pay from them, so in order to survive, the ordinary soldiers robbed the local villagers. The commanders also stole money by adding the names of long-dead people, or of men who had never even existed, to the soldiers' payroll.

The soldiers stole gasoline and supplies from the barracks, and illegally traded them at the local markets. They even stole uniforms and guns from the army stores and sold them to envoys from the guerrillas they were fighting against. They risked their own lives for profit, by trading in bullets that could end up hitting them in battle.

"For too many people war has become a way of earning a living," said

202 -◦- WOJCIECH JAGIELSKI

the archbishop of Gulu, the Reverend John Baptist Odama. "So it's not surprising no one's trying to put an end to it. If it ended, they'd lose everything."

The story in Gulu was that no one had made as much money out of the war as a certain colonel in the intelligence services. The Acholi Inn, the town's biggest and best hotel, was just one of the things he owned. The colonel had apparently bought it for a song at the very start of the war. He had become such an important figure in the town that whenever they mentioned his name, my interlocutors lowered their voices and cast nervous glances over their shoulders. They whispered that the colonel made sure his soldiers never captured or killed any of the Lord's Army officers, and also that they never let any government ministers from Kampala persuade them to hold peace talks. Apparently, he had broken at least three cease-fires.

But there were also rumors circulating in Gulu that the families of the rebel leaders were getting rich on the war too. The guerrilla officers' relatives ran stores where they sold war booty, goods plundered during raids and ambushes. Jackson once told me that one of the stores in Gulu belonged to a son of Joseph Kony. He also said that the rebel leaders, who kidnapped children from the villages to make them into killers, sent their own sons and daughters to be educated at the local schools.

I had an Acholi proverb written down in my notebook. "Where two elephants fight, the greatest victim is the grass." I think I heard it from Nora. First thing the next morning I was going to see her. And Samuel. This was going to be the start of dealing with unfinished business.

As I left the hotel bar, the music was still playing; the partygoers had moved onto the grass, under the trees. I could hear the merry voices of the soldiers' wives coming out of the darkness.

-◦-

She was sitting at her desk, in her office where the door was always open, wearing a light dress. When I stopped in the sunlit gateway, she looked up, as if hearing someone calling. From afar I saw her smile broadly and joyfully. She got up from her desk and, raising her arms twined together, she straightened her body, stretching like a cat, trustfully, without restraint. For a while she stared at the floor helplessly, trying to find her shoes, then gave up, came out of the office barefoot and walked across the gravel courtyard toward me. She held out a hand to greet me, briefly hesitated, and then gave me a big hug, throwing her arms around my neck.

"It really is you," she said, taking hold of my hand and leading me like a child. "So you did come back."

"I said I'd be back, didn't I?"

"I thought that was just talk. Other people who've come here have said that too. But you really have come back! Well, well, who'd have thought it?" She asked if I'd like a coffee. "Well I never!" she exclaimed, putting on the kettle. "First I'll run and fetch Samuel. He has classes now, but I'll call him out in a moment."

Still barefoot, she ran out into the yard and disappeared from view.

The room was strewn with documents, cardboard folders, and Nora's clothes. In the tiny kitchen, I noticed a toothbrush next to the sink, a thick comb, and some cosmetics. So she had been here when I got back to Gulu last night. If I had called, maybe she could have persuaded the security guard to let me in. One of her slippers was poking out from under the sofa bed. I heard her voice.

"See for yourself. I told you he'd come. Pity I didn't make a bet with you."

Samuel seemed a little ashamed, but was clearly pleased.

"He didn't believe me when I said you were here," said Nora. "Well? Is that him? For real? Touch him, because you still don't believe me."

I gave the boy my hand, then awkwardly patted him on the shoulder. He didn't say anything.

Nora put the kettle on and bustled about the room, picking up the pieces of clothing that were scattered about the furniture.

"Christine and I are the only ones here," she said. "I can't dig my way out from under the paperwork, and she can't get out of the classroom. I don't know which is better. We hardly ever see each other, although I'm spending the nights here."

204   ⊷   WOJCIECH JAGIELSKI

She turned to Samuel, as if she had suddenly remembered about him. "Hurry off to your classes now," she reminded him. "Afterward, this afternoon you can have a chat. I'm going to have him to myself now."

The boy lingered, as if trying to find an excuse to stay, but he couldn't think of anything off the cuff and gave up. He waved and turned to leave.

"Sam! Please shut the door after you," called Nora. "So no one will disturb us."

⊷

I stayed for the rest of the day. I had no other plans, nothing to do. Apart from dealing with unfinished business. Making ends meet.

"Will you have some lunch?" asked Nora. "Have you tried our food?"

The girls in orange skirts were cooking a meal on a bonfire in the yard. In some big pots black with smoke and soot, they were preparing *matoke*, a dish of green bananas cooked to a pulp and mashed, then baked and pepped up with beans, sauce, and sometimes bits of meat or fish.

We ate lunch in Nora's office, on her desk, once she had moved the documents spread all over it onto the floor. We ate in silence, watching the girls bustling about by the bonfire through the open door. Nora ate with her fingers, dripping with thick brown sauce. Pensive and absent, she was scooping *matoke* from her plate, kneading it into balls, dipping it in sauce, and putting it in her mouth.

"How do you like it?" she asked in amusement, glancing at my bent aluminum plate.

"I've had *matoke* before," I said. "How do you make it?"

"Me?" She was choking with laughter, pointing at herself. "Me? Oh no, I've got no idea about cooking. And I've no intention of learning."

"That's interesting. So how will you find a husband?"

"How do you know I'm looking for one?" she replied quickly, brusque as ever, as soon as she saw the opportunity for a bit of verbal fencing with some oblique remarks and ambiguities.

Silence fell. The girls in the yard finished serving lunch and started tidying up, sweeping, scrubbing the black cauldrons with yellow sand,

and putting the dishes away in rough jute sacks. When they had finished their kitchen work and raked the bonfire, they gathered in the shade of a roof propped on wooden poles where a class was being held. They sat down at some shabby desks and started working some old, pedal-powered sewing machines, on which they made bedclothes out of white linen, to be put out for sale in one of the local stores.

◄○►

Apart from sewing, the girls at the center also learned to cook and bake bread, and how to run a store or market stall. These skills were going to help them return to the world they had been stolen from years ago.

They were still children when they were abducted from their family villages and homes. They hadn't been old enough to know what a man's love, or love for a man, or desire meant. Handed over to guerrilla offi-cers as wives, they had borne them children while still being children themselves. They had become mothers before they had stopped need-ing their own mothers' care.

They were still very young now—the oldest ones were sixteen. Yet almost all of them already had children of their own. Obedient to the strict orders of Joseph Kony, his men summoned the wives to their huts on nights when they could father children by them. Only the youngest, too small to fall pregnant, came back from the bush as little girls, not teenage women.

As the wives of guerrilla officers and the mothers of their children, at least they didn't have to take part in combat or go on endless marches, or attack villages and kill people. But now, returning to their old life was much harder for them than for the former guerrillas. The children they had given birth to in the bush were a heavier millstone and a more painful stigma than any of the crimes they might have had on their consciences.

Pointed at and derided as "Kony's lovers," they had little chance of finding new husbands and starting their own families, or even of rejoining their old ones—to compound their grief, their parents often rejected them.

"Those sewing machines are the only hope for them," said Nora, lick-ing sauce off her fingers. "We give them the machines so they can set up a tailor's shop, and we help them to open market stalls or bakeries. They only have to earn their first shillings and our men instantly forget about their past, and there's nothing in their way anymore. The men aren't even bothered that the girls have someone else's children. They fall for them and want them to be their wives."

One of the girls in the yard started singing. In a while, several more had picked up the song too. However, the singing soon stopped. Embar-rassed, or maybe because they didn't know the words or the tune, one after another the girls fell silent. Finally, we could only hear the one who had started up the singing. Soon she went quiet too.

"Our men are useless," said Nora. "They're good for nothing."

I had heard these words before—the same ones, uttered in exactly the same tone, with a note of shame, regret, despair, and impotence, but there was also a hint of imploring prayer in them.

I had heard them a year earlier at a settlement called Uad el-Bashir outside Khartoum, where I had gone to see some refugees who had fled the war in southern Sudan. I was particularly interested in the Dinka, as I'd heard lots of stories about these African giants, the tallest people on the entire continent.

Uad el-Bashir didn't look like a refugee camp, but more like the typical slums to be found in the suburbs of most African and Asian capitals. There were dwellings made of rust-colored clay, streets covered in dust, more like country lanes than urban highways, goats and stray dogs lying about, and fetid, steaming mounds of garbage set on fire for fun by bored kids.

Apart from the people in the mud huts, and some government snoop-ers, there was nothing in Uad el-Bashir. There were no stores or schools, no hospital or medical center, no police or fire service. There wasn't even a bus stop. Few visitors ever came here, and the local men rarely headed for the big city.

Only Dinka were living at Uad el-Bashir, representatives of the big-gest black African tribe in southern Sudan. They were farmers and herders, driven to Khartoum by the war that had been raging in their territory for ages.

They had arrived here twenty years ago. The old men, who spent all day in conversation or in silence in a large tent pitched by the main road, could still remember their old life and former existence. But their sons remembered very little of it, or nothing at all. They had spent most of their lives in exile at Uad el-Bashir.

The old men only knew how to till the fields, so there was nothing for them to do in the suburbs of Khartoum. And they had been doing nothing—quite literally nothing, for twenty years now. Their sons didn't do anything either, because they didn't know how to do anything. They had never had the chance to become farmers, and their parents hadn't enough money for them to become anything else. They tramped to the city in search of casual work for a few pennies, but they had no qualifications and weren't fit for any profession.

There are probably no places as desperate as refugee camps. I've seen dozens of them, although I've generally tried to avoid them, in Congo, Kenya, Uganda, Pakistan, Iran, and the Caucasus. Refugees are people who may not have lost their lives to war, but their existence has been robbed of its meaning. War has taken away all their faith, hope, dreams, and energy.

As they brood on their misfortune, the refugees rapidly lose all sense of reality; immersed in pain, they come to the conclusion that the injury they have suffered is a sufficient reason to expect others to provide compensation and care. From victims they metamorphose into passive parasites, full of grudges, regret, and anger at everyone, including—perhaps most of all—the rare few who help them and are concerned about their fate.

They haven't the courage to admit that every element of their former life has gone forever. They haven't the strength to shake off their misfortune and stand on their own feet. Increasingly dependent on help which enables nothing but continued existence, they have the mentality of slaves deprived of all expectations, aspirations, or ingenuity.

When I met with them, the older Dinka men, who were large and gnarled, lounged on some broken chairs set out in a circle. The younger ones, who had nothing to sit on, stood behind them. I didn't see a single woman at Uad el-Bashir. At dawn, as every day, they had set off on foot along the country-lane-urban-highway to Khartoum, some to cook, clean, or mind children at the houses of rich Sudanese, others to make sweet tea at the city's markets and sell it to shoppers and traders. They were the only ones who earned more than just the handouts their husbands received from charitable foreigners.

For convenience, lots of the women stayed the night in the city, with relatives or quite often at their employer's house. This filled the men of Uad el-Bashir with alarm, because of rumors that at night many of these women sold themselves for money. The Dinka were worried by this gossip, but they didn't really know how to verify it. Or whether to verify it at all.

"Our men are useless," said Nora. "All they can do is get drunk and brawl."

One day, at one of the refugee camps outside Gulu I witnessed a funeral. A woman had died, the mother of three children. Her husband, high on *warangi*, the strong spirit distilled in the local homes, was sitting on the threshold of his hut, weeping.

"What am I to do now?" he sobbed. "How will I manage with three children?"

Everyone there felt sorry for him. When I told Nora about it, she just laughed. No one ever asks a single mother how she's going to support and raise her children.

I had heard stories in Gulu about wives who sprinkled poison in their husbands' meals to get rid of these scroungers—then they could apply for benefits paid to widows by the foreigners. I had also heard of husbands who abandoned their wives and numerous offspring for their own convenience. According to orders from the authorities in Kampala, free sacks of maize flour or sugar were distributed among the individual huts at the refugee camps. Widows or women living on their own were entitled to the same share of these goods as the large families living in the huts next door. Deprived of occupation and income, the men were happy to abandon their wives and children to go and enjoy comfort, plenty, and a carefree life, at least for a while, living with a widow, even an elderly one.

Those who decided to stay with their wives robbed them of the money they had earned by the sweat of their brows, beat them and forced themselves on them; it was as if only through violence, by inflicting pain and harm, could they restrain something beyond their control which was causing their former world and old way of life to slip away before their very eyes.

"Our men feel threatened, and the more frightened they are, the weaker they become," said Nora. In her view, the country's endless wars were partly to blame, but at least some of the fault also lay with the government, which had decided to give women the same rights as men, and had started employing them in jobs where once you could only have found their fathers, husbands, and brothers.

This was how Specioza Wandira Kazibwe became Uganda's first female vice president. A doctor from Iganga, she was one of the first women in all Africa to be promoted to such high office. But even though she held an important, eminent post, in private she was beaten by her husband, who was unhappy that she came home so late, wasn't caring for the children herself, and was associating with men he didn't know. For eight years on end the vice president had put up with her husband's scenes before daring to petition for divorce.

The authorities had also revoked a law under which only women were thrown in jail for adultery. A wife betraying her husband with a married man had been subject to a punishment of up to six months in prison, but for adultery with a bachelor it was up to a year in prison and a fine. An unmarried male adulterer had also been punished with a fine. But the old law did not regard an affair between a married man and an unmarried woman as a crime. A regulation had also been introduced that made widows the direct heirs of their deceased husbands. According to the old laws, a husband's estate had passed straight to his relatives in the male line.

"On top of that, the war here has changed our men," said Nora. "They have not only failed to defend us against it, but they haven't managed to protect the children who have been made into guerrillas. Small children have been exposed to all the weakness and evil that was lying in every one of us who lives here."

Nora said she understood the causes of the anger that filled the local men, and that she even sympathized with them. But she immediately added that it simply confirmed her conviction that if she didn't get away from here and was obliged to spend the rest of her life in Gulu, she shouldn't tie herself to any man.

"Our men are useless," she repeated once again, sighing softly.

◄∘►

That evening at the hotel I ran into the men who had terrified Samuel when I took him for a walk and invited him there for lunch and ice cream. Just as on that day, they were sitting at a small table under a mango tree by the fence.

As I passed their table they turned in my direction and greeted me like someone they knew. Surprised, I responded with a bow. The oldest of them, with the snow-white hair and light clothes, smiled and nodded politely.

While we were in Kampala, Jackson had told me about the guerrillas who lived at the hotel. Since returning to Gulu I hadn't seen him once. True, I had been spending my time with Nora and Samuel, but before the trip to Kampala I had run into Jackson at every step—in the street, at Franklin's bar, and outside the radio station building right next to the hotel. But now, although I kept asking for him, no one had seen him anywhere—he had vanished into thin air. Worried, I decided to visit him at his home, but no one at the radio station could tell me where he lived.

As I gazed at the men under the tree, I was sorry he wasn't with me. He would definitely have known who they were, and how best to approach and persuade them to open up. Noticing me watching them, the white-haired man turned round and smiled encouragingly. I took it as an invitation.

He was called Kenneth Banya and for many years he had been Joseph Kony's deputy in the Lord's Army. He had the rank of a guerrilla brigadier. When he was taken captive by the government troops—though many claimed he had given himself up—Vincent Otti had taken his place.

The man sitting next to him was Sam Kolo, one of Kony's confidants and closest advisers, who had at one time served as his envoy during rare and always unsuccessful negotiations with the government. The long-haired peg-leg introduced himself as Major Jackson Acama. He said he was one of the top commanders in the Lord's Army. His leg had been blown off by a shell fired from a helicopter that had tracked his unit in the savannah.

The last of the men who shook my hand was called Alfred Onen Kamdulu. He said he had been one of Kony's most loyal commanding officers until he had grown disenchanted with him and started to lose faith in what he said. He had decided to surrender when he realized that the Lord's Army would not bring his Acholi compatriots liberation or expiate them of sin, but was condemning them to even greater suffering and eternal wandering. By then he had realized Kony was a false prophet, not the messiah he claimed to be.

Having changed his mind, Kamdulu had secretly sent messengers to the troops stationed nearby. As proof of his sincerity and serious intentions, he had surrendered his three guerrilla wives to the soldiers.

As well as Banya, Kolo, Acama, and many other Lord's Army officers and guerrillas had taken advantage of an amnesty announced by President Museveni. Under the terms of the amnesty, anyone who surrendered and renounced further fighting was freed of all responsibility and cleared of blame.

These men were the Lord's Army's adult officers, under whose command the children were made to fight. So they were also their guardians, teachers, educators, and masters. They had wrinkled faces, gnarled hands, and tired, bloodshot eyes.

"So where's your friend got to?" asked Banya.

"Jackson?" I asked automatically.

"I mean the little boy you once brought here."

Intrigued by the conversation, his companions stared at me inquiringly. I remembered what Samuel had said about them—that they talk to spirits and nothing is hidden from them.

"Oh, him," I said. "He's my friend's son. I brought him here for ice cream one Sunday."

"That's very kind of you," replied Banya, still smiling. "It's good to have friends like that."

"It was nothing."

"Really?"

It was getting late, and apart from us there was no one else in the restaurant garden now. The waiters were clearing the tables and folding up the white tablecloths. There were just a few other people sitting in front of the flickering color TV in the bar.

"I'm a journalist," I said. "I'd like to talk to you about the war and about Joseph Kony."

Banya nodded, as if to say he understood and assented.

"First you have to ask permission from the military."

"Whom should I ask?"

"That officer, for instance," he said, pointing at the men on high stools at the bar. "The one in the red shirt."

When I approached him, the soldier gave me a searching look and asked me to show him my press card. He examined the photograph, the stamps, and the rows of words whose meaning he couldn't understand. He took a cell phone out of his pocket and called a number.

"Which one do you want to talk to?"

"Maybe Kenneth Banya?"

He nodded.

"Banya," he snapped into the receiver.

I was to wait for the white-haired Banya the next day at noon in the hotel restaurant, he said.

"What about today? Couldn't I talk to him now? Seeing he's already here."

"Today? It's too late today," he said, shaking his head. "He's coming back to the barracks with us. He lives there, didn't you know?"

"I was told they live here, at the hotel."

"Some of them do, but not him. He lives at the barracks."

"Couldn't he go back later?"

"On his own? That's a good one! Have him walk through town on his own at night? Haven't you seen what happens here at night?"

"You mean the children? One of your superiors has already warned me about the children here."

"The children . . ." he said, as if to himself, and then remembering me, added: "No, you needn't be afraid of them. But lots of people in this town truly detest Kenneth Banya and would love to see him die in agony."

"So maybe today I could talk to one of the guys who live here, at the hotel?"

"But you asked for a meeting with Banya. That's already arranged."

"What if he doesn't come? How will I find him? Where should I look for you?"

"He'll come, he'll come. He'll find you himself."

At that I gave up. When I got back to the garden, the table under the mango tree was empty.

Back in my room, I fetched my notes out of my pack. I knew the names Kenneth Banya and Sam Kolo from newspaper articles and agency reports. I hadn't heard of Acama or Kamdulu before. Looking through the clippings and the notes I'd made, I came across a report saying that all Joseph Kony's brothers who hadn't joined the rebellion but had stayed in their native village of Odek had been murdered; their killers had never been caught.

I also found an article from a Ugandan paper about the former guerrilla officers who lived in Gulu. To keep an eye on them, the army, which never fully trusted them, gave them accommodation in the barracks and at the Acholi Inn Hotel. The journalist wrote that the former guerrillas rarely went out, and were always escorted by soldiers. But when one of the converts had gone to town on his own at night, he had been so badly beaten up that they had only just managed to save his life.

The name of commanding officer Kamdulu appeared in the clippings too. According to the Ugandan press, he was the commander whose unit had attacked a funeral procession in the Agoro Mountains, on the border with Sudan, and had forced the mourners to cook and eat the corpse they were taking to the cemetery. When he surrendered to the army and was then taken into it as an officer, the guerrillas had attacked Alokulum camp not far from Gulu, where his mother lived. Their plan was to kill her, in revenge for her son's treachery.

I decided that after the conversation with Banya I would ask for permission to meet with Kamdulu as well. But when I inquired at the local garrison, I was told he had left town.

◂◦▸

The next day at noon Kenneth Banya was waiting for me under the mango tree, drinking lemonade.

Before becoming a guerrilla commander he had served in the Ugandan army, where he reached the rank of major. Idi Amin, who was in charge in those days, had even sent him to the Soviet Union to be trained as a helicopter pilot. He had left the army when Museveni came to power by deposing Generals Tito and Basilio Okello, who were from the Acholi tribe.

Many Acholi officers and officials had resigned from the Ugandan army and administration at that point. Some did it because they were outraged by Museveni's perfidy—he took Kampala from the Okellos by force, although he had previously promised to negotiate with them. Others were afraid the victorious guerrillas would now take revenge for the cruelties Acholi soldiers from the government army had inflicted on their compatriots during the war.

The richest and most influential left the country and moved to Kenya or Sudan, then further afield, to Great Britain, Germany, Canada, and the United States, from where they plotted against Museveni, devising plans to return and be revenged. They also sent money for weapons to all the guerrilla factions that were rebelling against Museveni's government in Acholi-land.

After quitting the military in Kampala, Banya had gone back to his hometown of Pader in the north. That was where Joseph Kony's envoys had found him.

"One day they came to my house and said their commander was summoning me to come and see him, and if I refused they had orders to kill me and my entire family. What would you have done in my place?" he began, when I asked him to tell me his story. "I went with them. Anyway, I didn't know what they wanted from me."

He had spent seven years in the guerrillas. The longest years of his life, he assured me. He was approaching sixty. With his white hair, his polite smile, and his smart pale suit he looked more like a respectable retired city dignitary than a savage rebel from the bush. "I am an old man whom life has put through the mill," he kept saying, sucking warm lemonade through a straw. Then he asked the waiter to bring him some tea with milk.

When Kony sent his soldiers to fetch Banya, he was only just starting his rebellion, and his troops weren't called the Lord's Army yet. He needed people like Banya, trained officers, experienced, seasoned fighters. Banya was the highest-ranking military officer to join Kony's guerrillas. Kony told him to train the army and teach them everything they needed for war. Then he also sent him off to Khartoum for talks with the Sudanese generals.

However, Banya refused to acknowledge the crimes that were being blamed on the Lord's Army guerrillas.

"It's true I was Kony's adviser and I trained his army. But I didn't do it of my own free will. I was abducted, just like the children who were kidnapped. They came out of the bush to get me too. I remember it well—dusk was falling, and I was having my dinner. They said Joseph Kony had summoned me. I asked if I could wait until morning to make the journey. They refused and said I must present myself to Kony that same night. Would you like a drop more milk with your tea?" he said, offering a small china jug. "He told me to teach the kids how to handle guns. Anyway, he soon realized that what I was teaching might be good for a regular army, but not for guerrillas. He also told me to go to Khartoum and secure weapons supplies for his people."

The military force Kony created wasn't really like any army before it, either a regular one or a guerrilla force. It never captured, stormed, or besieged anything, nor did it even try to take control of any villages or districts. Nor did it court the civilian population, as other guerrilla movements did, or try to win them over to its cause. It didn't fight battles or take on recruits. Eventually it wouldn't even accept volunteers who wanted to join it.

The Lord's Army soldiers were almost exclusively children, and the terror they inspired through their cruelty and cold, inhuman ruthlessness was their one and only, yet fail-safe weapon. They also prompted fear because they were regarded as sinister forces, creatures possessed, transformed, and different from anything at all familiar.

The violence they seemed to relish only looked like madness on the surface. It was enough for a small guerrilla unit to attack one of the villages, murder its citizens, set their huts on fire, and abduct their children, and at once news of the raid sent terror throughout Acholi-land. It was enough for them to hide in the long grass by the roadside and shoot at a military patrol, and immediately the army raised the alarm and declared an emergency. It was enough for them to kneecap or cut off the foot of a villager they had caught breaking their ban on cycling along the road (the guerrillas wouldn't let the peasants do that, because it gave them a quick way of informing the army that rebels had been seen in the area), and for weeks on end no one dared to disobey them. The roads, both surfaced and unsurfaced, went dead. The guerrillas didn't even have to post patrols on them.

Nor did they have to attack to keep the powerful adult army in check, though it was several times larger than their own. The same went for the hundreds of thousands of terrified villagers, who were convinced the guerrillas, impossible to defeat or to capture, were everywhere, and could appear and strike in any place at any moment. Instead of fighting pitched battles, the Lord's Army paralyzed its enemies with terror. It took away their courage and will to resist, and enslaved them like a snake hypnotizing its victim with its gaze. "We kill people to make them afraid of us"—somewhere I read this statement by one of the Lord's Army commanding officers.

"Why does Kony treat the Acholi like his worst enemies? Why does he hate them so much?"

"It wasn't always like that," replied Banya. "Joseph Kony thinks the Acholi have betrayed him."

When he became leader of the uprising, his compatriots, the Acholi, were already so agonized by the wars devastating their land that they were ready to agree to peace even if it was unfair to them. They had not only rejected the rebellion, but had actively opposed it. Formerly, the tribal chiefs had always incited the young men to revolt against what they saw as wrongs inflicted on the Acholi by the government, but now they refused to support the guerrillas. Instead they reported them to the army, and even formed an armed militia within the villages to deal with the rebels when they came to ask for food and recruits. Worse yet, remembering the defeats suffered by Alice of the Holy Spirit and her father Severino, the Acholi didn't believe in Kony's power or in the idea that he had been chosen as their leader by God Himself. They saw him as yet another false prophet, a usurper, or maybe a madman.

At this point Kony had flown into a rage. He had ordered the guerrillas to attack Acholi villages and take away their children. He threatened to massacre the Acholi and cobble the roads with their skulls. By refusing to obey him, they were disobeying the Holy Spirit, who spoke through him. Thus they were committing a sin and deserved to be annihilated.

"If you seize your bow and arrows and turn against us, and we hack off your hand, who is to blame? If you inform on us to the army, and we cut off your lips, ears, and noses, who is to blame?" he ranted. "You are! You are! And you alone!"

He often quoted the Bible.

"If your hand causes you to sin," he would say, "cut it off." "We do not kill," he would say. "We cleanse people so that only the good ones remain. 'I will direct my jealous anger against you, and they will deal with you in fury. They will cut off your noses and your ears, and those of you who are left will fall by the sword. They will take away your sons and daughters, and those of you who are left will be consumed by fire.'"

He also used to compare himself to Moses, who brought people God's commandments and would lead them to the promised land. "Moses had to kill too," Kony would say, and add that he too was not destined to enjoy happiness in the promised land, but that instead of him a twelve-year-old boy would reach it and lead others there.

He said it was Lakwena who ordered him to kill all the Acholi and fill the world with his own children and foster children—they would have the chance to rule Uganda and the world. But before then he had to get rid of all the fallen sinners, and those who dared to make their own distinctions between good and evil.

"Everyone who is too old to distinguish good from evil should be killed, even the old men," Kony called after the guerrillas he sent out on military expeditions. "I will create a new nation."

It was meant to arise from the village children he told the guerrillas to kidnap, and also—perhaps mainly—from those born at the Lord's Army camps. They alone would be saved on Judgment Day. So he wasn't taking children away from their parents, as he was accused of doing, but was saving them from doom and damnation. To fill the world as quickly as possible with the new chosen nation—his own children—he had made several dozen girls his wives and fathered over a hundred children with them. Fearing the mysterious killer virus transmitted during sexual intercourse, he only chose virgins to be his wives.

"Joseph Kony has a great weakness for children. He spends all his time with them and likes to give them presents. He even takes the other commanders' children and keeps them at his own camp. I've been told he is good to his wives too." Banya seemed to be getting more and more tired of our conversation about Kony and his guerrillas. "People think of him as a wild beast, but he is an ordinary man. I know him well. More than once he invited me to dine with him. He's a very devout man, kind and good. He likes to joke and he knows a lot of jokes. Just sometimes he can be unpredictable. And then he gives orders for even his closest advisers to be shot, if he starts to suspect them of anything."

Once the waiter had removed the empty lemonade bottles and the tea set, Banya said that in his view Kony had been unfairly blamed for all the evil done by his soldiers.

"He himself has never killed anyone. He simply gives the orders," he said. "His words are often bizarre and convoluted. The commanding officers don't make the effort to understand them, but just kill and inflict suffering on people, wrongly believing that's what he expects them to do. They think they'll get into his good books by doing so."

It was obvious he wanted to stop talking now. Once again he emphasized that he had served Joseph Kony to be able to serve the Acholi people too. He had fallen out with Kony when he started turning his rage on the villagers, attacking their homes and kidnapping their children.

"I never believed all those fairy tales about magic power or holy water protecting you against bullets," he smiled pitifully.

Kenneth Banya's guerrilla odyssey had finally ended when Kony had sent him into Uganda. Government helicopters had tracked down his unit near the village of Okidi on the river Unyama, near Gulu. As soon as the first shots were fired, the old major had ordered his soldiers to drop their guns and raise their hands in the air.

I asked if he had done anything that he now regretted.

"I never did anything wrong," he said, shaking his head. "Everything they say about me is lies. I never took girls for wives. There were just a lot of women and children serving in the unit I commanded."

Since the government had pardoned him, he had been living at the army barracks in Gulu. He sometimes spoke on the local radio station, Mega FM, urging guerrillas still out in the bush to abandon Joseph Kony and stop fighting. He had also undergone a ceremony which, so he claimed, the Acholi have practiced for years to reconcile victims and their oppressors and compensate for wrongdoing.

"This ritual is called *mato oput*. If you ever get the opportunity you should definitely see it," he said, gently squeezing my hand in farewell. "I asked for forgiveness, and I was forgiven. I can show you the official document certifying it. Now I live among my own people, free and without fear. The Acholi are different from other people. They don't believe in revenge, but in life."

The next day when I told Nora about my conversation with Banya, she virtually steamed with indignation.

"Sure I believe him!" she cried. "And who, if not he, came and pestered us at the center to give him a girl with a child whom he claimed was his wife from the guerrillas? We sent her to school in Kampala. She was about fourteen, she was still a child. Like every important commander, he had the right to possess wives chosen from among the abducted girls. And they say Banya willingly took advantage of the privilege."

That day for the first time since I had known her, Nora was wearing pants—pale blue, figure-hugging jeans. Before now I had only ever seen her in dresses. I even suspected her of wearing them not by preference, but as a way of emphasizing that she wasn't the same as the girls from Gulu, who were only too keen to squeeze into pants that showed off their curves. Nora's dresses were her trademark, a statement. They cried out: I'm not like you people, I don't belong to this town and I'm not going to stay here.

As if to spite her, she looked great in pants. The flares concealed her slightly too solid calves, while the tight material showed off her round buttocks and narrow, petite hips. She spotted that I had noticed the change in her appearance, and she was clearly pleased about it. There was a hint of flirtation in her look, her voice, and her husky laughter.

Samuel, who appeared every time I came, hardly said a word. He sat on the steps outside Nora's office, listening in on our conversations, or played nearby, casting us glances through the open door. He liked it when we talked; silence seemed to take away his sense of security. But with time, silence stopped bothering him too, and when it fell, we didn't feel awkwardness either, or an embarrassing need to keep up the conversation at any cost.

"Sometimes I feel terribly lonely here," sighed Nora, blinking in the sunlight that flooded the steps. "As if I were the only person here. Do you know that feeling? When even though you're talking the same language, no one, absolutely no one, can understand you."

She once said she didn't resent journalists, because she knew they asked questions not out of a macabre obsession with a nightmare, but for a professional need to find things out. But she admitted that personally she had long since lost the desire to know things. At first she had listened to Samuel and the others telling their stories, to at least try to understand what they had experienced. But their stories wouldn't let her sleep at night—they haunted her dreams and took away her peace and grip on reality.

In time she got used to it, but now she kept saying the last thing she needed was a conversation about a nightmare, and that she only talked to the children in order to heal them. When they spoke aloud about their horrific ordeal, describing it in ordinary words, they stripped it of power and got it out of their systems, which meant they were free of it. So it was really the children who needed the conversations.

"But if it's going to work, you absolutely must not, under any circumstances, lie to them," she would say. "That confuses them."

Sometimes, however, she seemed to lose her faith in everything she had earlier claimed to believe in.

"We encourage them to tell us about their experiences in order to

heal them," she said, drawing her knees up to her chin. "So we tell them
to go back in memory to all the things they'd most like to forget."

"Maybe there's no other way. Maybe they have to go through that to
be able to start again?"

"How should I know? Sometimes I think not everything can be fixed
or put together again. Everything has its time. Nothing will be the way
it was before. I don't know what to think anymore. Did I tell you that
lots of the girls who have been through our center and then gone home
to their villages have run away back to the bush, to the guerrillas? If
they're better off there, how terrible must our world seem to them?"

I noticed that almost all the children hanging about in the yard were
girls. Apart from Samuel, who was playing at the bottom of the steps,
I could only see three other boys kicking an old rag ball against a wall.

"Where have the rest of the boys gone?"

"They've left, gone back to their families and villages. Their treatment here had come to its end. There was nothing more we could do
for them. But whenever I see them leave, I feel as if there's something
I haven't finished."

"Dropped loose ends?" I muttered.

She looked at me in astonishment.

"Do you know what I'm talking about?"

I shrugged, not knowing how to answer.

"What about Samuel? What will happen to him?"

"Well yes, we're going to have a problem with our Samuel."

◄◦►

Outside the building housing the boys' dormitory there was a green
pickup truck in which Mike, the driver for the center, brought vegetables, sacks of maize flour and sugar, and yellow cans of oil from the
market in town. Now the truck was filling up with brand-new shiny
pots and pans, bowls, old blankets in neat rolls, quilted mattresses,
stuffed white sacks, and sheets of blue plastic folded into squares, the
kind which people living in refugee camps use to cover their roofs and
shield them from rain.

I noticed four boys buzzing around the vehicle, including Samuel. I waved to him, and he responded with a broad, happy smile. He and his friends were carrying parcel after parcel out of the building and loading them into Mike's truck. Two of the boys, taller and clearly older, were wearing white shirts and light, well-ironed pants. Maybe it was the clean, fresh clothes that were making them move rather stiffly and awkwardly.

One of them, Christopher, was seventeen, and had spent eight years in the guerrillas. He came from the village of Gere Gere and had been kidnapped from it during a night raid by the rebels. Christopher was asleep when shots rang out in the village; the guerrillas had started setting fire to the straw thatched huts and herding people into the main square. He didn't even know who had dragged him out of the hut—his father or the guerrillas. But he had a perfect memory of the fear and pain, and also that men in military clothes and rubber boots had driven him and the other children into the bush beyond the village.

In the guerrillas he was constantly beaten. His hands, arms, back, torso, and face were marked with scars from the blows he had received for being slow, for lack of discipline, insufficient enthusiasm and faith, and for trying to escape. However, he was strong and resilient—he had endured the difficulties, managed to keep marching for days on end, and carry heavy loads. Nora said that as he had survived, he must have killed too. But in her view he wasn't fit to be a guerrilla and had only killed when he had to, because his own life depended on it.

Christopher had run away from the guerrillas while his half-starved unit was wandering the deserted villages around Kitgum in search of food. He had escaped with a rifle and surrendered to the first military patrol he ran into.

At roughly the same time the soldiers had found sixteen-year-old Geoffrey hiding in the bushes near Gulu. Like Christopher, he had spent eight years in the guerrillas. With him was fourteen-year-old Richard, abducted barely two months earlier. Both of them came from Amuru.

Once they left the center, Samuel and Richard, who was a year older than him, would be the only boys still there. They hadn't taken any new boys for a long time. The soldiers brought no one but girls, the wives of commanders and mothers of their children, whom the guerrillas had sent home to save them. In town this was seen as confirmation of rumors that the Lord's Army was getting out of Acholi-land for good and moving far beyond the Nile, into Congo, or maybe even Chad. People were tentatively starting to suggest that the war was fizzling out.

The building housing the boys' dormitory was empty. I had never looked in here before. There was a long, dark room with a high ceiling, furnished with rows of now empty bunks. It didn't look cozy or friendly. Despite the fact that the door and windows were wide open, it was stuffy in there. From the next building, where the girls slept, came the loud wail of a baby.

Samuel's bed was at the far end of the room. It was separated from the other occupied bunk, belonging to Richard, by several rows of bed frames made of metal bars and springs. Any day now Richard was going to be sent home. His parents and siblings were waiting for him in Amuru. No one was waiting for Samuel; he had no one. He had no one and nothing to go home to.

—◦—

Christine was in charge of sending the boys home. She was the same age as Nora, and maybe that was why I thought they ought to be friends, or at least to get on well. In fact they had a strong mutual dislike and tried not to get in each other's way.

Christine came from Kitgum and was locally regarded as a beauty. Tall, strong, and straight as a reed, she not only stood out among the Gulu women for her shapely figure and aristocratic, slightly proud allure, but also her milky brown skin, a rarity here. She was aware that men found her attractive, but she dressed simply and modestly. She was also sparing and unemotional in her words and gestures.

Nora annoyed her, not only with her unrestrained way of expressing her feelings, but with her attitude to life in general. Christine thought you shouldn't expect too much from life, that you should be glad of everything that came your way and never stop being grateful for this mercy.

I often ran into her at church, during the service, but also in the presbytery, where after mass I usually dropped in for a chat with the priests over a cup of tea; Christine helped them keep the parish books. Sometimes she also brought her sons to the presbytery, three quiet, polite boys, shy in their white Sunday shirts.

Christine had a husband too. He had married her in church, and they had moved from Kitgum to Gulu, where he owned a house. Later, he had sold it and left for Kampala to open a store, while Christine and their sons had moved into his mother's house.

Nora flew off the handle whenever the conversation turned to Christine. She said she couldn't understand how you could willingly let yourself be enslaved, and renounce your last vestiges of freedom and dignity. The rumor in town was that Christine's husband lived with another woman in Kampala and had children with her too. Christine gave no credence to the gossip. After all, every two or three months her husband came to Gulu, bringing presents. It was true he had sometimes asked Christine for money, but usually he brought some himself and gave it to his mother for housekeeping.

"When he comes home, he spends the whole time with the boys. They simply adore each other," she told me one day. "The people who spread all those lies about him should see that—they'd immediately stop wasting their breath."

In her turn, Christine couldn't understand why Nora, her contemporary, hadn't got herself a husband yet, had no family, and lived alone in Gulu like an orphan. Or like a leper. To her, anyone condemned by a twist of fate to be alone was the most unfortunate wretch imaginable, deserving nothing but pity. She regarded being on your own by choice as contrary to the natural order—a form of heresy, or blasphemy.

That was also how she understood the purpose and meaning of her work—it was to restore the natural order, rebuild and preserve the community, recover the children stolen from it.

"We convince them they are not to blame for the crimes they committed in the guerrillas," she once told me when I dropped in on the classes she ran at the center. "It's not they who are to blame, but we ourselves. It's the parents who bear the guilt for having brought their children up badly. It's not the guerrillas who are to blame for inciting the war, but the government for letting it come to this. So in fact it is not they who require treatment, but we adults."

She also said that blaming the war for everything wasn't a proper explanation; the war was an effect, not a cause, of the evil latent inside people, and this evil, let loose by a lack of faith and disobedience toward sanctity, had broken the circles of life. That's how she put it—the rule of the twice-broken circles of life. In her view, human existence occurred within a structure of circles, at the center of which, as an extension of the species and of life, were the children. The first, closest of the circles surrounding them was the immediate family. That circle was situated inside a larger, extended family circle, which in turn was inside an even bigger, neighborhood circle, and that one was inside a tribe circle. Further circles represented the community, the state, the world, and the laws regulating international order.

The structure of circles, which guaranteed security and order, had been smashed to bits in Acholi-land like an old, cracked gourd. Parents, relatives, neighbors, the tribe, the police, the army, officials, international regulations—everything and everyone had been a letdown, and no one had been capable of protecting the children from misfortune. Worse yet, after having come apart at a time of trial, the broken circles had re-formed again, blocking the way back even for those children who had managed to escape captivity.

International law, which had finally recognized the leaders of the Lord's Army as criminals and outlaws, had now put a ban on forgiving them. However, many Acholi were convinced they could only put an end to the war by letting everything be forgotten. And peace, they argued, was more important and more badly needed than justice. The Ugandan authorities regarded the children incorporated into the guerrillas as rebels and gave the army orders to fight against them. The runaways who had managed to save their own lives were being denied the right to come home and remain there because the neighbors objected to them. Quite often the closest circle of all, the immediate family, was also closed and hostile to them.

And so many former guerrillas encountered mistrust and hostility after returning to their villages, and were rejected. For the neighbors, and even for their own cousins, they weren't victims who deserved sympathy and help, but killers and criminals who should be punished and condemned. The girls who had given birth to the rebel commanders' babies in captivity were now branded as whores by their own fathers and mothers, and driven out of their homes.

"Yet none of these children started killing of their own free will," said Christine. "What they need most now is to be released from a sense of guilt. Otherwise they'll go mad and become a danger or themselves and others. So we keep telling them from dawn to dusk that although they committed some appalling crimes, they aren't to blame for anything and they aren't evil. And they deserve love."

In her view the ultimate aim of the therapy at the center was not just to cure runaways from the bush or cleanse them of a sense of guilt, but to restore the structure of the circles of life, and make it possible for them to function properly again. The center was only meant to serve as a bridge, by way of which everything could return to its place.

She believed in this, and often said that everyone should believe in something.

◄◦►

"*Kidogo!*" she called out to Samuel.

In Swahili *kidogo* means little boy, but also "nonessential trifle," something totally insignificant. It's also what children incorporated into the guerrillas are called in this part of Africa.

"Boy! Run and fetch Father Remigio," she said. "We should leave now, but at this rate we won't get going until evening."

Christine and Father Remigio were taking the boys back to their villages. Christopher was to get out first in Olwal. Geoffrey was going further, all the way to Amuru.

"Can I come with you?" I asked.

"Do you want to?" she said, feigning surprise. "I thought you preferred to stay with Nora."

She didn't approve of our friendship. She saw it as too intimate. However, she clearly didn't lay the blame for that on me, but on Nora. Whenever she came into her office, she ostentatiously knocked at the open door, and from the threshold, with studied concern, insisted she didn't want to disturb us and that she'd only take a moment of Nora's time.

"I'd like to come. As long as there's room for me."

"We'll make space somehow," she said, nodding. "*Kidogo!* Also tell Nora the journalist is coming with us."

The boys got into the bed of the pickup truck. Christine sat next to the driver, and the priest and I sat behind.

The town ended suddenly, just round a bend in the dirt road we had driven down from the main street. Further on, bumping over potholes and sending up clouds of rust-colored dust, we drove along a narrow red road, among elephant grass rippling in the wind, with only some gnarled mango trees protruding above it.

"I hope they don't fall out," said Christine, looking at the boys through the back window. "Just a week or two and there'll be no one at the center."

"So that's a good thing?" I asked.

"Sure it is," she replied.

"God willing," added the priest.

Before setting off, Christopher and Geoffrey had said goodbye to Samuel and Richard. They had shaken hands, clapped each other on the back in an adult way, and burst into loud, nervous laughter. Like my son's school friends when they part ways for the summer vacation.

"Do you still remember the first girls the army brought us, Father?" asked Christine.

Father Remigio nodded.

⤚⟡⤜

That day heavy rain had fallen on the town. The army truck bringing the children had rolled slowly down the main street, splashing through the puddles. Despite the cold, lashing rain, lots of people had come to the marketplace. Most of them were drawn by curiosity, wanting to see for themselves these monsters, werewolves, forest creatures the children had been changed into. But there were also some who had come to find out if their own sons or daughters were among those brought in from the forest.

In the marketplace the soldiers had chased the children out of the truck, lined them up in a column, and herded them along the main street toward the center. Now people could get a better look at them. Dirty, with matted hair, ragged, barefoot, and wild, they didn't look human. At first the rubbernecks lurking in the arcades had stared at them in silence. Finally someone had shouted the first curse, followed by a torrent of abuse. People bad-mouthed, maligned, hurled insults, and shook their fists. The road to the center where their sins were going to be absolved seemed endless.

In the courtyard, behind the wall fencing them off from the hostile town, the children were told to undress and throw their rags in a pile, which was set on fire. Washed, wrapped in blankets, and dressed in new clothes, as if bewitched they stared into the flames consuming their old attire, and with it their old incarnations.

At first they behaved fearfully and mistrustfully, like captured wild animals. If they were called, they immediately came running and froze to attention, giving a springy salute. They were afraid of everything, and expected danger at any moment from any direction. Nora told me she had to eat their first meals with them so they could feel sure no one had sprinkled poison in the pot. When she stayed on night duty, she slept with the girls in their dormitory. She told the boys to leave the door of their building open so she could hear every noise.

She never slept through a single one of those nights. She kept being awoken by the children's screams and moans as they had nightmares. Senseless with fear, they would leap out of bed, throw themselves to the floor in convulsions, or try to run away or break free of something. They said afterward that at night the spirits of the people they had killed came to haunt them. Others said nothing, just whimpered softly, squeezing their eyes shut to block out the light. She explained to them that inside the walls of the center they were safe, and that here the spirits couldn't get to them. But she hated and feared those nights. She felt as if with each passing day the curse the children placed in her care were casting off was snaring and enslaving her instead.

The best medicine to provide reassurance and security turned out to be routine—daily, mechanically repeated activities, such as the morning washup, gymnastics, cleaning, breakfast, classes, therapy, prayers, dinner, and the night bell. They just had to make sure nothing disturbed the order of events, and that there was never a moment of inactivity.

✦

It looked as if the entire village of Olwal had come out onto the road. People were lined up on the hard shoulder as if to welcome a minister or a provincial governor.

They must have been waiting a long time, because the tiredness was plain to see on the faces of the mothers chasing romping children off the road. Curious faces, piercing stares, and nervous smiles flashed past the car windows. Motionless figures standing on the hard shoulder suddenly came to life and followed the car, banging their fists on its metal body. The fastest ran ahead to show us the way.

Olwal was no different from Palenga and the other refugee camps. It had the same grayish round huts with thatched roofs, the same muddy, stinking yards. The paths were covered in refuse, with hens, goats, piglets, and dogs rooting about in it.

Mike turned off the main road and wove his way slowly among the huts. Attracted by the commotion, more of the locals came crawling out of them and joined the growing crowd that was right on our heels. Finally the car stopped on the dirt floor outside one of the huts, and Mike switched off the engine.

Christopher jumped down from the truck bed and nervously glanced at the people surrounding him. Besides the marks from the whipping he'd received in the guerrillas, his arms and neck were covered in terrible scars. He had been badly burned during the fire at his family's hut when the guerrillas had attacked their village. "Fire dripped on me," I read in his memoirs, shut in Nora's safe. The flames had got to him before someone pulled him from the blaze and saved his life. Rescued from the fire, he had ended up a captive of the guerrillas.

"They're all covered in scars," said Christine, noticing me inspecting the boy. "As if branded."

She went up to Christopher and put an arm around him.

"So now your home will be here," she said.

The boy nodded, and replied with a timid smile.

"Take your things out of the car. Geoffrey, give your friend a hand," she called.

The boys hauled out the equipment Christopher had been given for the start of his new life and put it outside the hut. The assembled villagers stared hungrily and voraciously at the growing pyramid of treasure, murmuring in delight at the sight of the brand-new blue mattress, the sumptuous red quilt, and the shiny pots.

The bystanders suddenly made way to let two breathless boys through. At the sight of them, joy finally appeared on Christopher's troubled face. They fell into each other's arms and patted each other on the back.

"Those are his brothers," said Christine.

The crowd parted again, and a weeping woman ran into the yard, immediately followed by an older man in a dirty jacket thrown over his bare chest. Wailing loudly, the woman pulled Christopher into her embrace. She kissed him on the hair, cheeks, and eyes. At one point she raised his hands to her lips and kissed them. The man stood by and wept, without emitting a sound. He wiped his bloodshot eyes with large, dirty fists as the tears rolled down his face.

"He's drunk again," snapped Christine angrily. "He could have refrained today at least."

Christopher's father, as the man in the jacket turned out to be, had started drinking after the guerrillas had stolen his son. But not at once, and not out of despair. He had started boozing in earnest and stealing money from his wife for drink when the army told them to leave their huts, fields, and graveyards and move to a new place. Here in the guarded camp at Olwal the men had nothing to do anymore, apart from tormenting their wives and getting drunk on *warangi*.

Eventually Christopher's mother had left him, and she and her two other sons had gone to live with another man, the owner of the biggest store in the village. She had borne him two daughters. The new husband was furious that she hadn't given him boys, as she had her previous husband. He often beat and abused her, and drove her sons out of the house, telling them to go back to their drunkard of a father. The next day, or at most a few days later, his anger would pass, and then he would let the boys back into the hut. But when he learned that Christopher had been found, the third son of his new wife, who had borne him nothing but daughters, he announced that no way was he going to play nursemaid to other people's children and take yet another scrounger under his roof.

Christopher's father had found himself a new woman too. He hadn't married her, but he had let her move in with him. They had no children, and it wasn't at all clear what they lived on, because both of them seemed to be permanently drunk.

Christopher, who as a captive of the guerrillas had been dying of terrible homesickness for his parents, knew none of this—the first time he heard that they had broken up and that he no longer had a home was from Christine, in Gulu. Luckily his old paternal grandmother had agreed to take him in. At first she had turned up her nose at the idea, but she had stopped grumbling when she found out the boy would be coming home with a valuable dowry.

Although she'd been sent for as soon as we arrived, she was the last to come and welcome her grandson. She had the furthest to walk, because her fish stall was right by the road. As wrinkled as a dried fig, with her gaze fixed on the ground, she listened to what Christine was telling her and nodded her assent. She rarely asked a question, spitting out her words from a toothless mouth and absently wiping her hands on the folds of her shabby dress.

She opened the hasp of a small door made of planks and let Christine go in. It was dark inside the windowless hut. The only light fell in a stream through the small doorway. On the round dirt floor near the entrance there was a hearth, with some sooty pots, a bowl, and some bent tin plates lying next to it, and also a bucket of water. Apart from an old mattress and two small stools, there was no other furniture in the hut.

The grandmother showed Christopher a place by the wall, opposite her shakedown, where he could put his mattress and bedding, and his suitcase full of clothes. With a greedy eye she inspected the kitchen utensils he had brought, and told him to put the can of oil and the sacks of flour and sugar beside the hearth.

Still stiff and awkward as he tried not to dirty his new clothes at any cost, Christopher sat on a bench with his brothers, who never left his side for a moment. The villagers watched them from a slight distance. Christopher didn't look like a miraculously rescued castaway or a wandering beggar, but a long-lost cousin who has come from the big city to visit his poor relatives in a village forsaken by both God and man. He looked like someone from another world—but not the one he had actually been in.

Christine filled in a report, which the grandmother signed by marking a cross. When they came outside, Christine went up to Christopher to say goodbye. I thought she would embrace him, give him a hug, but she just held out her hand.

"Everything will be fine," she said.

He nodded.

She fetched her wallet out of her purse and took several banknotes from it.

"This is from me. Buy yourself some candy," she said, pressing the money into his hand.

The boy smiled cheekily.

"Well, all right, spend it on whatever you want, but on your own. Just don't buy cigarettes with it. Or beer."

As we drove away, I thought I could see him waving goodbye. In his white shirt, ironed pants, and above all his clean sneakers, among the barefoot, dirty villagers dressed in rags he almost seemed to radiate light. He remained visible from afar for ages, a bright point, a small light in the thickening darkness.

◄•►

"What will happen to him?" I asked, when he finally disappeared from view.

"What do you expect?" Christine shrugged, without turning around in the front seat. "He'll live like the others. No one ever said it's going to be easy for him."

"Have they got a school there?"

"No, the nearest one is in Gulu, too far to get there every day."

"Will he go to work? He doesn't know how to do anything, does he?"

"Like most of the people here. Even so Christopher has had luck. He can help his grandmother to sell fish at the market."

From Nora's accounts it emerged that living in refugee camps, where there was absolutely no form of occupation and life was reduced to daily, hopeless vegetation, often proved a far tougher challenge than surviving in the bush.

"Apparently some of them run away?"

"Lots of children who have been through the guerrillas find it very hard to adapt to their new life," put in Father Remigio. "It's true they don't all succeed. Maybe because the home life they find is so horribly different from the one they were so badly missing."

The villages they were abducted from had ceased to exist or had moved to new, unfamiliar places. Their huts had been taken over by other people now, and their parents had sometimes broken up and had new children. On coming home from the bush they made the painful discovery that their tragedy wasn't the most vital concern of all for their closest relatives, and that it hadn't really changed anything. The void they had left behind them had soon been filled, and contrary to their belief, time had not stopped, but had run on at its usual steady pace.

Not everyone was pleased by their miraculous survival and return to the world of the living. Some of the neighbors didn't even try to hide their nasty looks, didn't trust them and dogged their every step—just like the commanders at the guerrilla camps in the bush.

Whenever a former guerrilla happened to do something strange or behave differently from everyone else, the neighbors glanced at each other knowingly, recognizing his or her peculiarity as proof that he or she was still possessed by evil spirits. So these children were shunned and not allowed to play with the others, and conversation stopped as soon as they appeared. Feeling rejected, unwanted, and unloved, the

234 -o- WOJCIECH JAGIELSKI

children from the bush quite often responded with anger and violence. They easily got into furious, aggressive fights, flew at their tiresome younger siblings with their fists, and even ganged up in secret robber bands, which looted the village stores and huts by night.

"Father, do you remember the girl who smothered her sister because she wouldn't stop crying?" asked Christine. "Another one leaped up at night and attacked her mother in her sleep, killing her with a knife."

"Well, those who know the meaning of pain usually know how to inflict it too," replied the priest.

"They've been through so much, they've put such an effort into surviving, kept so much hope alive. And just when they think they have finally reached their goal, and that this is the end of their ordeal, it turns out to have all come to nothing," said Christine. "Maybe it really does happen because of spirits? It must be an unclean spirit that lures them back into the bush."

"They run away to the guerrillas?" I asked.

"You can hardly believe it, can you?" she answered with a question, turning her head.

"It's a shame to have to admit it, but it does happen," added the priest. "They feel safer among the guerrillas. Though what we recognize as good is called evil there, and evil—good, in the bush they have clearly defined limits, they know what is allowed and what is not, there are rules in force and a familiar order. Whereas here they come to believe nothing is certain, nothing is constant. They can't even be sure of the love of their own parents. Out there, in the bush, at least they have a sense of the meaning of life and of belonging to a community."

"Geoffrey won't run off anywhere," said Christine, cutting the conversation short and glancing through the back window.

When she found his parents, she told them their son was alive, but ill, and that they couldn't see him yet. Geoffrey didn't know how to express his gratitude to her for that. Finally free of the guerrillas, he felt relief, but he didn't want to return to his village immediately, because he wasn't ready yet.

He wanted to stay in Christine and Nora's care for as long as possible. Here he felt the way he used to feel at home—safe. Only here and only now, among boys and girls who had been through the same experience, to whom he didn't have to account for anything, and who understood and forgave him without the need for any explanation.

During one of their visits, Christine had told Geoffrey's father there was no certainty the boy would ever be ready to return to his old life. A few days later the father had come to Gulu again. He declared that once his son was ready, they would go away together as far as possible, best of all to Kampala. In the big city no one would ask questions and it would be easier to hide away.

Geoffrey knocked on the back window. We had reached Amuru. From afar we could see white ribbons of smoke rising above the village.

❖

The village looked abandoned. There was a strange, intense silence, the kind that falls at moments of great anticipation. The weather looked set for a downpour. There were storm clouds gathering on the horizon, and the sky appeared to be moving.

We passed several empty homesteads surrounded by low fences made of thorny branches. We were almost at the center of the village when we saw the first human being. An old woman was slowly wobbling along in front of us, leaning on a stick. When we drew level with her, Christine asked her the way. The old woman straightened up, shook her cane in the air, and pointed ahead of her.

"*Mato oput*," she said. "*Mato oput*."

I had heard those words before somewhere. I scoured my memory for their source and meaning. Suddenly it came to me—it was Kenneth Banya, the converted Lord's Army commander, who had told me about the ritual the Acholi called *mato oput*. It was a ceremony of absolution and expiation of sins. A ceremony for reconciliation and liberation from spirits and evil forces; enraged by people's arrogance, they had invaded their lives and turned them into a hideous nightmare.

"You're in luck," said Father Remigio, adjusting his clerical collar, gleaming white against his black skin. "It's rarely performed around here nowadays."

"Chasing away spirits?" I asked.

"In our part of the country people believe that after death their souls do not entirely leave the earth and the world of the living. Or at least they can still come back here."

I asked Christine if she believed in the spirits of the dead.

"I believe in the Holy Spirit," she replied drily.

In the square, a large crowd had gathered under a huge old mango tree. The village elders were sitting in the middle on wooden stools, at a long table covered in oilcloth.

A case was being heard which had occurred three years earlier, when one young man had fatally stabbed another during a drunken brawl. The killer had been caught by the police, and a judge from Gulu had sentenced him to two years in prison. The remorseful boy hadn't caused any trouble, and probably really did regret what he had done, so he had been released after only six months, on probation.

But once he got back to the village, strange and terrible things had started to happen there. That same day his two brothers were killed in car crashes, each in a different place, but at almost exactly the same time, in the evening, just before nightfall. Another time the hut in which the boy lived had suddenly gone up in flames in broad daylight. His youngest sister, a girl of only about five, had started to complain of nightmares.

The family elders had immediately gone to the village chief, who after conferring with the *ajwaka*, or healer, who was able to talk to spirits, said there would have to be a *mato oput* ritual; this would allow the families of the killer and the victim of the old, drunken brawl to be reconciled. If they reached agreement, the evil forces would no longer be able to reach them, and the old order and harmony would return.

For sixty days the chief heard statements from witnesses to the fight, and considered all the circumstances, with a view to issuing a just verdict. Finally he announced that the killer's family must give the victim's relatives eight goats and eight sacks of maize flour as compensation. He also set a date for the ritual of expiation and reconciliation.

In the past, to recompense for loss caused by murder, the killer's family used to give the victim's family a young girl. She would then marry his brother or cousin, and when she gave birth to a son, the child would be named after the victim and regarded as his—and also as his new incarnation. Gradually the Acholi had dropped this custom, as more and more outsiders came to their lands, foreigners to whom they would also have had to give away their women. And although many chiefs still believed it was impossible to speak of atonement and reconciliation until a new life had replaced the old one that had been cut short, the Acholi realized that a more appropriate form of compensation would be to pay damages.

Ever since, they had paid for a death with cattle or cash; the chiefs made sure the victims' families didn't waste the fine on drink, or try to increase it through risky investments, but used it to pay for a wife for one of the victim's relatives.

At first the damages were mainly paid in the form of cattle. But when foreign invaders looted the Acholi's herds, they had to use cash instead. The wars that had chosen to plague Acholi-land had finally stripped them of the last vestiges of their property, and driven them out of their villages into miserable refugee camps. To complete the ritual needed for harmony and resolution, the chiefs had reduced the fines, and now let them be paid off in goats or sheep instead of cattle, or even in hens. To those who grumbled that human life had become awfully cheap, the chiefs responded that, just like reconciliation, the fine had a symbolic side to it. It should be high enough for the culprit's family to feel it, but at the same time payable without condemning them to poverty and adversity. They also said that compensation, making peace, and wiping sins from memory were more important than even the fairest punishment—however just, it could never right the wrong that had been done.

The criminal's entire family collected the sum which the chiefs had decided was due to the victim's relatives. Sometimes it took them several years, but they bore the guilt for his deed and assumed the responsibility of making sure he never did harm again. They frankly admitted the crime he had already committed, and truly regretted it.

Every reconciliation ceremony started with the criminal confessing his guilt and asking for forgiveness, not only from his victim's relatives, but also from his own cousins, on whom he had brought shame and trouble, if not danger.

Once the killer had confessed, shown remorse, and asked for forgiveness, and the chiefs had set the sum and form of the damages, no one could stand in the way of reconciliation, oppose the settlement, or spoil the ceremony of atonement.

"What if the culprit refuses to admit it, or thinks he's innocent?" I asked Father Remigio. "Or asks for forgiveness without really meaning it, just because his relatives are insisting on it?"

"That sort of remorse doesn't count, and sooner or later the deceit will come to light," he replied.

"So is it impossible to hide anything?"

"Fear of the most shocking truth means nothing when you're dealing with spirits."

"Do you believe in them, Father?"

"In fact, I don't think you can look at it in terms of belief."

⟶

Among the Acholi, the dead do not leave the world of the living. Death does not mean the annihilation of the human being. Although the dead person's soul is separated from his or her body, it retains the features and properties of the deceased, his or her personality, social position, and gender. The person dies, but in a way goes on living, continuing to take part in earthly life. He or she becomes one of the countless spirits that fill the universe.

Apart from the spirits of dead people, and also of the races, tribes, clans, and families to which they belonged, there are spirits of nature too: of rocks, lakes, rivers, and streams, wildernesses, wild animals, and seasons of the year. Altogether they are the main active force in earthly life. They guarantee security and the natural order. They guard the border between good and evil, and they ensure perfect harmony between people, nature, and the extraterrestrial world. It is an extremely important task, the most important of all, because any disruption of this harmony immediately causes human life to be changed into cruel, unbearable torment.

The state of harmony, the only one in which a happy, worthwhile life is possible, demands coexisting peacefully and keeping the rules of life in the community. In the world of the Acholi an individual means nothing, but a community of people—the immediate or wider family—is everything, the most sacred thing of all. The community answers for the deeds of all its members, who understand in turn that by yielding to temptation and committing crimes they do harm and bring condemnation and punishment on their entire family.

Each crime, every human infringement of the natural harmony instantly provokes the anger of the spirits of nature and the spirits of the ancestors. To punish the culprits, force them to correct their mistakes and compensate for their wrongdoing, these spirits inflict all sorts of misfortune and disaster on them—wars, plagues, floods, and droughts. Suffering is understood to be a punishment for violating the order, which is associated with purity. The enraged spirits can change from guardians of order into bringers of misfortune. Merely if a funeral ritual is not completed, the angered spirit of the dead person will wander the world of the living, disturbing, tormenting, and harming them.

In fact, this is the case not just in Acholi-land but in other African countries too. Many of the Zulus in South Africa believe that the cause of the fratricidal wars destroying their country is the spirit of King Chaki, who was buried without all the proper rituals. Their neighbors, the Xhosa, ascribe the reason for their troubles to the anger of King Hintsa, whose head was cut off by the British and taken away from Africa as a macabre trophy. Ever since, Hintsa's spirit has wandered the world, bringing calamity and misfortune on his tribe. If the king's head were recovered and buried with the rest of his remains, his spirit would finally rest, and peace would reign in the land of the Xhosa.

The spirits of the ancestors also appeared in the dreams of Liberian commander Prince Johnson, telling him there would never be peace in Liberia until the remains of President Samuel Doe—whom he had personally tortured and then had killed—were burned, and the ashes taken to Mecca. Johnson quickly gave orders for the body to be dug up and placed on a pyre; eyewitnesses to the exhumation claimed that two years after his death, President Doe looked as if he were alive, which was clear proof that his spirit was enraged.

When the mysterious epidemic caused by the Ebola virus erupted in Congo, the locals ascribed that to the anger of the spirits too. It all started with the greed of the doctors at the hospital in a town called Kikwit, where a man called Kimbabu had reported with stomach pains; he was a treasure hunter who had just come back from Angola. The doctors cut his stomach open and found a very valuable diamond in there. The wretched man had forgotten that he had swallowed this treasure to hide it from customs men at the border. But Kimbabu had died, and the doctors had appropriated his diamond. The treasure hunter's infuriated father had then paid some sorcerers capable of communicating with spirits, and the spirits had sent the plague on the town.

The worst, most dangerous spirits are of people who weren't duly buried or fully mourned. As they haven't been sent off to the next world properly, they angrily thirst for revenge, and bring misery and disease not just on those who took their lives, but also on those who haven't shown them enough respect since they died.

This sort of furious, vengeful spirit persecutes its offender, possessing him, terrifying him with nightmares, and driving him mad. It can also harass his relatives, or even the entire community. It can make itself felt instantly, straight after death, but it can also wait years for its revenge, or even pass from the parents to the children, making their heirs pay for the sins and crimes of a different generation. More than once I heard comments in Gulu that the children of the Acholi were being abducted and changed into cruel killers because evil spirits had sworn vengeance on their fathers and grandfathers.

The Acholi gave a wide berth to places where people had been killed during the war and their corpses abandoned without a proper burial. They were afraid that the victims' spirits gathered in the vicinity of massacred, gutted villages, where they lay in wait to enter lost, ignorant travelers and make use of them to exact their revenge. The Acholi also avoided the bush, where their children had been transformed into monsters.

The revenge and anger of the ancestor and nature spirits were not only provoked by killing, but by any deviation from the norm, any breach of harmony—such as a marital quarrel or betrayal, contempt for one's elders, or a dispute between neighbors. One Acholi chief recited to me a whole litany of deeds and behavior that disrupt the harmony of the community, described in minute detail. It included crimes such as flinging money or food at someone in anger, refusing to eat a meal prepared by your wife, or even giving birth to a handicapped child—any behavior that was different from the accepted norm.

"The spirits don't intervene out of malevolence or an innate desire to do harm or destroy. The spirits of the Acholi are neither good nor evil," said Father Remigio. "But they can serve both good and evil. They can serve to cure illness, but also to kill."

"What does it depend on?" I asked.

"On people. On what people want to use them for."

The Acholi even regard traveling abroad, or spending a long time away from your home area, as a deviation from the normal order. For the wanderer to be accepted back into the community, he has to undergo a purification ritual to free him of any offenses he may have committed far from home. And also to release him from the foreign spirits he may have brought back with him from the outside world. The Acholi regarded the children kidnapped from them years ago who were now coming home from captivity in the bush as arrivals from a remote, unfamiliar world. Not knowing what to do with them, they subjected them to the same ritual as the travelers and exiles.

Quite often, after the children's return home a separate ritual was performed to chase away spirits. First, the possessed individuals spent some time in the care of the elders, and sometimes the shaman too. At sunset, under the leadership of the elders, all the inhabitants gathered in the main square, and shouted at the top of their lungs, beat drums, calabashes, tin bowls, pots, or anything that could make a noise so terrifying and unbearable that the evil spirits would abandon their victims and take to their heels. Jackson told me that when Gulu was attacked by the Ebola virus, for a few days they had sounded an alarm to chase away the spirits that had brought the epidemic.

As a way of exercising caution, chasing the spirits away proved the simplest and most effective method. Many Acholi and even some Kampalans believed that this was how Uganda had been freed from Obote and Amin. Both of them were possessed by evil forces, and both had been expelled from the country to live out their days in exile. When news went round in Gulu that Joseph Kony and his underage guerrillas had abandoned their hideouts, not just in Uganda, but in Sudan too, and moved away, into the marshes and jungle of Congo, the Acholi gave each other knowing looks, with joyful hope in their eyes.

·◦·

That day, the purification ritual was being conducted just outside the village of Amuru. A site for the ceremony was usually chosen at a point located halfway between the homes of the criminal and the victim. Like this, in order to reach agreement and be reconciled, both sides had to come an equal distance and make the same effort.

By the time we arrived in Amuru, the fine had already been paid and deposited with the chiefs, and the victim's and culprit's families were submitting to the reconciliation ritual. The ceremony was in full swing, and no one seemed to notice our arrival. However, people made way for us and let us get closer, almost into the center.

The ceremony was being conducted by three chiefs, who were sitting at a table in the middle of the square, like a board of examiners. Two of them were monitoring the correct procedure for the ritual, and the third was instructing the participants what to do. As soon as he gave the signal, the victim's relatives started hurling abuse at the killer's cousins, while shaking their fists and sticks at them. Meanwhile the women raised a lament. Then the chief conducting the ceremony asked whether they were willing to forget their injury and forgive the culprit, if they were given due compensation. When they said yes, the chief turned to the killer's cousins. If they would pay for the harm done by their relative and ask for forgiveness, he said, his crime would be wiped from memory and everything would be the same as it was before. They too willingly agreed.

Then the chief placed three hen's eggs on the well-compacted ground, and the killer's cousins taking part in the ceremony, two women and two men (there were also two women and two men representing the victim's family), crushed them with their bare feet, each using the right foot, as required. This signified a break with the past and the start of something new. With their feet smeared in crushed egg, the men also walked across some sticks with forked ends that had been laid on the ground, the kind used to barricade the entrances to granaries in the villages.

"The egg symbolizes innocence—it is pure, intact, and perfect," Father Remigio explained to me. "It has no mouth, so it can't speak evil or blaspheme. It is delicate and fragile, but its hard shell protects it from all impurities. Crossing the sticks that barricade the granaries represents agreement to return to the community and an invitation to communal meals. To cleanse the wrongdoer of evil you can also tell him to stand under a stream of water trickling from the roof of a hut where an innocent child lives. Or else you can sacrifice a hen. Except that it must be a white one."

The crowd parted to make way for some boys, who dragged two young goats wearing halters into the middle of the circle. In normal circumstances the killer's family was meant to bring a lamb as a sacrifice, and the victim's cousins a goat, but in view of the general poverty and the chaos of war they chose whatever animals were at hand for the sacrifice. Sometimes they even used a rooster instead of a sheep or goat, or just ordinary hens. The goats destined for the reconciliation sacrifice had their legs bound and their muzzles tied with straps.

"That's so when they're slaughtered they won't let out a moan that could startle the spirits and unsettle them," said the priest quietly, and after pausing for thought he added: "The killer is meant to bring a lamb whose blood is cold, and thus better able to cool the anger of the evil forces."

At a signal from the oldest chief, who as the closest to death and the world of the ancestors was in charge of the ceremony, the killer's and victim's cousins slit the animals' throats with large butcher's knives. The blood splashed out, liberally spattering the ground. Then the animals were beheaded, skinned, and cut in half. The killer's relatives handed half of their goat to the victim's family, who gave them half of theirs in exchange.

The women cut out the butchered animals' bleeding livers, then chopped them into small pieces and roasted them on a bonfire lit in the middle of the square. When the meat was cooked, they threw the chunks into a communal bowl and, spearing them on long spikes, served them in turn into the mouths of the representatives of both families, who had gathered in a circle.

"The liver is removed because it collects the bile, and thus all the evil hidden inside a person," I heard the priest whisper. "And also the blood, which is the source of life."

The mild, natural way in which the priest took on the role of guide and interpreter reminded me of my first meeting with Jackson, just after my arrival in Gulu. He had accompanied me on the journey to Kampala when I decided to go there, and he had come back to Gulu when I decided to return. And then he had disappeared, vanished into thin air, just as unexpectedly and suddenly as he had appeared. I kept dropping in at the radio station where he worked, and into Franklin's bar, where formerly we had spent our afternoons. But no one had seen him, and no one had any news of him, as if he had never existed, as if he were purely a figment of my imagination.

Father Remigio was from near Kitgum. While Gulu, being nearer to Kampala and surrounded by fertile land, earned a living from trade and agriculture, the only thing to do in godforsaken Kitgum was to get away from the place by joining the army or the police. Or, like Remigio, by devoting yourself to the service of God. He had been sent to his parish in Gulu after graduating from a seminary in Kampala. As he talked about spirits and ways of dealing with them, he often referred to the customs of his native parts. "At home in Kitgum we do it differently," he would say.

"At home in Kitgum they often conduct a spear-breaking ritual too," he put in now, as he gazed at the women bustling around the bonfire. "The spear isn't actually broken—it rots, but it comes to the same thing. It is meant to signify that the period of war between the families is over once and for all. This ritual can also be applied when there are wars between entire tribes. Years ago, when Amin was deposed, the Acholi were reconciled in this way with his compatriots, the Kakwa, from across the Nile."

Years ago, long, long ago, the Acholi were capable of dealing with spirits. They were familiar with them, they knew what to expect of them, how not to offend them, and how to placate them on the occasions when they did flare up in anger. They also knew how to drive away evil forces, expiate sins, and atone for crimes, even the very worst ones.

They were always fighting wars in which they killed their foe. Inflicting death on the enemy was a source of pride, and the bravest warriors were revered as heroes, famous throughout the region. But after each battle they too had to undergo a purification ceremony, to appease and compensate the spirits of their victims with sacrifices. So after the fight, the warriors came back to their villages, bringing the heads of their enemies as war trophies, and also to enable them to find and communicate with their spirits.

The natural order and harmony had been disrupted as soon as the first foreigners appeared in Acholi-land from the outside world—hunters and slave traders, merchants, missionaries, and soldiers. Along with them, foreign spirits came wandering into Acholi territory too. If the outsiders died here, in exile, the Acholi didn't know what to do with their spirits, how to avoid offending or angering them, and how to calm their fury.

The number of foreigners had kept increasing, until finally they had declared themselves the masters of Acholi-land, of all Uganda and half of Africa. Now the Acholi had to serve them. More and more Acholi had become possessed by foreign spirits. They had started to dress and behave like foreigners, cut their hair like them, speak their dialect, dance to their music, drink *kwete* out of glasses, and eat with knives and forks.

Then the foreigners had made the Acholi set off for distant countries to fight in their wars, which were called world wars. Many Acholi were killed abroad, and their cousins and neighbors went crazy wondering whether they had been buried and sent off to the other world as necessary. And what would their spirits do so far from home? How would they find the way? What would happen if they didn't return, and what if they came back enraged?

But the really bad times were only just beginning. The civil wars that hit Uganda like a plague of locusts meant that once again thousands of Acholi fled the country, and thousands of others were enlisted in various armies. These were especially violent and bloody wars. People were not just killed like vermin, with no pity or scruples, but in ways designed to inflict the worst possible suffering on them before death. No care was taken either to give them a proper funeral or any mourning ceremonies.

At first the war was fought in the land of the Bugandans, on Lake Victoria, but in time it moved to the right bank of the Nile, into Acholiland. First their compatriots from the government army massacred the population of the villages around Luwero and Kampala, which were supporting the guerrillas. Then, defeated by the rebels, they rushed off to hide from vengeance in their own villages on the other side of the river.

But they came home changed, wild and bloodstained, with madness in their eyes, like beasts. The crimes they had committed proved too terrible for them to be able to confess them or make them public. Without doing so, they couldn't attain purification, or break free of the avenging spirits tormenting them, which they had dragged after them into the world of the Acholi. Possessed by evil forces, they went on killing and injuring, merely increasing the number of victims and their stray spirits thirsting for revenge.

Until finally, in the very middle of the war, the army told the Acholi to get out of their villages and move into guarded camps close to the bigger towns. Split up and crowded together, in the confusion the Acholi lost their chiefs and leaders, abandoned their cemeteries and chapels, where the old, good protector spirits lived; they stood and watched helplessly as evil forces inflicted more and more curses on their land—epidemics, floods, droughts, and wars. Many Acholi believed that evil spirits were exacting revenge on them, changing their children into bloodthirsty, merciless, insensitive soldiers—killers.

Some chiefs predicted a holocaust. They claimed that the ritual of purification and reconciliation with the spirit of a killed opponent is only possible when the warrior knows who he killed, or at least has captured a trophy from his victim enabling him to identify and find his spirit. During today's wars, however, the soldiers and guerrillas fired whole volleys of bullets at each other from modern, long-range machine guns, quite often from so far away that they had no idea whom they had killed, or even if they had killed anyone. So they didn't know if they should be guarding against any spirits or not, and if so, how to get rid of them.

The vast and still rising number of spirits—lost, restless, vengeful, and dangerous—prompted many of the Acholi to exploit the dark and evil forces to their own advantage. They paid shamans, who had the gift of healing and could talk to spirits, to set them on their enemies or neighbors and bring them misfortune. So the spirits' chosen favorites, who until now had healed people, started exploiting their gift in order to kill.

As anyone could go to the shaman and ask him to cast a spell, unleash a malicious spirit, cause a sudden death, a mysterious illness, infertility, madness, a lightning strike, poverty, or a cattle plague, the Acholi lived not just under constant threat, but also in a state of eternal suspicion, in a heavy atmosphere of endless accusations. No one trusted anyone else anymore, and the effects of witchcraft were seen in everything. Even in ordinary, peaceful times the Acholi believed that nothing happened without a reason, purely by accident or a twist of fate. Even when they were killed fighting, they didn't think death was caused by their enemies, who merely fired the lethal bullets in their direction, but by the spirits who guided them.

Now the Acholi world had collapsed, they had lost their sense of community, and the despairing chiefs were prophesying the approach of Judgment Day.

◄◦►

Christine didn't believe in spirits, or in village rituals to make truces and pacts with them.

"It's nonsense," she said, shrugging. "Superstition, quite outrageous."

She resented Father Remigio's feverish excitement, which wasn't appropriate for a clergyman; nor was his interest in and knowledge of pagan rites, and she certainly didn't approve of the fact that he was explaining their meaning to me. She was also offended that her superiors allowed village chiefs into the center in Gulu to tell the children about their traditional beliefs and customs.

Nora had nothing against it. "It means nothing to me," she said. "But if it can help the children, then why not? We should try everything."

"Father, how can you say such things?" said Christine, unable to restrain herself as Father Remigio was telling me about people who were possessed by spirits.

We were talking about the spirits that fought for Alice of the Holy Spirit, and also for Joseph Kony.

"So they say, though I don't think they are the same spirits," said the priest, shaking his head. "The ones with Alice were helping her to fight, and above all making sure her soldiers lived a pure life. They say that over a hundred thousand spirits served in Alice's army. She was also helped by animals, snakes, and even bees. Everything that had been wronged by people."

"I heard that the spirits protected Alice's soldiers from enemy bullets so they could attack standing up straight, and didn't have to crouch," I said.

"But only the ones who hadn't committed any shameful acts, and had undergone a purification ritual before the battle," he replied. "And as they were going into battle they recited special prayers."

"Is that possible?" I said, after a short pause. "Do you believe prayer can stop bullets?"

"Do you?" he replied with a question. "Would you be prepared to admit that if you believe strongly enough, a bullet aimed straight at your heart will turn aside at the last moment?"

"I believe it's possible to believe as strongly as that."

"That's not the same thing."

◂◦▸

The most important moment in the ceremony had come. In the middle of the square, between the representatives of the feuding but now reconciling families, the women put out a large clay pot, which they had filled with beer made of millet and sorghum. Then one of them took a small bottle of strong homemade hooch from the front of her dress and mixed it in with the beer.

Next, one of the chiefs went up to the pot and poured in some juice pressed from the leaves and roots of the *oput* tree, which tastes so bitter that without the alcohol the drink would be impossible to swallow. Finally the women added a few drops of blood from the sacrificial goats. The reconciliation drink was ready. The culmination of the *mato oput* ceremony was approaching.

The sour juice from the *oput* tree was not chosen for this purpose by accident. According to an Acholi legend, the *oput* tree once saved two quarreling tribes from war. Armed with spears, bows, clubs, and shields, the two sides were already heading toward each other to fight a bloody battle when suddenly a large old *oput* tree crashed down between them. The chiefs of the tribes saw it as a sign. They called off the battle, and instead of killing each other, the warriors went home to their villages. Ever since, trees of this species have been revered among the Acholi as a symbol of concord. Once they discovered what a bitter, tongue-tingling flavor its juices have, the Acholi believed that anyone who drank this foul stuff could give no stronger proof of sincerity in aspiring for peace; it was also the perfect reflection of the bitterness caused by crime, suffering, mourning, and hatred.

The representatives of the feuding families came up to the pot in pairs. They knelt on the ground with their heads drooping, holding their hands folded behind their backs, and at the same time they bent forward and lapped up the reconciliation drink. Before bowing down they lightly touched their foreheads, as a sign that they were making peace and becoming a community again.

When the clay vessel had been drained to the bottom and the participants in the ceremony, now rather intoxicated, had sat down around it, the chiefs announced that the crime and injury had been forgiven and forgotten once and for all.

Then the eating and drinking began, as the whole village sat down over gourds full of food prepared for the celebration, hooch, and beer. Everything had to be eaten and drunk on this site, because if anyone at the feast took just a small piece of meat home to his hut, the entire reconciliation ritual would be invalidated.

Some dancers ran into the square wearing feather headdresses, costumes made of skins and strips of leather covered in shells that rattled as they moved. As if unable to see them, the old women from both reconciled families, who were tipsier than anyone else, started wailing dirges. If not for the storm and the downpour that suddenly fell from the sky onto this deeply self-absorbed village, the peacemaking feast would have gone on all night around the bonfires.

⤙⤙

When the first, heavy raindrops fell, it suddenly went dark under the cloud-covered sky. Disappointed that such promising entertainment should end so suddenly, the old women went on sitting there in spite of the weather, the circumstances, and common sense. They continued to drink hooch straight from the bottle, closing their eyes and enjoying their inebriation, oblivious to the streams of rain pouring down their faces.

Stumbling on the uneven road and slipping in the mud, we headed for the pickup truck, which we had left in the village. The oldest of the chiefs who had conducted the reconciliation ritual was standing by the car, leaning on a stick. He said his name was Jeremiah, and asked if we could find room for him—he wanted to come back to Gulu with us.

"The king has given me an audience for tomorrow," he said, squeezing into the backseat between me and the priest. Still annoyed and offended, Christine did not respond from the front seat.

"The king?" I asked. "Do you have a king here?"

"Indeed we do. Our *rwot* Acana may not be as rich and powerful as the Bugandan Kabaka, but for us he is a very important person."

"And he lives in Gulu?"

"Where else would he live? His homestead is on the hill, right next to the children's center," said Father Remigio.

"Is it possible to visit him?"

"Of course. Why not?" said the chief. "You should definitely go and see him."

"Is it true that former guerrillas from the Lord's Army are subjected to purification rituals, and only then are they accepted back into their families and villages?"

"It's not as simple as that. The *mato oput* ceremony can only succeed if the body of the victim is found and identified, and his family is found too. The relatives of the killer have to be there too, because they are the ones who must take responsibility for him and pay the compensation."

"And what about those who don't even know whom they have killed? Or those who have no family?" I asked.

"You should ask the king about that. He knows the most about it all."

We spent ages weaving our way through a labyrinth of alleyways, occasionally asking directions from villagers fleeing the rain, until the driver finally found Geoffrey's parents' hut. They had been waiting for the boy since noon, and hadn't even gone to watch the purification rite for fear of missing their son's return. Wet from the rain, cheerfully chatting and patting each other on the arms now and then, they unloaded Geoffrey's luggage from the bed of the truck.

Christine asked Geoffrey's father if he had found a house and a job in Kampala yet. He eagerly said yes. He asked if we would like to have dinner with them, but Christine refused.

"It's already late. Time we were on our way," she said firmly.

We said goodbye to Geoffrey with relief.

"They are leaving for Kampala," I heard Christine say from the front seat. "Seven more days and they'll be gone from here."

No one said a word. We drove in total darkness, only illuminated by the beams of car headlights. The air was sticky with humidity.

"What will happen to Samuel?" I asked Christine.

"That boy of Nora's?"

"But you know him. He hasn't got anyone. Does that mean he'll never be freed from the spirits?"

"So it would seem," she said, "if you believe in all that."

"So what's going to happen to him?"

"On Monday they're taking him to the orphanage in Kampala. Unless of course someone is found before then who would come and fetch him and look after him," she replied. "He's too small to go to boarding school.

If he were two or three years older, then maybe. But they won't take him now."

Silence fell. Fat raindrops drummed on the car roof. There were two days left until Monday.

"Didn't Nora tell you?" wondered Christine.

⬩⬩⬩

The Acholi king was called David Onen Acana II, and his court was more like a shabby provincial post office than a royal palace. It was on a green hill, in a suburb. As a result, whenever the *rwot* addressed his subjects to mark some extremely important event or especially big festival, he looked down on them from above.

In another African kingdom, Swaziland, on the slopes of the Drakensberg Mountains, the court chamberlain of His Gracious Majesty Mswati III warned me to crouch in the king's presence; I was to be careful not to accidentally or absentmindedly create a mutually unpleasant, awkward situation where I would be looking the monarch straight in the face. Someone might think I considered myself his equal.

King Mswati III had just convoked an important conference on the constitution, and according to custom had summoned everyone to his *kraal* in the village of Ludzidzini. That day the herdsmen had driven the royal cattle to the mountain pastures to make room for his subjects in their empty pen, on grass littered with cow dung, as well as for the foreign ambassadors and correspondents whom the king had invited, in order to demonstrate his progressive views. As no seats were provided, and court etiquette forbade standing up straight in the presence of the king, all the foreigners spent the two-day conference in an uncomfortable squat.

The Acholi king's office was not far from Christine and Nora's center, which I had to pass on my way there. Through the open gate I saw the girls in their orange skirts buzzing about in the yard, and heard the hubbub of their voices. Samuel must also be in there somewhere, and Nora too for sure. I knew I must ask her about the boy, and about what Christine had told me on the way back from Amuru. I had decided to come back here after my visit to the king. As I passed the gate, I quickened my pace.

The Acholi king was a tall, well-built man approaching forty. The entire furnishings of his office consisted of a big, heavy table with a computer and several constantly ringing cell phones, a large armchair that looked like a throne, and two rows of chairs, set against the walls for guests.

He wasn't a real king, just a chief. The first among equals, but still just a chief. The Acholi, who came to these lands centuries ago from southern Sudan, were a race of nomadic shepherds, hunters, and fishermen. Before they took up cultivating crops, as eternal nomads they had made do without kings, judges, police, and official posts. All they needed were chiefs, whom they chose from among themselves to lead them on journeys across the savannahs, bravely command them in battle, act as wise judges to settle their disputes, make sure the old laws and customs were observed, and take care of the protector spirits who guaranteed security and plenty.

Usually the role of *rwot* passed from father to son. So indeed, after his father's sudden death, David Acana II had inherited the throne; his compatriots had summoned him home from the British city of Birmingham, where he was training to be a hotelier. In view of the new *rwot*'s young age, some experienced chiefs were selected as his deputies, Atuka Otinga and George William Lugai.

I found the king in his office, in conference with Chief Lugai. They had just come back from a trip to Garamba jungle, where on the border of Sudan and Congo they were supposed to be meeting Joseph Kony to persuade him to surrender and give up the fight. They had taken not just some other Acholi chiefs with them on the journey, but also Kony's older sister, one of his former wives, and his uncle.

However, Kony had not turned up, and hadn't even called to give warning or to explain himself. His guerrillas, who guided the chiefs to the secret meeting place, did not even offer them water. Chief Lugai's explanation for this was that Kony was extremely suspicious as well as hostile toward the Acholi elders. He regarded them as traitors and was taking revenge on them. He claimed that years ago, when he set off for war, they had given him their blessing, but later they had disowned him and turned their backs on him, though according to Acholi tradition, once given, a chief's blessing could not be removed or withdrawn.

The chosen few whom he admitted to his presence related that Kony had had enough of war by now, and that he was struggling with illness; apparently he was weak and had started spitting blood. However, he was more afraid of prison and the trial he would be made to face than he was of death, homelessness, endless flight, and condemnation. He would never agree to be tried in Kampala, and was even less willing to face the court far away in The Hague, from where warrants had been issued for his arrest. He knew what had happened to Charles Taylor, whose ambition to be president of Liberia had led him to provoke an equally bloody, sinister war. Years later he had let himself be seduced by the persuasions of foreigners, and had resigned his post in exchange for the promise of safe asylum in Nigeria. But when he no longer had any power, friends, or soldiers, he had been abducted, transported to Europe, and shut in prison.

Joseph Kony also knew what fate had befallen the defeated and captured Iraqi ruler, Saddam Hussein. The mayor of Gulu had brought a film of Saddam's execution into the jungle for him. He had watched it over and over, as the executioners maligned the once mighty tyrant, showering abuse on him as he made his final journey, then as they tightened the rope around his neck, and he struggled in the noose. So Kony had sworn not to surrender, not to disband his guerrilla army, and not to stop fighting until President Museveni had pardoned him, and the international tribunal in The Hague had withdrawn its arrest warrant. Only then would he be ready to talk about peace or to leave, go away and never look back, let them forget about him.

The Acholi were ready to forgive Kony his crimes, and so was the president in Kampala. The Acholi chiefs wanted to judge his case in their own way, according to their laws and customs—if only to make him undergo a *mato oput* ritual, be cleansed of evil forces, compensate for his crimes, be reconciled, and forget about everything. But the judges from Europe were insisting that their law took precedence, and that once an arrest warrant had been issued they couldn't retract it, and once an accusation of crime had been made,

they couldn't revoke it—just as the Acholi chiefs could not withdraw their blessing.

"So what are we to do?" asked King Acana, spreading his arms helplessly. "You are concerned about justice and punishment. For us it is
more important to stop the war, so our children can come back from the
bush and we can have order again."

"They say we're trying to save a criminal from punishment, and that
by wiping all the evil he has done from memory we will only encourage
others to do the same," added Chief Lugai. "But what would happen if
Kony were arrested and put in prison in Amsterdam or Stockholm? After
twenty years in the bush would a cozy cell with a TV, good meals, security, and comfort be such a great onus for him? And what benefit would
our people get from that? Joseph Kony is fighting his war on our land and
the Acholi are its victims. That is why I think we should be allowed to
judge the crime and decide the punishment according to our laws."

"After everything he has done, could Joseph Kony really return to his
village and start to live an ordinary life, like others?" I asked.

"No one knows what lies in Kony's soul. Or maybe he hasn't even got
a soul?" said King Acana. "Kony is an evil, but he is still one of us."

Chief Lugai nodded.

"When I was a child I too was abducted into the forest," added the
king. "I was their prisoner too—for some time I was one of them."

"Is it possible to cleanse yourself of all those evil forces? Are there
appropriate rituals for every kind of evil?"

"Sometimes if matters go too far, there's no longer a way to do it,"
replied Chief Lugai. "It's not good if there's too much killing."

Many chiefs insisted that the *mato oput* ceremony should only be conducted when the hostility between the embattled sides had ceased, so
it couldn't be held while the war was still going on. Nor did the laws
of the Acholi stipulate punishments for crimes committed during war.
The Acholi had never experienced such crimes before, nor had small
children ever turned out to be violent murderers until now.

Some of the chiefs did not believe that underage guerrillas asking
for forgiveness would openly confess their sins without being forced
to do so. The crimes they had committed in the bush were so terrible

that not even adults were capable of describing them. Other chiefs were convinced that the truth would not bring any release, but on the contrary, would stir up new killing and suffering. Nor did they believe that genuine forgiveness was possible after everything that had happened.

"People have already forgotten what it is to forgive or to confess their sins openly," sighed King Acana. "This war has destroyed everything. It has already cost us two generations. Our rites and traditions are vanishing from memory. And if we're unaware of them, we don't really know who we are."

There was a soft knock at the door, and a moment later one of his courtiers came into the room. At this point, Chief Lugai hauled himself up from his chair and, leaning on a cane, started to make his exit. He bowed to the king, and as he pressed my hand in farewell he explained that now he was going down to talk about Acholi history and customs to the children who were brought to him by teachers from the local schools.

As Lugai was telling me about Kony and forgiveness, the king had been glancing at his computer screen, which had some color photos flashing across it. Once we were left alone, he gently pushed away the keyboard and lounged back in his chair.

"There aren't many chiefs like Lugai," he said. "This damned war and the modern world are finishing them off."

Those who had managed to escape from their villages to the big cities and gain an education had long ago flouted the chiefs and the ancient village laws and customs, calling them superstition, an embarrassing relic testifying only to backwardness. Christian priests and missionaries spoke out against the chiefs, those depositaries and guardians of tribal traditions, and so did the Muslim imams. They anathematized them as heathen, and put the young people off them, insisting that the right path was faith, not tradition. The position of the chiefs was being further undermined by officials, teachers, judges, and policemen, who bit by bit were gradually eroding their authority, and inevitably their respect among their fellow tribesmen too.

When the war erupted and the soldiers told the Acholi to leave their villages and move into the camps around the cities, the chiefs ceased to have any significance. Sometimes a chief from one of the tribes was put in one camp, and his kinsmen and subjects in others. As a result of the guerrillas moving about the area, the roads weren't safe, so people from the widely dispersed camps never traveled unnecessarily and didn't visit each other.

The Acholi villages were built with the chief's hut at the very center, surrounded by his subjects' homesteads. It was bigger than the others and there was more open ground around it so the chief could rest and think about things without hindrance. In the refugee camps there was so little space that the huts, including the chiefs' ones, were on top of each other, with no regard for protocol or good manners.

Poverty and war had even made nightly gatherings around the bonfire impossible. Once upon a time the entire village had come and sat around the fire, to listen to the chief's tales about events from the past, about good and bad spirits and how to defend yourself against them. Now even firewood was in short supply, and in any case the soldiers wouldn't let them burn fires at night to avoid attracting the guerrillas.

Deprived of any sort of occupation or importance, the chiefs had been replaced by camp directors appointed by the army and charity workers who supplied food, medicine, clothing, and blankets. Many of the chiefs sought oblivion and a refuge from idleness in drink. The richer ones, who were more accustomed to a comfortable life, fled the camps and moved to the cities.

As a result the Acholi didn't know their own chiefs anymore, and the young people had no idea what their purpose was. Sometimes they passed them by without showing respect or even greeting them.

"Once fathers and mothers made sure their children were well brought up, and those children knew they owed the chiefs respect," said King Acana. "But ever since the war began, the parents haven't had the time or can't be bothered to educate their children properly, so they're growing up like wild trees in an orchard. They don't respect their elders, because they don't even know they should. But it's also because they see what they have come to, and how helpless they are. And the children whose parents have been killed and who have no one left grow up completely wild. No one knows what will happen to them."

"I have been told it's the chief's duty to take care of the orphans. And that he substitutes for their family during the ceremony to cleanse them of evil forces. Without going through this rite they can't return to their villages."

"That's true, but there's nothing to be done. Everything is upside down. Children are turning against their parents, and parents are disowning their own children."

"Is there really nothing that can be done about it?"

"Nothing, until the old order returns. There are good people who, although they're outsiders, are prepared to take our orphans away with them and bring them up as their own. They come here from as far away as Kampala. The children who don't find new homes, but haven't been cleansed of evil so they can't return to their old ones, are sent to orphanages, across the river."

At noon I said goodbye to the king and headed down the dirt road toward the town. I passed an old, spreading mango tree, where I saw Chief Lugai, surrounded by a circle of children in green school uniforms. He was telling them how the Acholi used to live.

◆►

"I'm not disturbing you, am I? I've just come for a moment."

Nora looked up, and for the first time I noticed anxiety, and an unfamiliar, unpleasant coolness in her eyes.

"Right," she said, straightening up in her chair. "I was expecting you yesterday."

"It was late when we got back from Amuru."

"Apparently you saw that ritual—Christine told me."

"You didn't tell me Samuel was being sent to an orphanage."

"You never asked. You haven't been talking to him at all lately. You come when he's not around. You leave as soon as he appears," she said, and paused, as if waiting for something.

"He's already told me everything."

"So what have you come for?"

I shrugged.

"Are you really going to send him off to the orphanage?"

"What am I supposed to do?"

"I thought you'd take him."

"Me? Why should I take him?"

"You already devote such a lot of time to him, you sit here day after day. He likes you."

"And who'd pay for our keep?"

"I could arrange something. Send money . . ."

"And I thought you were going to take him, he likes you too."

"But I've already got a family, my own children."

"So have I. I have a child too."

Nora's confession threw me off course and scattered my thoughts about Samuel.

"You have a child?"

"Yes, a daughter. She's big now, she goes to school. I was sixteen when I had her. The boy who got me pregnant was terrified and ran away."

"You never said a word. Does your daughter live with you?"

"Of course not! She's at my mother's place, in Lira. I wouldn't bring her here for anything. You can see what happens to children round here."

I felt relief when the phone rang. Although I was standing right next to her, I didn't listen to what she was saying.

"It's Mark. I must go and see him," she said. Mark was the head of the center. "Will you come by later? Or maybe you'll wait?"

"I have to go," I replied. "I have an appointment."

"An appointment?" she said in surprise. "You said you had nothing else to do today."

"I've just remembered."

"Will you come again?"

"Sure."

◂◦▸

I followed the road downtown. On the main square I turned left, to a red-brick church visible from afar, so immense you could fit a small town inside it. On the wooden terrace outside the presbytery there was a barefoot girl doing the cleaning. Only when I got closer did she look up in surprise, and I saw her mutilated face. Her mouth was mangled, as if it had been crushed, exposing her white teeth in a strange grimace. I asked to see Father Carlos, and the girl silently disappeared behind the presbytery door.

Father Carlos Rodriguez was the local priest, a missionary. I had read about him in the papers. He was not sparing with his words of condemnation for both the government troops and the Lord's Army guerrillas. He had once provoked Kony into telling his soldiers to blow up all the churches in Acholi-land and kill all the priests.

"This war seems pointless and is just feeding on itself. It's not about oil, or diamonds, and the guerrillas are guerrillas only because they always have been, and are incapable of being anything else," Father Carlos had once said. I wanted to ask him if in that case the war that had hit the Acholi was simply a war of good against bad—evil in its purest form.

The door opened, and there stood a small white man with extremely sparse hair, wearing a gray shirt of the kind worn by clerics in these parts.

"Father Carlos?" I asked.

"No, I'm Father Cosmas," he replied, sounding piqued. "But I'm quite accustomed to everyone asking for Carlos. Unfortunately, he's left for Europe."

He agreed to talk to me, and said something to the girl in the Acholi language.

"Can you speak their language, Father?"

"I've been here so many years now that I'd have to be deaf not to have learned it."

"You've been here that long?"

"I've been here from the very start."

He had taken on a parish in Kitgum when Alice of the Holy Spirit started her uprising. In the letters he had sent to the curia he had warned the bishops not to be deluded by the name the rebel woman had given to her faction. He was sure the Holy Spirit Movement had nothing holy about it—quite the opposite. He had explained that the rebellion and its leader were a shady business, but they hadn't listened to him; they hadn't understood what he was talking about or what he was warning them against.

And he said that maybe Lakwena was a spirit, but certainly not the Holy Spirit. After all, the Holy Spirit is a call for belonging and for unity—it guides you to the Father's House. Thanks to it, we know what road will take us there. But Lakwena? Lakwena and his servants—Alice, Severino, and above all Kony—had tangled up the paths of the Lord.

"Alice and Severino did not serve the Holy Spirit, but Satan. And Kony . . ." he said, lowering his voice, "is Satan. Satan is Joseph Kony. The fact that he and his companions have brought suffering and death on so many people still isn't the greatest evil they have committed, nor is the fact that they have forced children to do the most terrible things. The greatest evil they have committed is to make them believe they were doing it in the name of the Holy Spirit."

Father Cosmas never took his eyes off me, as if wanting to check what impression his story would have on me. He talked of the cold terror he felt when he heard that as they set off on their nocturnal expeditions ending in bloodshed and slaughter, the Lord's Army guerrillas prayed and sang the Christian psalms that are chanted at church services. And that they strung rosaries on their rifles and machetes, just like the ones used for prayer.

"They take a person off into the bush, and there they unleash all the evil that's latent in him," said Father Cosmas.

The barefoot girl with the mutilated face brought lemonade and cookies.

"Kony tells them to kill, and himself plays the role of a kindly father, a caregiver, their only defender in the cruel world which he himself has created. He fills them with horror, but they also worship him. They will do anything he demands." The priest wiped beads of sweat from his brow with a large checked handkerchief. "He tells them he's going to be president, and that they'll be masters of the entire country along with him; he says he's the messiah, the true Christ, who has come down from heaven, the Lord God himself. And those kids believe him, because if he has dared to do all this he must be God. Or Satan."

Every evening after the service, Father Cosmas went to the center run by Christine and Nora to pray with the rescued children, sing hymns in praise of the Lord with them, and hear their confessions. As long as he lived he would never forget the boy who revealed to him that he had killed his father and younger brother, and many, many more people after that. And here he was, asking for repentance and absolution. The priest admitted that never before or since had he been so overcome with doubt and helplessness.

"Is there any repentance that could atone for such terrible crimes? How can you give absolution for that? But then comes the thought that these cruel killers are just children, after all. Maybe it is we who should be asking them for forgiveness. They ask for repentance and absolution, but what they lack most is consolation and love. So we keep telling them: It's not your fault, it's not your fault."

The girl cleared the glasses and plates from the table. She asked something quietly, indistinctly, as if ashamed to move her mutilated mouth.

"Would you like anything else? Coffee, perhaps?" asked the priest, and seeing that I refused, he said to the girl in English, "That's all, Elizabeth. May God requite you, my child."

The girl was seventeen, and until quite recently had been regarded as fortunate. She had been pretty, healthy, and strong. She came from a good, well-to-do family of teachers. Her parents had taken care of her education and planned to send her to college in Kampala. In Gulu she was considered an excellent candidate for a wife and mother, and had been surrounded by admirers.

It all came to an end in an instant, one evening when she was on her way home from a visit to a friend who lived on the edge of town. Lost in thought, she didn't notice the guerrillas, who sprang up in her path. Just as greatly alarmed as she was, they threw her to the ground, beat and kicked her. Only then did they cool down, but their commander, a boy who looked the same age as she was, took a knife from his belt. She begged for mercy and swore she wouldn't tell anyone about the encounter. The commander just shook his head, told the soldiers to hold her down, and sliced off her lips. Elizabeth's injury was meant as a warning to others, not to dare report to the government army.

The girl had lost her mind. Her parents took her out of school and kept her shut in an empty room because she had tried to take her own life and kept attacking others, biting and scratching like a wild animal. A doctor was fetched from Kampala, who prescribed pills that calmed her down, and then her parents, who were known in the town for their piety, decided to place her in service at the presbytery.

"If her insanity doesn't return, they want Elizabeth to enter a convent," said Father Cosmas, as he led me to the gate. "I talk to her every day. I've got used to the sight of her face. She says she has forgiven those who did it to her. Yet every morning she looks in the mirror. Do you think it's really possible to forgive something you can never forget?"

◄◦►

Nora was waiting in her office. Serious and distant.

"Where have you been? I thought you'd forgotten about me," she said, with a welcoming smile.

"I'm leaving," I said.

This idea had only just occurred to me, to my own surprise too. But when I said it out loud, it seemed obvious, the only possible thing to do.

"So soon?" Nora was clearly surprised. "Stay to the end of the week at least. On Monday they're taking Samuel away. He'd be pleased if you came to say goodbye to him."

"I really must go," I answered quickly. "I still have something to see to in Kampala."

"Why did you bother to come back here?"

"I had some unfinished business here."

"What was it?"

"Well, for instance, I wanted to clarify what would happen to Samuel."

"And now you've finished it all?"

"So it seems to me at least."

We usually spoke on top of each other, interrupting one another, not letting the other one get a word in. Now the conversation wasn't taking off, but was getting harder and increasingly tiresome.

"Why did you bother coming here at all?"

"For my work. That's my profession."

"What is?"

"Well, writing about important things that are happening in the world."

"I'm curious to know what exactly you wrote about Gulu. What important thing has been happening here in our town?"

"Do you think what I do is of no significance?"

She gestured impatiently.

"Others have come here too, asked the children questions and then gone away, and at least it was all cut-and-dried. But you came back. I thought it was going to be different. What did you come back for? For your work! For your work! Is that what I'm to tell Samuel when he asks? You barged into our lives, and now you've got cold feet. What are you afraid of? You got too close to us, right?"

I started getting ready to leave.

"I'll come and say goodbye, okay?"

She nodded.

"Tell me, did the fact that I have a child change something?"

"What would it change?"

"I don't really know . . . Everything? Anything . . ."

◄-◦►

I was already on my way back to the hotel when I remembered Severino, the servant of Satan, who was the father of Alice of the Holy Spirit and the uncle of Joseph Kony. According to Father Cosmas, he lived at his own church in a poor part of town, not far from the hospital. The priest said I only had to ask the way, and anyone would point it out to me. No one here acknowledged Severino openly, but they all knew where to find him. Although people had lost faith in the old man's powers, Father Cosmas claimed that the spirits still haunted him.

He was possessed for the first time when he was still a boy. It happened while he was reading the Bible. He heard a voice telling him that God had chosen him as a favorite son. If he were obedient, lived without sin, and did as God told him, He would give him a trade and income, a wife and children. The voice sent Severino to a district where he did in fact find work as a carpenter and met his wife, Iberina, with whom he had a small flock of children. But as soon as he had started to do well, he prayed less and less often, indulged his desires and weaknesses, and committed sins. God became angry with Severino and inflicted death on his four sons. Finally He knocked him off a roof he was trying to repair.

Severino lost consciousness, and the angels and spirits took him on a journey into the world beyond. This time he encountered the Supreme Being Himself, His Son, and the prophets. At the end of the visit Moses handed him the stone tablets with the Ten Commandments and told him to take them back to earth. In his vision Severino also learned that one of his children had been chosen by God too.

The chosen one proved to be Alice, who on the advice of the spirits had incited an armed rebellion. The envious Severino had immediately set off for Kitgum to take away his daughter's leadership. But the possessed Alice told him to get lost. He went away with his tail between his legs and never saw his daughter again.

Meanwhile, her cousin, Joseph Kony, came to see Alice for advice and help; he had an army too, and was fighting at the head of it against the government troops. However, Lakwena, who had entered the girl, started belittling the newcomer, claiming that the spirits possessing him would make him at best a healer, but not a warrior and leader. Deeply offended, Kony took to his heels and swore vengeance.

Once Alice had been vanquished outside Kampala, Severino banded together soldiers from her defeated army to create a new guerrilla force. However, he suffered an even more crushing defeat than his daughter, without ever having won a victory. In an attempt to besiege Kitgum that lasted for three weeks, he lost almost five hundred men.

Thoroughly routed, he fled to Gulu, where Kony was fighting. His soldiers soon caught Severino, beat him and tied him up, then led him before their commander, who warned him that no one but he, Kony, had the right to talk to the spirits. He imprisoned Severino, had his chapel destroyed, and burned the wooden chair on which he sat whenever he let the spirits possess him.

However, Severino had managed to escape. He hid among the Alero waterfalls, where he fasted and prayed for many days. There he was found, barely alive, by soldiers from the government army, and ended up in jail again. When he was released, he came back to Gulu and built a new church.

I had no trouble finding it in the labyrinth of alleyways, puddles, and gutters filled with garbage. Severino's church was made of clay and straw with a thatched roof. It differed from the other churches in the area, as it was bigger and had whitewashed walls. There were two entrances. The main one, designed for the congregation to use on Sundays, was now locked shut. The other one was near the altar and led into a chapel.

Inside the church it was dark. The shutters were closed, so only thin shafts of light could squeeze through chinks in the roof. With a cross hanging on the wall behind it, the altar stood in the brightest part of the church; it was austere and modest, typical of the ones I had seen here. It was decorated with flowers and liturgical vessels, and there were some green glass bottles standing on the floor around it. These bottles were filled with some miraculous concoctions that helped chase away evil forces, as well as cure infertility, wounds, headaches, and leprosy.

As I was approaching the altar, wondering if I should genuflect, I heard some noises coming from near the locked main door. There was someone there in the darkness; I could hear someone clearing his throat, a weak, low coughing noise, and an old bed creaking.

"Is there someone there?" I called.

I jumped as I felt a hand touch my arm.

Right behind me stood a young man in a light shirt. I hadn't noticed him come in, and he hadn't made the slightest sound as he approached me.

"I scared you," he said. "My name is Martin and I work here in the church."

"Oh, so you're the priest."

"I am the chaplain," he explained.

Something moved in the darkness in front of the main entrance. Martin left me by the altar and vanished into the gloom, then reappeared, leading by the arm a naked old man with long hair, a beard, and bloodshot eyes.

"This is Severino," he said, leaving us in front of the altar.

The old man smiled toothlessly and held out a welcoming hand. His grip was weak and his bones were as delicate and fragile as a child's.

Martin brought a chair and a white robe. He placed the chair under the cross behind the altar, led the old man there, and handed him the robe. He disappeared again, and soon after I heard him opening the shutters. The interior of the church was flooded with dazzling white light. Only now did I notice a bamboo bed set against the wall by the main entrance.

"Soon Lakwena will enter Severino, please be patient," said the chaplain, putting some of the green bottles on the altar. "You have come to see that, am I right?"

The old man pulled the flowing robe over his head and threw back his long, sparse hair, then hung a large rosary around his neck.

"Will I be able to ask him some questions too?"

"I think he'll be happy to talk to you," replied the chaplain. "As soon as the spirits have left him."

I had been told that the spirit of Lakwena possessed Alice at seven in the morning and seven in the evening. For Lakwena to enter Severino's body, the old man only had to sit down on a wooden chair behind the altar, holding one of the glass bottles.

Severino folded his hands as if to pray and froze still. I failed to sense the descent of the Holy Spirit or any other kind of spirit, but suddenly the old man shuddered, rolled back his eyes, and announced that now Lakwena was talking through him, transmitting the words of God the Father Himself.

"Please take note," advised Martin the chaplain.

◀◦▶

Severino spoke in the Acholi language, and Martin translated his words into English for me.

"First Lakwena taught him how to heal people . . . He sent him to cure people of illnesses and of madness, but then he told him to stop, because people were blind to everything. He kept healing them, but they were immediately at each other's throats again, killing each other in wars so much that the spirits, the hosts of spirits of those killed, could not find peace, so they went on haunting people, getting vengeance. Only he, Severino, knew how to control the spirits, because God had chosen him as His son . . . His messenger on earth. And he was to lead the Acholi people to the promised land. And he would sacrifice himself for their salvation.

"So he went to the nature reserve at Paraa and conferred with the wild animals, with the water and the rocks . . . Alice was with him. They fetched water for purification and stones to change into grenades and bullets. But those were not the most important thing, no, they were not. For victory lies in purity of heart. Without sin. Sinners perish, their hands are torn off or their eyes are put out. And that is just, because they have sinned against God. That is proof that they are guilty. For every battle fought by His army is the day of the Last Judgment. The very Last."

Suddenly Severino fell silent. He looked as if the life had drained out of him. The chaplain examined him closely for a while, then said Lakwena had left the old man's body.

"Just a moment and he'll recover," he added. "Then you'll be able to ask him your questions."

He put a small gourd down in front of the altar, with some coins jingling at the bottom of it. I took a few banknotes from my wallet and shoved them inside it. He nodded to show his gratitude.

"And those were all the words of Lakwena?"

"A man who is possessed by spirits loses his wits. He ceases to be himself, has no control and can't remember anything, neither what he did nor what he said," he replied, glancing at Severino, who was flopping feebly on his chair. "That is why to find out what the spirit that enters a man wants, you need someone there who will understand and memorize his words."

I thought of Jackson. He had been with me during almost all my meetings in Gulu and had interpreted almost every word for me. I had spoken to lots of people, but I only knew from him what they had really said.

"So only someone to whom the spirits have no access can be an interpreter?"

"Not necessarily. Sometimes the spirits also enter the interpreter, but usually they assign him a different role to perform," he explained. "Are you making do here without an interpreter? Without a guide?"

I told him about Jackson. He didn't know anyone by that name. I said he had accompanied me when I first came to Gulu, then he had been to Kampala with me and we had returned here together—since when he had disappeared without a trace.

In his full-length, crumpled robe Severino came down from the altar and smiled, like an artiste embarrassed by the compliments after a successful performance.

"Well, maybe he has already played his part and stopped being needed. He took you from here to Kampala and brought you back again," said the chaplain. "Maybe he did what he had to do and then he was gone. That happens here."

⟶

Toward evening I went to say goodbye to Nora and Samuel. Sunday was ending, the holy day. Tomorrow I was leaving Gulu for Kampala. I asked Nora where I could find the boy.

"They're praying in the chapel. Father Cosmas is with them. Will you wait?"

"I can't. I'm just about to leave for Kampala. Tell him I was here."

"But the last bus has already gone."

"I met someone at the hotel who's going by car. He's taking me with him. We'll make it across the Nile by nightfall."

"Do you know what they say here? That the truth is only told when there's no alternative left," said Nora, smiling. "Here among us only old people speak the truth. They have no reason left to lie."

"I'll call from Kampala."

"Yes, please do. Without fail."

⟶

In Gulu the day was ending.

Heated to blazing, the town was dropping, starting to cool down and go quiet. It was hurriedly preparing for sleep, as usual in the rainy season, trying to get everything done in time before the storm erupted which had been gathering in the darkening sky in swollen, angry clouds, only waiting for dusk to release all the rage accumulated during the scorching day.

At Franklin's bar I asked about Jackson. The waiter looked at me in astonishment, as if he didn't understand what I was on about, then shrugged. I sat down at a table under the arcade.

The imminent cloudburst was already palpable. It was as if heavy drops of warm rain were hanging in the air, ready to fall at any moment onto the dusty red earth and change it into slippery mud the color of blood. The sky was thundering louder and louder, bolder and nearer, and short, bright streaks of lightning were cutting across the clouds as they closed in on the town.

The storm was circling above Gulu now, waiting for the right time and place to lunge and stun it with thunderclaps, lightning, and lashings of rain. The town was frozen still, as if afraid of being too distracted by the usual hustle and bustle to notice the tempest's first strike. Crushed by its own weight, the sky was sinking lower and lower, as if trying to touch the ground.

Suddenly the wind, which was tugging at the palms just in sight beyond town, remembered about Gulu, and through a chink between sky and earth it blew sand along the main street. Abruptly animated, shreds of old newspaper, bits of colored plastic, and yellowed grass went whirling across the cracked asphalt.

I froze motionless, holding my breath.

The waiter poured beer into a glass.

"Did you see that?" I asked.

He shrugged.

"But he flew past just over your head," I said.

"Who did?"

Soon after, spattering noisily on the roofs and on the ground, the first raindrops fell.

TIMELINE OF EVENTS

1894	Uganda becomes a protectorate of the British crown
1962	Independence, with Kabaka Mutesa II as honorary president and Obote as prime minister
February 1966	Obote deposes Mutesa and declares himself president
1971	Amin deposes Obote
1979	Uganda-Tanzania war
1980	Obote returns to power. Start of Ugandan Bush War
1985	Obote deposed by General Tito Okello
1986	Museveni comes to power after victory in bush war of National Resistance Army. Start of armed resistance in Acholi-land
1996	First presidential elections—landslide for Museveni
2001	Second presidential elections, Museveni wins with 69 percent of the vote, Besigye takes 27 percent
February 2006	Third presidential elections, Museveni wins with 59 percent of the vote, Besigye takes 37 percent
February 2011	Fourth presidential elections, Museveni wins with 68 percent of the vote, Besigye takes 26 percent. Besigye said the polls were marred by widespread bribery, ballot box stuffing, and intimidation. He called for peaceful protests which resulted in riots in Kampala that were compared to street revolts from Arab countries.

ABOUT THE AUTHOR

WOJCIECH JAGIELSKI is a journalist at *Gazeta Wyborcza*, Poland's first and biggest independent daily, where he specializes in Africa, Central Asia, the Trans-Caucasus, and the Caucasus. He has been witness to some of the most important political events of the end of the twentieth century and is a permanent observer of developments in Afghanistan. He is the author of *A Good Place to Die*, the result of several years of travel to the Caucasus in the era of the Soviet Union's collapse and of the emergence of new independent states; *Praying for Rain*, the bestseller chronicling Afghan regimes; and *Towers of Stone*, a book about the war in Chechnya and the bitter history of that region. Jagielski is the recipient of the most prestigious awards for excellence in journalism in Poland. In 2008, *Towers of Stone* received the Letterature Dal Fronte Award in Italy.

ABOUT SEVEN STORIES PRESS

SEVEN STORIES PRESS is an independent book publisher based in New York City. We publish works of the imagination by such writers as Nelson Algren, Russell Banks, Octavia E. Butler, Ani DiFranco, Assia Djebar, Ariel Dorfman, Coco Fusco, Barry Gifford, Hwang Sok-yong, Lee Stringer, and Kurt Vonnegut, to name a few, together with political titles by voices of conscience, including the Boston Women's Health Collective, Noam Chomsky, Angela Y. Davis, Human Rights Watch, Derrick Jensen, Ralph Nader, Loretta Napoleoni, Gary Null, Project Censored, Barbara Seaman, Alice Walker, Gary Webb, and Howard Zinn, among many others. Seven Stories Press believes publishers have a special responsibility to defend free speech and human rights, and to celebrate the gifts of the human imagination, wherever we can. For additional information, visit www.sevenstories.com.

967.61044 J24 ·   INFCW

Jagielski, Wojciech,

The night wanderers :Uganda's

children and the Lord's Resistance Army
CENTRAL LIBRARY

09/12